## BOOKS BY DARD HUNTER

My Life with Paper: An Autobiography (1958)
Papermaking: The History and Technique of an Ancient
Craft (1942, 1947)

*These are Borzoi Books*
*published in New York by Alfred A. Knopf*

# MY LIFE WITH PAPER

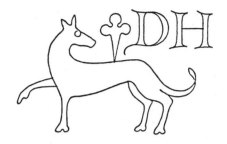

# MY LIFE
# WITH PAPER

An Autobiography

By

Dard Hunter

ALFRED A. KNOPF · NEW YORK · 1958

© Dard Hunter, 1958

THIS IS A BORZOI BOOK,

Published by Alfred A. Knopf, Inc.

FIRST EDITION

L. C. CATALOG CARD NUMBER: 58–9672

# Foreword

In 1941 the Rowfant Club of Cleveland published an octavo volume of 120 pages entitled *Before Life Began*. This book was designed by Bruce Rogers and was printed on Lime Rock handmade paper in an edition of 219 copies—a book for each member of the Club. This small volume was my autobiography covering the first forty years—1883–1923. The title was, of course, based on that of the popular book *Life Begins at Forty* by Walter B. Pitkin, which gained the top of the best-seller list of non-fiction when in 1933 the total sales reached 164,000 copies.

In the present volume the original text of *Before Life Began* has been augmented and extended, with thirty more years added, making it the story of my first seventy years—1883–1953. From the year 1923 onward, the book deals almost entirely with my journeys and experiences in the Far East. These Asiatic travels were undertaken for the specific purpose of assembling information, photographs, tools, and specimens of the ancient craft of making paper by hand. This material resulted in the compilation and illustrating of numerous books, pamphlets, and articles, and, in 1939, in the establishment of the Dard Hunter Paper Museum, originally at the Massachusetts Institute of Technology, Cambridge.

Although more than a dozen of my books have been published and four universities have given me honorary Doctor

# FOREWORD

of Literature degrees, I do not think of myself as an author. My utmost ambitions have not been in the field of writing.

The manuscript for this book was revised and amended during the winter of 1957 while I was living in the West Indies, where I was fortunate in having the criticism and help of Helen V. Tooker of *El Mundo*, San Juan, Puerto Rico, and for her assistance I am grateful.

Santurce, P.R.
*April* 1957

# Contents

Contents

# Illustrations

# ILLUSTRATIONS

# ILLUSTRATIONS

# ILLUSTRATIONS

# ILLUSTRATIONS

# MY LIFE WITH PAPER

# I

DURING the past fifty years the world has undergone a more radical transformation than any in a like period of history. The change is usually called "progress," from which there is apparently no escape. It has been my fortune, good or ill, to have lived through this half-century and to have seen the changes that have come, one upon another. The machine age has unfolded before my eyes, a prosaic period that has not appealed to me. I have long been an advocate of hand craftsmanship and have struggled against mass-production methods, but my efforts have been no more effectual than the exertions of a lone termite in a petrified forest. The discovery of oil in the ground, which made the gasoline engine possible, was the turning-point. Before the advent of automobiles—and the natural sequence of airplanes, tanks, bombers, and guided missiles—the world was more at ease. There is no gain in quarreling with machines, science, and technology, but the question persists: have they brought more peace and contentment to the world?

Had the choice been given me, I would have placed the beginning of my life during the latter part of the eighteenth century and its termination before the year 1830. Had the choice of place in which to live this span of years been mine, I would probably have selected rural Scotland, the seat of my forebears.

Not being accorded the privilege of selecting birthday and birthplace, I came into this world in the unromantic year of 1883 in a small agricultural and industrial town in eastern Ohio. In Steubenville my father, William Henry Hunter (1852–1906), was owner and editor of the Democratic daily newspaper, the *Gazette*. Before taking up life in this Ohio River city, he had worked for his father and brother-in-law on the four-page *Sentinel*, a weekly newspaper in Cadiz, Ohio, a sheep-raising community in the rugged hills of Harrison County. Cadiz was thirty-one miles from Steubenville, and when the journey was made by horse and carriage this was not an insignificant distance.

Besides being financially interested in the Cadiz *Sentinel*, my grandfather, Joseph Hunter (1804–1886), conducted a cabinet shop and a small brass foundry. Pieces of his mahogany furniture are still preserved, as are a few examples of brass door-knockers and andirons. One of my grandfather's employees—the boy who turned by hand the great wooden wheel that actuated the wood lathe—was George Armstrong Custer, who, history tells us, became an Indian-fighter and attained success and acclaim in that unholy field. Apart from his ability to work in wood and metal, Grandfather Hunter had studied law with Edwin M. Stanton, who later became Lincoln's Secretary of War. During his years in Cadiz, Stanton had his law office over the Hunter furniture shop. Grandfather was Associate Judge under the old Constitution, and in the family genealogy it is stated that he could repeat from memory much of Shakespeare and all of the poems of Robert Burns.

My grandmother on my father's side was Letitia McFadden (1815–1886), a mild little Irish woman who had been born in County Cavan. Joseph and Letitia, stanch Presbyterians, died within a day of each other, the old gentleman preceeding his patient wife. They were buried on the same day, side by side, in the old Cadiz graveyard. The double obituary in the Cadiz *Sentinel* stated with unconscious humor: ". . . Joseph Hunter was never sick a day in his life, he was hale and hearty to the last breath. . . . Letitia Hunter's death was due to the long strain of nursing her ailing husband." All of the family were born collectors with a penchant for saving everything, which accounts for the preservation of the bills for Joseph's and Letitia's funerals in April 1886: "Robert Wood, undertaker, $137.00; Eliza Bancroft, making shrouds, $3.50; George Creswell, digging two graves, $10.00; carriages at funeral, $19.50." Besides the old family residence, with its adjoining cabinet shop and showroom, and various other properties, there was $21,377.28 in cash which Grandfather Hunter could not take with him.

My mother, Harriet Rosemond Hunter (1856–1925), a delicate although beautiful woman, was the only daughter of William Courtney Browne (1824–1899) and Margaret Rosemond (1830–1856), both born in Ohio. In 1859 Grandfather Browne moved to the East, where he was a wool-and-grain merchant with offices at 1328 Vine Street, Philadelphia, and 48 Broad and 76 Pearl streets, New York. After the Civil War he returned to Ohio and established a private bank.

My earliest remembrances of Steubenville are of a large brick-and-stone house built for my father in the seventies. It overlooked the Ohio River, with the rocky hills of West Virginia and Pennsylvania in the distance. I recall the place as a romantic setting, with sloping lawn and wide-spreading trees. At the foot of the wide gravel path leading from the house to the river stood an iron lamp-post with glass globe and natural-gas burner. Each night at dusk, scarcely tall enough to reach the window sill, I would watch for the man who came on horseback to light the lamp with his flaming torch. Our house was heated and lighted by natural gas, and as gas was plentiful and we were in the newspaper business, no gas bills were ever presented. Passes on all railroads and river steamboats were ours for the asking. A newspaper-owner was a citizen of influence, and it behooved the various companies to treat him with generosity.

In later years the lawn and the flower and vegetable gardens were in my care. I also had to feed the numerous chickens and gather the few eggs they consented to lay. These duties were decidedly chores, but when the care of my father's two spirited horses was finally entrusted to me I found that task no hardship, as I have always been a lover of horses. The *Gazette* printing-office was about one mile from the house, and when I was not cleaning the stable and currying the horses or hoeing corn and cutting grass, I was occupied at the printing-office or my father's pottery. The Lonhuda art pottery was established by my father and two other enthusiasts about the year 1886. The name Lonhuda was derived from the three sponsors: Long, Hunter, and Day. For me, working days started early in life; my parents were filled with energy and could not tolerate indolence. My brother, Philip Courtney Hunter, two years my senior, and I were busy from morning until night—indeed, on some nights when the great kiln at the pottery was being fired with the white-hot gas flames, father and we two boys did not return home until the small hours of the morning.

The printing-office had been built about the year 1845. It was a rambling brick-and-stone building with a beautiful mahogany spiral staircase to the third floor. In earlier days the structure had served as a tavern or hotel. My father had purchased the old building and with innate ability and artistic talent had converted it into a most unusual printing-establishment. It had the type of façade still to be seen in Blackfriars Street or the Canongate in the old section of Edinburgh. The first floor housed the counting-room and the reporters' quarters. Well toward the back on a lower level were located the newspaper press and folder and three job presses. On the second floor was the composing-room with its thick stone slabs supported on heavy wooden tables. It was on these stones that the pages of type were made ready for the press. Six wooden type-stands with their rows of type-cases stood by the front windows. The third floor of the building was used for the storage and setting of wood type, some of the founts containing letters eighteen inches high and giant figures two and three feet in height.

In connection with the daily and weekly newspapers and job-printing office my father operated a show-printing shop and had contracts for printing date-lines for circuses, fairs, and traveling theatrical companies. These date-lines were set in the huge wood type and printed in red on yellow poster paper. The business of the printing-shop and pottery was prosperous, and although the family never "splurged," we had everything our simple tastes required. Our most enjoyed possessions were the team of sorrel horses and the natural-wood surrey with heavy brown fringe around the top. When my father would let the horses have their way on the dirt road along the river, the deep fringe would blow in the wind, giving a sensation of great speed. The carriage had ornamental side lanterns, and at dusk on rare occasions we would light the candles and drive through La Belle Avenue, past the home of the editor of the Republican newspaper, much to his envy, we hoped, and to the delight of my father, whom the opposition newspaper always mentioned editorially as "Wild Bill." My father must have been a mild counterpart of John Baskerville, the eighteenth-century English type-founder and printer who took pleasure in appearing on the streets of Birmingham with coach and four and all the trappings of nobility.

I was eight or ten years of age when Mr. Feckey, foreman of the *Gazette,* instructed me in the art and mystery of type-setting, and it was through the humor of this genial old printer that I was introduced to "type-lice." One compositor was a deaf-mute, and "Dummy," as he was called, could "stick" more type than any of the other compositors. The five or six typesetters who could hear and talk were usually gossiping about the news stories that were sent up from the copy room, via pockets in an endless canvas belt, by Chauncy Waite, the star reporter. This reporter looked for all the world like an unkempt white leghorn rooster. In fact, we had just such a scrawny old rooster that we called "Chauncy Waite" because the two resembled each other so closely. All of our nondescript chickens bore names of leading local characters: the roosters were named after the businessmen of the town and the hens were called after the members of the Ladies' Aid Society of the Methodist Episcopal Church, of which we were regular attendants and contributors.

In this old square brick church I was baptized after my father and mother had given much thought to the ceremony. I will not mention the name of the minister who sprinkled the few drops of water upon my curly blond head, for only a short time after he performed this symbolic rite the saintly gentleman was made treasurer of the missionary society and, the responsibility proving too great a temptation, the kindly old soul absconded with all the funds. He was convicted and died in the state penitentiary. After the scandal became known, my parents gave serious thought to having me "done" again by a more worthy exponent of the gospel. For some reason the repetition never materialized, so I have the dubious distinction of having been baptized by a convicted malefactor.

The pressroom of my father's printing-establishment was under the jurisdiction of Jim McPherson, a cantankerous old Negro who had long been in our employ. The press-feeding was dexterously done by a thin, toothless old spinster with the unlovely name of Mag Wheeler. At two thirty every weekday afternoon Jim McPherson would fire the boiler and get up steam for printing the evening edition. Mag Wheeler would stand at attention on her bench behind the press, sheets of blank paper fanned out on the inclined press-table ready for printing as soon as the pages of type were locked in the bed of the press. Mag was an expert press-feeder, and each time the cylinder revolved she would be ready with a sheet of paper, giving it a little toss in the air and allowing it to glide gently against the guides that would pull it around the cylinder to be printed. Jim McPherson made all of the printing-rollers used on the newspaper and job presses. On Saturdays I would often help him pour the sugarhouse molasses, bone glue, and gelatin into the long, round iron moulds. Those were the days before printing-rollers were readily procurable and before the general use of stereotyping, the linotype, telegraph service, comic strips, cartoons, syndicated editorials, and columnists—before small-town newspapers became standardized, with every daily built on precisely the same pattern as all the others.

My mother and brother were much interested in newspaper work, but I could not adapt myself to the speed necessary to the publication of a daily paper. I was fat and rotund, and had a lackadaisical disposition; a slow and easy way of life was more to my liking. I recall my embarrassment when my father ordered two pairs of trousers for me from a Philadelphia tailor. When the enormous pants were completed they were displayed in the clothing-store window with a placard reading: "For a ten-year-old Ohio boy."

My brother had no such handicap. Starting at the age of twelve, he wrote every week and set in brevier type a column entitled "The Garden." The type was composed in our house in an upstairs room fitted with type-stand and cases and a proving-press that I had constructed. When the column was ready for the Saturday edition, I would carefully place the galley of type on the back seat of the surrey and drive to the newspaper office, where Mr. Feckey had reserved a place in the chase for its inclusion. After the evening edition was printed, the type would be taken home for me to distribute into the case, to be reset by Phil for another column of "The Garden" for the following week's paper. My mother also wrote her "copy" at our house, but it was put in type at the newspaper office and always by "Dummy," as my mother felt that he could set "cleaner" type than the other compositors. My father seldom prewrote any of his editorials, but, standing erect at the type-case, would compose the material as he placed the types, one by one, in the composing-stick. A newspaper composing-stick held about two inches of type—fifteen or sixteen lines. My father would always refer to the length of an editorial or any set matter as so many "sticks." At noonday lunch I have often heard my mother ask about articles that were to appear in the paper that evening. For instance, my mother would say: "Did they have a large funeral for old Joe Basler?" and my father would answer: "One of the largest this year, about eight and a half sticks." And then in an offhand manner he would comment: "The Stark-

Huscroft wedding, so much talked about, was not such a magnificent affair after all, only about two and a quarter sticks."

Aside from father and mother, numerous uncles, aunts, and cousins were engaged in newspaper or magazine work. As years passed and father had more leisure, he became interested in Ohio history and wrote a number of books, chief of which was *Pathfinders of Jefferson County*, a two-volume work published by the Ohio State Historical Society in 1898–9.

It was in the upstairs office of the old Cadiz *Sentinel* that I saw for the first time a machine for setting type. The apparatus was known as a Thorne typesetter, and my uncle, who edited the *Sentinel,* had no end of difficulty in making the contrivance function. The machine, invented in 1888, was eventually discarded, and the old and tried hand method of typesetting resumed. During my father's ownership of the Steubenville *Gazette* all type was set by hand.

My brother and I had a well-filled childhood: the printing-office, the pottery, the gardens, and the horses—never an idle moment. Everything was of interest to us. The only thing that was obnoxious to me was school, especially in the overheated schoolroom during the winter months when I was required to wear long underwear in which there seemed to be embedded every minute thorn and brier that the woolly sheep had picked up in the pasture. My father had two fads: the detestable wool underclothing that would have made a hair shirt of the ancient monks feel like velvet, and a peculiar although sensible idea about food. During my entire home life nothing sweet was tolerated in our house; cakes and pies were taboo, and only at Christmastime were we permitted to have candy—even then only one piece each of a hard clear candy moulded in the form of a red or amber elephant or camel.

There was little sickness in our family, but when some minor ailment came along we had the needed remedy. In exchange for an advertisement in the *Gazette,* my father had accepted one of the medical chests compounded and sold by Dr. Humphrey, a highly publicized New York homeopathic physician. The chest was of polished walnut, with neatly fitting lock. Within the box there were one hundred small compartments, ten one way and ten the other. Each compartment held a small glass bottle of white sugar-coated pills, and each individual bottle had a cork stopper with a number stamped on the top; there were no labels on the bottles. Along with the chest Dr. Humphrey supplied a catalogue listing one hundred diseases and ailments, each sickness followed by a number that referred to the numbers on the corks: a simple and ingenious method of prescribing for the sick. All the pills in all the bottles were probably the same, but all members of our family accepted the medicine as an antidote for every slight illness. My father was always fearful that the corks in the bottles might become interchanged, more especially the bottles containing pills for constipation and diarrhea.

In 1893, when I was ten and my brother twelve, the family left by train for Chicago to visit the World's Columbian Exposition. I vividly recall the over-elaborate Pullman sleeping-car, with its carved, shiny mahogany, pressed-plush seats, and long row of hanging oil lamps with decorated glass shades which the porter lighted with a wax taper held in a curved metal holder. We were especially interested in the Fair, for a number of pieces of Lonhuda pottery and several examples of father's wood-carving had been accepted for display. This made all the exhibits more vital to us. Perhaps my father's work would be given a medal; even a ribbon of honor would be acceptable. Father had studied wood-carving with Benn Pitman, an ingenious gentleman who, along with his brother Sir Isaac Pitman, received recognition for the invention of a system of shorthand. Father was influenced by the exhibits of craftsmanship at the Fair, and on his return to Ohio he wrote and set in type a column article advocating the teaching of drawing and manual training in the Steubenville public schools. Although his idea was not then accepted in the local schools, the article was reprinted in *The Times* of London, and through its influence drawing was made a part of the curriculum of some of the English schools. Later, through this same influence, drawing was introduced into many of the public schools of America. Both father and grandfather were capable draftsmen, as attested by work still preserved.

When I was eleven I had a harrowing experience that carved a permanent groove in my memory. As I have said, our house faced the Ohio River, with a sloping lawn that extended to the dirt roadway along the water. Our barn, exercise lot for the horses, and garden were in the rear of the house, with a private drive to the stable. As I was family hostler, much of my time was occupied with the horses in and near the barn. One cool spring morning while I was brushing the horses in the barnyard I saw, to my horror, a young girl enveloped in flames running down our driveway toward the river. Her thin cotton dress was burning furiously, the fire reaching well above her head. She was screaming: "The river, the river!" Ordinarily my mind worked slowly, but this was an emergency. I reached for a horse blanket and ran toward the terrified girl. I threw the blanket around her frail body and gently laid her on the ground and smothered the flames. The poor girl was terribly burned; nothing could be done. She died in my arms. Little did I think that in years to come, in far-off Indo-China, a lovely young Annamese girl would expire in my arms in much the same manner.

Our neighbors were elderly gentlemen, their wives, and maidservants, who never deviated from their leisurely habits, so my services were always in demand. If a cat fell into a well or a stray horse or cow roamed aimlessly over the connecting lawns, I was the one to summon. No other person, according to our neighbors, was so competent at extracting a cat from a well or capturing stray animals. On one side of us dwelt Captain and Mrs. Cope. The Captain had long since retired as master of the Ohio River steamboat *City of New Orleans*. Captain Cope, in his eighties, had suffered a stroke and got about in a wheelchair. When wheeled by his nurse under the shade of the great russet apple tree in the garden, he was always cautioned to remain quiet. But when the nurse would turn her head for a moment, he would hop out of his padded chair and attempt to walk. Invariably he would fall to the ground and there would be a great calling throughout the neighborhood for me. I was the only one with sufficient strength to pick up the old codger and place him in his accustomed seat. Mrs. Cope, unlike her frail husband, was heavy and rotund. A little later she also suffered a stroke of paralysis, which confined her to bed. It became my duty every morning to lift the corpulent woman from her couch so that the nurse might arrange the dear old lady for the day. After a week I rebelled against this distasteful chore, but not until I had devised a plan for which my strength would not be needed. With some oak timber, rope, and a windlass I constructed a derrick. This cumbersome contraption was bolted through the brick wall of Mrs. Cope's room, and with wide linen bands slipped under the patient's huge body the nurse was able to raise and lower her charge at will. The neighbors praised me for my ingenious human lifting device, and from all over town curious people came to see my apparatus gently swing Mrs. Cope above her bed. The old lady was confined to her room the remainder of her life, and every day my derrick served its useful purpose.

All these things were, however, merely incidental: my real interests were the horses and boyish experiments in the printing-office and pottery. Of my many chores one that gave me decided pleasure was the periodical trip with the horses to the blacksmith's shop up the narrow lane behind the old Congregational church. The bearded smith, Alonzo Huscroft, fascinated me: his great hairy chest, his immense arms, and his captivating technique in chewing tobacco made me envious. He dressed in a thick woolen shirt and heavy homemade pants, and a split leather apron hung from his middle. In the winter months when the doors of the blacksmith shop were closed, I never tired of watching the sparks fly from the anvil in the darkened room. It was my task to pump the great leather bellows, the long wooden handle of which reached eight or ten feet across the shop. On the end of the lever was fitted a cow's horn that made a convenient handle. In the woodcut of *Der Schmidt,* so handomely depicted by Jost Amman in the German *Book of Trades* published in Frankfurt-am-Main in 1568, a cow's horn is used in precisely this same manner. The period of my childhood had not yet begun to undergo the mechanical changes that were eventually to transform the universe; many ancient customs and old ways still lingered.

The family delighted in long journeys with the horses and surrey over the country roads and lanes from one village to another. For packing our clothing father made two cedarwood boxes, each fitting under one of the seats of the carriage. We had waterproof curtains that could be fastened around the surrey for rainy weather, and coverings for the horses. The horses had cotton headdresses and pantaloons as precautions against the sharp-biting horseflies. We had one horse named Queen who would stop still at the first fly bite and would not budge until her headgear and pantaloons had been put on and adjusted. Mother had an insatiable humor, and took delight in making fancy hoods and pants for the horses, using the most bizarre color schemes and patterns. Some of our journeys in the surrey would extend over many miles, and we would stay away from the newspaper office for a week at a time. About twenty-five miles was the limit for a day's jaunt over the narrow, grass-grown dirt roads, and we would stop at night in a country inn or at the home of a relative or newspaper acquaintance. In the evening the horses would be put in a sweet-smelling country barn with plenty of oats and hay so as to be ready for the following day's drive.

The countryside of eastern Ohio was rugged and hilly, with stretches of woodland, cultivated fields, and pastures, interspersed with brooks and grassy lanes. For a short evening drive, after father had seen the newspaper to press, we had favorite roads—up through the villages of Nineva and Holliday's Cove, or over the Alakana road past the mossy wooden watering-trough embedded in ferns and trailing arbutus, with the clear spring water dripping over the cool green rocks. The horses drank with such contentment. I have never returned to those scenes of my childhood, and it would be unwise for me to do so. This beauty exists now only in my memory. "Progress" has left no stone unturned, and the lovely haunts of my youth would now be a distressing and disappointing sight.

1. Great-Grandfather James Hunter (1777–1829), the third generation in America, and the first of the family to migrate to the wilds of Ohio, where he set up a printing-office in 1812.

2. Grandfather Joseph Hunter (1804–1886), editor-cabinetmaker, on the steps of his home and shop, which he built in Cadiz, Ohio, in 1830. From 1836 to 1839 Edwin M. Stanton, Lincoln's Secretary of War, had his law office over this shop, and here George Armstrong Custer, Indian-fighter, worked as an apprentice for grandfather. Photograph made about 1873.

3. William Henry Hunter (1852–1906), editor and publisher of the Steubenville (Ohio) Daily Gazette. Photograph dated May 17, 1889.

4. *Phil Hunter (1881–1908), magician. Photograph made 1900.*

5. *The Roycroft Printing Shop, East Aurora, New York. My studio was in the uppermost room of the square tower.*

6. As I appeared in 1903, the year I went to East Aurora.

7. Alice and Elbert Hubbard, the most natural photograph of them together that I have ever seen. Photograph made 1907.

8. The half-timbered, thatched mill near Marlborough-on-Hudson, which I built in 1913. The handmade paper used in printing several books was made in this mill.

9. The old Gómez house near Marlborough, where the two books for the Chicago Society of Etchers were made, 1915 and 1917, the first use of my paper and type. The type-foundry was on the second floor of the addition to the left of the main building, built in 1714 and 1772.

10. Workroom of the Mountain House Press, Chillicothe, Ohio, where the press was set up in 1919. Some of this furniture was made in grandfather's shop. The pottery above the doorway was designed and made by father, about 1889.

11. *Mountain House, where eight books on the subject of papermaking by hand were printed. The house was built in 1850.*

12. *Mountain House overlooking the town of Chillicothe. From a hand-colored lithograph made in Cincinnati in 1852.*

13. *Tongatabu, Tonga Islands. Pounding the inner bark of the mulberry tree into small sheets that were later combined to form large pieces of "tapa," used for many domestic purposes. Photograph made 1926.*

14. *Taviuni, Fiji Islands. Decorating "tapa" or "masi" by the use of leaf-cut stencils. The vegetable pigments were dull red and dense black.*

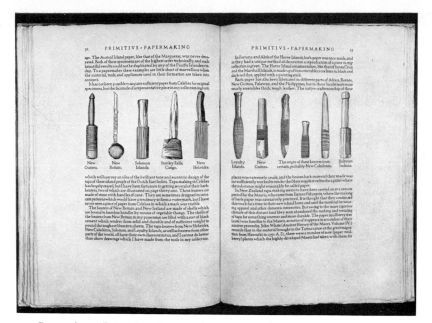

15. Pages from Primitive Papermaking, *printed by the Mountain House Press, 1927, following the South Sea Island travels. This was the third book on the subject of papermaking to be printed in my hand-cut and hand-cast type.*

16. The Lime Rock, Connecticut, *mill, lying precariously along the Salmon Fells Kill. The old English equipment for making paper by hand was housed in the basement of the wooden building, the drying-loft was on the third floor. The entire structure was demolished during the severe flood of 1955; not a vestige remains.*

17. *Robert Perry Robertson stands at the vat forming a sheet of paper in a hand mould, the method used in making all paper before the perfection of the paper machine during the early nineteenth century. Mr. Robertson and five members of his family came from Maidstone, Kent, England, to work in the Connecticut mill. (This "still" photograph and the four following were taken during the making of a color moving picture depicting the history of the American paper industry.)*

18. *Robertson stirring the beaten rag fibers in the vat, the earliest method of agitation. The second worker has just "couched" a moist sheet of paper, while the "layboy" stands ready with a felt to place upon the newly formed sheet.*

19. *Turning down the screw press on the "post" of paper and felts in the manner of the pioneer paper mills of America. This procedure extracted much of the water from the paper.*

20. *A worker removing the semi-moist sheets from the felts after the "post" had been pressed. The sheets of paper were then hung to dry.*

21. *The drying-loft of the Lime Rock mill with young lady workers and a gentleman visitor dressed in Colonial costume. The piles of paper were eventually used in printing the folio book* Papermaking by Hand in America, *completed in 1951. (The moving picture was made in 1945 by Springer Pictures, Incorporated, New York, for F. C. Huyck and Sons, Rensselaer, N.Y.)*

22. A cottage mill in Najio, Hyōgo Prefecture, Japan, where the workers sat at the vats while forming sheets of paper. Old Japanese woodblock prints depict this ancient custom. The European practice of standing at the vat is now almost universal.

23. The village of Ompei, Korea, spread out along the river, where every man, woman, and child was engaged in some branch of the craft of making paper by hand.

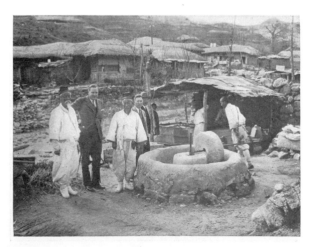

24. The proprietors of one of the Ompei paper mills stand at either side of their first American visitor.

25. Forming sheets of paper in Ompei. The workers were using the appliances and methods of hundreds of years ago.

26. Drying paper on the ground in Ompei village. The large sheets were later laminated together and used on the floors of Korean houses, in the manner the Japanese used straw mats.

27. The Japanese Technical Institute in Seoul, 1933. In the seventh century the Koreans introduced the art of papermaking to the Japanese, but in the twentieth century the Japanese were instructing the Koreans in the methods of Japan.

28. *Bangsoom, Siam. Pyn Niltongkum forming a sheet of paper on a mould floated on the stream. The beaten* khoi bark *was poured on the woven-cloth mould in the manner of the most ancient Chinese form of making paper.*

29. *The mould lifted from the surface of the water after the sheet of paper had been formed.*

30. *Luolin Niltongkum rolling the newly formed sheet of paper with a smooth, round stick which gave one side of the paper a surface suitable for calligraphy.*

31. *Each sheet of paper after being rolled was dried on the mould on which it had been formed, in the ancient Chinese manner.*

32. *Tym Niltongkum was too old for making paper, but he did prepare the ground charcoal used in dying the paper a dense black. The shaven, yellow-robed Siamese monks used the blackened paper for inscribing with yellow pigment.*

33. *A Chinese pulp mill which supplied several small paper mills. The bamboo and straw was beaten by stone rolls pulled around and around by blindfolded mules. The man in the octagonal trough was giving the pulp a final refinement by stamping with his feet.*

34. *"Spirit-paper" being made on a laid bamboo mould divided into three sections, thus forming three separate sheets of paper at one dipping of the mould.*

35. *After pressing, the sheets were separated and dried in the open fields. In the foreground, bundles of "spirit-paper" await bearers to carry them to the printers.*

36. *A paper shop in south China where all sorts of funereal and ceremonial papers were sold. These shops were in every Asiatic community where Chinese people had located.*

37. *Examples of the most common "spirit-papers," which were printed with woodblocks and burned at funerals and other ceremonies.*

38. *Tonkin, Indo-China. A Tonkinese worker preparing bark for papermaking during my visit in 1934 to the paper villages of Yên-Thai and Lang-Buoi, near Hanoi, Tonkin.*

39. *A young Annamese woman "couching," or laying, a sheet of moist paper after it had been formed on a laid bamboo mould. Each sheet was laid directly upon the others, without the aid of felts as in European papermaking. In all Asiatic papermaking by hand one worker acted as both vatman and "coucher."*

40. Pressing the piles of newly formed sheets of paper by means of a lever press. The pressure was supplied by placing stones on the hanging shelf at the end of the stout lever.

41. Drying the paper, sheet by sheet, on a plaster oven. The weather of Tonkin was so humid that drying was done by artificial heat. The fuel consisted of the outer bark not suited for making into paper.

42. *Kashmir, India. In Nowshera the papermakers' houses were typical of all Kashmirian architecture, built of mud blocks with heavy timbering. On the tile roofs grew grass and moss. In this house paper was made for my benefit as it was the cold season and the cottage mills were closed.*

43. *The old Kashmirian papermaker who was chosen by his fellow workers to go through the various papermaking processes for my enlightenment. A sheet of paper had just been formed by dipping his laid grass mould into the vat of beaten pulp.*

44. *The Nowshera papermakers who sold us paper for use as specimens in my proposed book. It was extremely cold in Kashmir during our sojourn, and the men wore small charcoal braziers underneath their robes.*

45. *Making paper in the Ma-mudeen Khagjee cottage mill in the Nekapura district of Sailkot, Punjab, India.*

46. *Drying paper near Sail-kot. The moist, newly made sheets of paper adhered to the plaster wall and fell to the ground when dry.*

47. *In Old Delhi when we fi-nally reached the Mohammed Sadrque Kaghzi paper mill the workers were in the streets celebrating a holy day, but they soon returned to the mill-yard and gave a demonstra-tion of their papermaking.*

48. The home of Mohandas Gandhi near Wardha, where I talked with the Mahatma about the crafts of weaving and papermaking.

49. The Mahatma Gandhi school of papermaking in Wardha. Young men from all parts of India came to this institute to learn the craft of making paper by hand. They then returned to their native districts and set up small mills for supplying local needs. The people were too impoverished to buy paper, and only by making it themselves were they able to have paper at all.

50. Autsahai, Bengal. One of the workers who had walked from the papermaking village of Kurmira to demonstrate the local technique of Indian papermaking. While in this remote district Mr. Rao and I lived in this bamboo-and-palmleaf house.

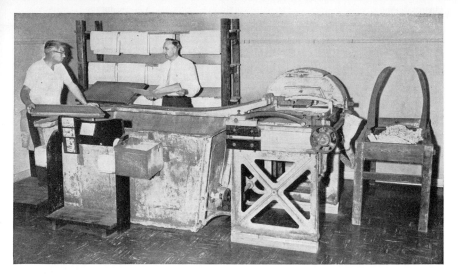

51. *The equipment for making paper by hand which I procured in Downton, Wiltshire, England, in 1920. These appliances were eventually set up in Lime Rock, Connecticut, where the paper for several of my books was made, including* Papermaking by Hand in America, *finished in 1951. This equipment is now in the Dard Hunter Paper Museum of The Institute of Paper Chemistry, Appleton, Wisconsin. The two men in the photograph were students at the institute.*

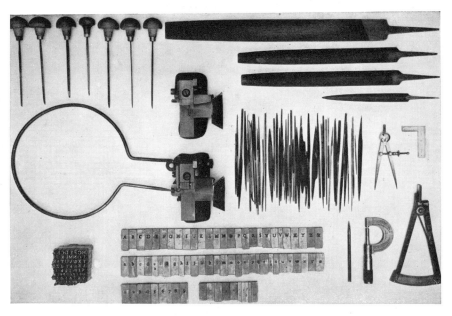

52. *The gravers, files, and measuring-tools used by Dard, Junior, in cutting his fount of type that was used in printing the folio edition of* Papermaking by Hand in America. *The steel letter-punches, the copper matrices, and a hand mould for casting type are also shown in this photograph.*

53. Dard, Junior, casting the type in one of the machines we had acquired from the defunct Boston type-foundry. Thirty or forty units of type were cast per minute by turning the machine by hand.

54. Setting the folio pages for Papermaking by Hand in America. The text of this book was composed in Dard, Junior's type and ornaments. We had sufficient type for setting three pages, all that was needed. This was my last typesetting.

55. *At the hand press during the making of* Papermaking *by Hand in America. Two pages were printed at each impression. The initial letters were cut in brass and printed in red ink simultaneously with the text in black. The Lime Rock handmade paper was dampened prior to printing.*

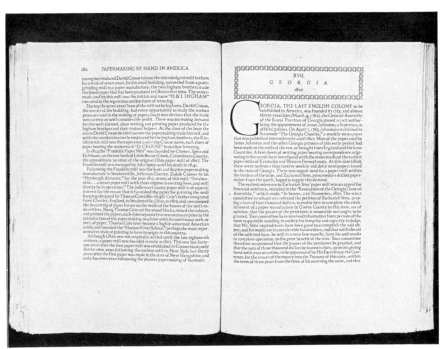

56. *Two folio pages of* Papermaking *by Hand in America showing Dard, Junior's type, which had required several years to make.*

57. The administration building of The Institute of Paper Chemistry, Appleton, Wisconsin, where the Dard Hunter Paper Museum was moved in 1954, after fifteen years at the Massachusetts Institute of Technology, Cambridge.

58. In the wall cases of this section of the Paper Museum are displayed paper-making appliances from China, Japan, Korea, Siam, and India, all procured in the places of origin. The table cases in this wing show material relating to the use of paper in both the Orient and the Occident.

# ❧ II ❧

IN 1898, when the Spanish-American War began, I was fourteen, but I was larger and stronger than most boys of my years. My brother being frail, the usual manual work of the household, which ordinarily would have been divided between us, fell on my shoulders, giving me added strength. War was a new experience, and after the sinking of the battleship *Maine* excitement and emotion became rampant. Pent-up patriotism gave way to passion, and every night torchlight processions marched the streets, the parade invariably terminating at the fair grounds with the burning in effigy of a Spanish general or admiral. My duty was apparent— I must enlist. Without telling my parents or brother Phil, I pulled my huge physique together, tried to conceal my youth, and left for the nearest recruiting-office, but not before I had said farewell to my beloved horses. I was going to war, perhaps I would never see them again. . . . I was not surprised when I was accepted at the recruiting-station; I expected to pass all physical examinations, for I was six feet tall and as muscular and developed as a regular-army man. I was fearful, however, that my juvenile expression might be my undoing, but when I solemnly said I was nineteen the officer did not even lift his eyes. He asked if I knew anything about horses. Well, I should say I did! I was assigned to the cavalry, given a uniform much too small, and sent off to a camp about a hundred and fifty miles away. I was put in a company under Captain McCrosley, a little dried-up officer who reached only to my shoulder. He looked me over and said I would make a mighty good soldier. I wholeheartedly agreed with him.

The first two days at the camp were well occupied with caring for the mules and horses, training, and cleaning saddles and harness. I was a little restless and depressed those two days—was I such a mighty good soldier after all? I had not communicated with my parents, but I had a suspicion that they were aware of my adventure. The third morning, when I looked out of the tent, I was shocked to see my father talking calmly with Captain McCrosley! I was called over to where the two men were standing, and to father I must have appeared comical, all fitted out as a United States cavalryman. He did not laugh, however, at least not noticeably. Father had come to take me home, but my embarrassment was somewhat softened when the grim old Captain called after us: "There goes the best man I had in my company."

When I was back home again, my parents showed wisdom by never referring to my exploits as a soldier. I could sense that my mother was overcome with a desire to tease, but her understanding was too great to subject me to ridicule. I took up my work where I had left it a few days before, and father was noticeably glad that I was back, as it had fallen to him to care for the horses during my absence. I entertained my brother by the hour relating my experiences at the camp, not omitting a fictional touch here and there to make my story impressive. I was the envy of all the boys in the neighborhood, but it was not long before the Spanish-American War was forgotten.

Previous to the breaking out of the war, my brother and I

had gone to Pittsburgh to see Herrmann, the magician. My brother was so impressed by this famous conjuror that he too wanted to become a prestidigitator. Phil, who was as brilliant in school as I was dull, began the construction of apparatus for a magical performance. He was far more successful than was agreeable to our parents, as they cherished visions of their one bright son going to college and becoming a writer or professor. In a few years my brother had developed into a first-class entertainer; at eighteen he was considered a professional performer. I was the assistant.

At first we played engagements in near-by towns, but the fame of "Phil Hunter, The Wizard" spread beyond state lines, and when he was twenty he was under the management of a lecture bureau in Cincinnati at the almost unheard-of salary of three hundred dollars a week. Our parents were worried, perhaps not so much on account of our having entered the shady theatrical profession as because we were both ignoring college. Also, Phil was far from robust, and they were anxious about his health. But we were determined to continue our work on the stage. During the winter months we played lecture-course engagements in Ohio, Pennsylvania, Virginia, West Virginia, Kentucky, and Tennessee. In summer we had widespread Chautauqua engagements under the management of a booking-bureau with offices in Maryland and Florida. My brother's fame continued to soar until it was not unusual for him to receive a thousand dollars for a week's work. Even so, our parents implored us to give up the trying work and enter college.

We were now away from home practically all the time, my brother being twenty and I "going on" eighteen. We traveled from one end of the country to the other, and many were our experiences. My cavalry days were nothing compared with the one-night stands in Nebraska, North and South Dakota, and other distant states, and week engagements in the Chautauquas from Florida to California. As stated, I was the assistant, and the job of magician's assistant was no sinecure. The unpacking and setting up of the apparatus fell to me. All manner of delicate paraphernalia was employed, and every one of the hundreds of objects had to be in perfect order so that the show would run smoothly. We carried about twenty trunks, several large packing-cases, and other heavy equipment. Then, too, there were rabbits, ducks, guinea pigs, canaries, doves, and goldfish. As I had been so successful with horses in my extreme youth, the livestock was entrusted to my care, and what a job it was! We traveled from one town to another by railroad, often on freight trains, and on several occasions by special train so that we might reach a town in time to be ready for the show. The evening performance would be over at about ten thirty; then the packing of the apparatus and equipment would require about an hour's time. We would often catch a train immediately after the packing had been completed, but many nights we slept in the stations, waiting for trains at two or three o'clock in the morning.

In the South and Northwest it was not uncommon to travel by wagon, the teams and drivers waiting at the stage entrance until the show was over. Then the trunks, packing-cases, cages of birds and animals, and pails of goldfish, to say nothing of the tired magician and his assistant, would be loaded into the lumbering conveyance to be driven by moonlight or in the rain to the next "stand," twenty or thirty miles distant. I vividly recall spending most of one night in an honest-to-goodness leather-hung stagecoach, buffalo robes and all, driving from Deadwood to Spearfish, South Dakota, over a road so rough and filled with deep ruts that we could scarcely retain our seats inside the swaying coach. Entertainment and transportation have undergone many changes during the past half-century.

My brother had several tricks that almost gave me heart failure every time he performed them. One of these was an "experiment"—as he called all of his feats—of borrowing a watch from a lady in the audience and putting it through a remarkable ordeal. The watch was placed in a paper bag, and then, apparently by mistake, the timepiece was crushed under the foot of the magician. In reality, however, the watch had not been put in the bag at all, but had been dexterously passed to me behind the scenes. The crushing sound in the bag, for all the world like the mashing of a watch, was made by treading on several lumps of sugar which had been put in the bag. The seemingly crushed watch inside the paper bag was next loaded into a huge blunderbuss which was fired at an oval mirror that stood on a carved gilt table in the center of the stage. The mirror was broken at the discharge of the gun, when I, unseen by the audience, pulled a black cord that released a piston, breaking the glass mirror from the rear. Directly back of the shattered looking-glass hung the borrowed watch, "not a penny the worse for its many vicissitudes"—the very words my brother always said after performing this trick.

This experiment did not always work smoothly. One evening in a town in Kentucky my brother, in handling the borrowed watch before passing it to me behind the scenes, had accidentally broken the crystal and twisted the delicate gold hands. It was an expensive timepiece. Phil signaled to me that something unusual had happened and commanded me to do something! For a fraction of a second my mind would not function. Then I realized that it was Saturday night and that the stores of the town would be open. I ran out the stage entrance with the watch to the nearest jewelry shop and had the hands straightened and a new crystal inserted. In the meantime my brother had gone on with another trick, purposely delaying the firing of the blunderbuss at the mirror until I could return to the theater. The watch, fully restored from being crushed in the paper bag (and from the more realistic mishap as well), was at last found behind the shattered mirror. When Phil returned the watch to the lady in the audience and spoke the customary phrase "not a penny the worse for its many vicissitudes," little did the audience or the lady from whom the watch had been borrowed realize the ordeal that the timepiece had been through. My brother did not often praise me for my work as his assistant, but he did that night.

Another feat of Phil's ledgerdemain which on one occasion had an unfortunate ending was a trick in which two doves were involved. This experiment in sleight-of-hand consisted of borrowing two diamond rings from ladies in the audience. The rings were seemingly mixed with eggs, flour, and other messy ingredients and placed in a nickel-plated chafing-dish; the concoction was then covered with alcohol and set afire. The lid was immediately put on the chafing-dish to quench the flames, and when it was removed two white doves flew from the dish, one leg of each bird held securely by a ribbon so that they could fly only a few yards. The borrowed rings, lo and behold, were suspended on red baby ribbons around the necks of the doves. This trick always received an appreciative "hand" from the bewildered audience. One delightful spring evening, in a town in Illinois, Phil was performing this trick. The borrowed rings had been passed to me behind the scenes and I had tied them with ribbons to the necks of the doves and concealed the birds in the false double lid of the chafing-dish, as was the nightly procedure. I do not know what happened to the retaining ribbons supposed to prevent the birds from flying, but the moment the dish was uncovered both birds, ribbons trailing behind them, flew to the dome of the theater, the borrowed diamond rings suspended from the short red ribbons around their necks. They then circled around and around until an open window invited them to flee into the soft spring air. Neither doves nor rings were ever seen by us again. After the evening's performance there was considerable embarrassment, but the following morning Phil and I, with the two ladies from whom the rings had been borrowed, visited a local jewelry store and, at the expense of several weeks of our earnings, purchased two beautiful diamond rings. The ladies were so pleased and so satisfied that we afterward wondered if the rings that went out the theater window on the necks of the doves contained genuine diamonds.

In 1900 my father sold the Steubenville *Gazette* and the family moved to Chillicothe, where he and my Uncle George continued the publication of the *News-Advertiser,* a daily newspaper; also a semi-weekly, the Ross County *Register* on Tuesdays and the *Advertiser* on Fridays. At this period my brother was doing remarkably well with his magic show, but our parents continued to implore us to return home and prepare for college. With a solid year of engagements before us, however, we could see no reason to give up traveling. In the interim I had developed a fifteen-minute "act" that placed me in the performer class, although I continued as magician's assistant. My act was known as a "chalk talk." With square sticks of colored chalk I drew pictures on large sheets of rough paper held upon upright easels, and at the same time carried on a line of "patter" supposed to be both humorous and instructive.

The summer Chautauquas were a great American institution, and we were usually on the same program with famous and forceful speakers. The lectures were invariably given in the morning, with our more generally popular type of show following in the afternoon and evening. One morning in a western Chautauqua, William Jennings Bryan was the speaker. As our show had to go on only an hour after the "Great Commoner" had finished speaking, I had set up our paraphernalia and adjusted the many intricate pieces of apparatus so that we would be ready to begin our performance on time. The magical equipment and my various pieces of colored chalk and easels were all concealed behind a series of dark-blue plush draperies that we carried with us. As Bryan entered the stage for his lecture, he unwittingly became entangled in the various strings, threads, and wires that were connected with our tricks. In a fraction of a second my patient work of setting up the apparatus was undone, but Bryan did not even apologize. I was provoked, as everything had to be completely rearranged. During Bryan's lecture I noticed his wide-brimmed hat lying on one of our magic tables where he had carelessly left it hidden behind the plush draperies. I was aching for revenge. The chalk and the hat gave me an idea. With my pocket knife I grated an entire piece of soft red chalk into the inside of Bryan's headpiece. It was a hot morning, and after the lecture Bryan placed the great broad hat on his perspiring head. The finely powdered red chalk mingled with the perspiration, and the classical face of William Jennings Bryan was literally streaked with bright-red pigment as he walked to the hotel. Several Republicans present told me with considerable satisfaction that the "Silver-tongued Orator" was infuriated by my childish prank.

If my quarter-hour "chalk talk" had no other virtue, it gave my brother a short rest during each performance. I had noticed that he had been losing weight and was pale and fatigued. But we went on from one town to another, with little sleep, tired and worn. Finally Phil became so exhausted that there was nothing to do but cancel the remaining dates and return home, where he remained under the care of a specialist in tuberculosis.

Other magicians were hired by the lecture bureau to substitute for Phil. I continued the "chalk talk" and acted as manager. I traveled one more year with such old-time necromancers as Clinton Burgess; the "Great Nicoli"; Joseffy; and one or two others. Joseffy was a Hungarian of middle age, tall and gaunt. A typical magician's mustache and goatee ornamented his wrinkled face. His most exciting and bewildering trick was his own invention, and was billed in newspaper advertising and on posters as "The Talking Hand, the baffling phenomenon that has mystified the great scientists of the Orient and the Occident." The experiment consisted of placing a lifelike artificial hand upon a foot-square piece of plate glass, which in turn was suspended by four silk ribbons secured through holes in each corner of the glass. At the magician's request the ends of the ribbons were held by four members of the audience, thus balancing the hand upon the glass in mid-air. There appeared to be no possible connection between Joseffy and the false hand. Members of the audience were requested to ask questions of the suspended object, and after each question the hand would reply by slowly raising its forefinger and tapping on the glass—two taps for "no" and three taps for "yes." This was considered a brilliant trick, and the spectators were usually spellbound. Joseffy was exceedingly jealous of his mechanical hand, and would never permit me to examine it. To prevent any exposure of his invention, he carried the talking hand in a small leather satchel and kept it by his bedside in his hotel room. He never knowingly permitted the satchel out of his sight. One day at a railway station, however, he left the satchel unattended for a moment, and I had an opportunity of at least ascertaining the weight of the hand. When he saw that I had touched the sacred satchel, he was furious and cautioned me never again to attempt to fathom the mystery. Aside from the dummy hand coming between us, Joseffy and I got along well for the three or four months that we were together. I was not easily perturbed.

I have never since heard from any of the performers who substituted for my brother, although a score or more years ago I read in *The New York Times* that the "Great Nicoli," his assistants, and magical apparatus had been lost in a shipwreck off Singapore.

# III

AFTER having toured the country with several magicians and illusionists, I was at last willing to give up any future connection with traveling shows and their accompanying hardships. Suddenly and forcefully a repugnance for a life of this sort came to me.

My brother continued to write a daily column for our newspaper, although he was suffering from the serious illness contracted in his youth and aggravated by traveling as an entertainer. My work was now wholly in the newspaper office, where I drew cartoons and news pictures for the evening edition. My drawings were made on "chalk-plates," an early and now obsolete method of reproducing linecuts. For this process one side of a polished steel plate was coated with about one sixteenth of an inch of a moist composition of powdered chalk. The chalk was baked on the plate, forming a soft but tenacious surface. With a set of steel points of various sizes, the picture was drawn in the dry-chalk coating directly through to the steel plate, thus forming a matrix. The chalk-plate with its line drawing was then placed in a casting-box and molten stereotype metal was poured upon it, forming a relief plate for printing.

On occasion I made cuts for lodges, stores, patent medicines, and politicians. One day an elderly horse doctor came to the newspaper office in the hope of finding a person who could draw the illustrations for a book he had written on veterinary surgery. The old gentleman was referred to me as the only "artist" in the establishment, and the foreman assured him that I was just the man he was seeking. "Can you make drawings and diagrams of the anatomy, diseases, and infirmities of horses, cows, pigs, and sheep?" he asked. With my usual willingness to attempt anything about which I knew little or nothing, I told him that I was a specialist in that very field. The illustrated edition of the veterinary book was made entirely in our printing-shop. Even now I shudder when I think of that job of bookmaking.

Later I became interested in the making of furniture and in wood-carving; my father, experienced in both crafts, was a patient and helpful instructor. At this juncture, father, also keenly interested in fine printing, purchased a book that had a pronounced influence upon me. This unusual volume, with richly decorative borders and initials, had been printed in England several years previously by William Morris, an artist and craftsman about whom I knew little. I became so fascinated by the book and by father's description of the Kelmscott Press that I was eager to visit England, where such books had been made. Father agreed that later I might go abroad, but said that first I should have more schooling. After quiet persuasion I consented to enter Ohio State University, provided that I could choose my own course of studies.

While attending the university in Columbus, I lodged in the home of William C. Mills, the well-known archaeologist, who was responsible for many of the great "finds" in the prehistoric mounds of southern Ohio. One summer I camped with Dr. Mills and his assistants during the exploration of the Baum Village Site, where many treasures now in museums were unearthed. I was also with him during the opening of the Adena mound, where he discovered a magnificent effigy pipe, one of the finest of all prehistoric American artifacts. A reproduction of this carved pipe forms the frontispiece in Gerard Fowke's monumental work *The Archaeological History of Ohio,* published by the Ohio Historical Society in 1901.

From time to time Dr. Fowke held editorial positions in our newspaper office, and he was a familiar figure to me, with his great shock of gray hair, his flowing beard, and sharply chiseled features; he wore soft leather boots that reached to his knees. John Bennett, of *Master Skylark* fame, was at one time editor of the Chillicothe *News,* and his brother, Henry Holcomb Bennett, author of *The Flag Goes By,* was city editor of our newspaper for many years. William Ireland the cartoonist received his training on the Chillicothe *News.* Percy Hammond, my father's sister's son, who in later years was dramatic critic on the New York *Herald Tribune,* wrote his first stories for our publication. For years the well-known anthologist Burton Egbert Stevenson was one of our reporters. The Chillicothe newspaper was a training-ground for a number of men who eventually became illustrious in their fields.

At the Ohio State University I examined additional books from the Kelmscott and Doves presses. My desire to visit Europe increased, but as I was enrolled in the university, it was best to continue my educational opportunities. In the meantime Phil had become absorbed in a little magazine, bound in butcher's paper, called *The Philistine,* edited by Elbert Hubbard, and I immediately became interested in the work of the Roycroft Shop in East Aurora, New York. I wrote to Mr. Hubbard asking if he could find a place for me after I was graduated from the university. His reply was genial, although discouraging: no additional help would be needed. With the coming of summer vacation, the colony in East Aurora appealed strongly; if I could not then journey to England to see the Doves and other private presses, I could at least go to East Aurora for a short stay and then return home for the remainder of the vacation.

On the morning of June 15, 1903, when I was nineteen, I awoke in a sleeping-car in the old dilapidated Buffalo railway station; the local train left within an hour for East Aurora, where I met Mr. Hubbard and his sons, Bert and Sandy. Later Mrs. Hubbard and her charming daughter Miriam arrived from Boston. Mrs. Hubbard was a most likable and agreeable woman. Mr. Hubbard did not impress me as unusual. Except for his long hair, flowing windsor tie, and abnormally keen expression, he might have been a prosperous Ohio farmer. Mrs. Hubbard seemed more strait-laced and puritanical than anyone I had ever known, and I supposed that this was the result of her New England background. She was tall, slight, and sunburned, and had almost kinky blond hair. Her thin, pleasant face was filled with minute wrinkles that bespoke a life lived in the open. She wore long, full, high-collared dresses in soft shades of brown with stiff white ruching at her neck. When she walked, she fairly swept along the paths, her slim figure giving the appearance of unusual height. In riding, she sat so erect upon her horse that she appeared to be in actual discomfort. There was little nonsense about the woman Elbert Hubbard called "White Hyacinths," but she was filled with kindly humor, forgiveness, and generosity. I shall always remember Alice Hubbard with respect and affection.

My first weeks in East Aurora were most agreeable, but I regarded my stay as little more than a summer vacation, a short respite from my studies at the university. I made one or two pieces of furniture, did a little wood-carving, and designed several objects in iron and copper for Pete Robarge to pound into form in the blacksmith shop. I liked the rugged little village of East Aurora and the surrounding country, and Mr. and Mrs. Hubbard treated me with understanding. At the end of the vacation period I arranged to return home, although I was not keen about continuing at the university. Schools and colleges frightened me; they seemed heartless and forbidding. When Mr. Hubbard asked me to remain at the Roycroft Shop, I was not surprised; it seemed a perfectly natural place for me to be. The Hubbards suggested that I continue to live at their Roycroft Inn and receive a weekly wage in addition to room and board. My parents thought that I should accept, as they looked upon the Roycroft Shop as a school—as indeed it was, although with too much leeway and insufficient direction.

In the rear of the inn, or Phalanstery as it was called, stood a one-story wooden building that had been a carriage house during the early days when Mr. Hubbard commuted to the Larkin Soap Company in Buffalo. I asked Mrs. Hubbard if I might convert this small building into a studio for myself, and she readily consented; neither she nor Mr. Hubbard ever opposed anything I wanted to do. The structure was at once renovated and transformed into a pleasant retreat, Mrs. Hubbard supplying furniture, rugs, and draperies. It was not long before the former carriage house became a meeting-place for the boys and girls of the shop.

I shall long remember two old people in East Aurora: Dr. and Mrs. Silas Hubbard, Elbert Hubbard's father and mother, who had come from their old home in Illinois to live in the New York State village. Like his son, Dr. Silas was of small stature; his short grizzly gray beard, his shiny black Prince

Albert coat, and his baggy trousers were those of a country doctor. Mrs. Silas Hubbard, a frail wisp of a woman, was the height of neatness and decorum, wearing black silk dresses and white lace collars, and a tiny kerchief upon her benign gray head. Dr. Silas was a physician of the old school of medicine: he gathered herbs in the woods and stripped bark from trees and compounded his own remedies and tonics. On several occasions I was taken ill with a minor ailment, and the good Dr. Silas would come to my room bringing a gallon jug of thick black medicine, always with the same terse directions: "Half a cup every two hours, and, mind, none out the window!" I took the ill-smelling concoction religiously, for I had unbounded faith in the dignified little Dr. Silas and I knew that anything he would prepare could not help but give relief.

Dr. and Mrs. Silas Hubbard, like Elbert and Alice, would be out of place in the world as it has come to be—they were of a simpler, more gracious, more moral age. When unknowing people mention the "immorality" and "free love" that they have been led to believe abounded in East Aurora, my mind goes back to those four puritanical individuals whose strict morality would now be almost incomprehensible.

I had been in East Aurora only a few months when I casually told Mr. Hubbard of my desire to learn the rudiments of making leaded-glass windows. I had often examined work of this kind in churches, and wanted to try my hand at the craft. Mr. Hubbard said that he would arrange for me to go to New York, where I could work in a stained-glass studio. Within a week I was off to the city with a letter to the firm of J. and R. Lamb, architects of church interiors. This firm was in Carmine Street in a picturesque old building that had formerly been a church. I was delighted with my reception in the studio, and, moreover, I was invited to spend some of the time in the home of Osborn Rennie Lamb, author and poet, a member of this old-established firm.

After a few weeks in New York I returned to East Aurora with many ideas and plans. I approached Mr. and Mrs. Hubbard with the suggestion that I make leaded-glass windows for the Roycroft Inn, then being reconstructed. In the long dining-room there were eight windows, each about nine feet in height and about three and one-half feet wide. I drew a full-scale design for the windows—clusters of tulips in many colors, with a blue-sky background—and laid the "masterpiece" before them. They were overjoyed, or at least they said they were, and gave me permission to order material and construct the windows. A pattern for each piece of glass was cut in cardboard from the original drawing; for this purpose we used a double-bladed knife, the space between the blades allowing for the width of lead. The glass was cut with a diamond Mr. Hubbard purchased for me in Buffalo. The bits of colored glass were leaded together by the method I had learned in the studio of the Lambs, but trouble arose when I attempted to solder the joints of the lead. The solder and lead were not so tractable as they had been in the New York studio. I went to Zeke Standeven, the Roycroft plumber, with my difficulty, and Zeke corrected my error. For flux I had been using a modern composition candle when I should have used an old-fashioned tallow candle or palm oil. The lead strips were often melted in soldering, and in cutting the varicolored tulips considerable glass was destroyed. My window-making was a costly project for Mr. Hubbard, but I was learning.

In six months the windows were finally completed. The effect was startling! The Roycroft workers came to see my embryo attempt, Mr. and Mrs. Hubbard said they were delighted, and even kindly old Dr. Silas gave my work a nod of approval. But the gay pink, green, purple, and blue windows never pleased me. At breakfast and lunch in the large dining-room I would look up at the clumsy glass tulips and feel ashamed that I could have designed anything so repulsive. When Mr. Hubbard passed the great round oak table, where I would be serving lunch to a dozen inquisitive visitors, he would tell the assembled diners that the windows were my work. They would exclaim: "How beautiful!" and I would have a sudden inclination to slide under the table. Several months passed; I could endure the sight of the gaudy tulips no longer, but what was to be done? Mr. Hubbard had paid for the glass and lead, and he had sponsored my trip to New York. Also I was on the payroll at two dollars and fifty cents a week. My conscience bothered me, but the design and colors of the tulip windows disturbed me even more than my conscience.

One November morning I arose early, took hammer in hand, and made my way to the dining-room. Standing on the broad windowsills, about four feet above the floor, I literally smashed to bits the windows I had made. Broken glass littered the floor; the twisted leads hung in grotesque shapes from the window frames; the windows were wrecked; but my pent-up feelings had been relieved. What would Mr. and Mrs. Hubbard say? I waited for them to come to the dining-room for breakfast. With bewildered expressions they looked at the window openings with the hanging, twisted leads, and at the broken glass on the floor. Then they saw me, hammer still grasped in my hand. I could endure the windows no longer; something had to be done, I explained. Elbert and Alice Hubbard stood rigid. Faint smiles crossed their surprised faces. Without the slightest anger or remorse, Mr. Hubbard said: "Evidently the windows did not please you. Better try again and make a design you will like." As he commenced breakfast in the room chilled by the absence of windows, he called after me as I was leaving: "Dard, if you feel inclined to smash your next set of windows, please wait until summertime." At once I drew a new design for a second lot of windows, and during the winter completed the work. These windows, with a design of conventionalized roses in subdued white and green glass, are still in the dining-room of the Roycroft Inn.

In the library of the Roycroft Shop were several examples of incunabula, a number of art books, and complete files of the *International Studio* and other English, French, and German art publications; two volumes from the Kelmscott Press graced a shelf in the big corner bookcase. I had become more and more interested in this Hammersmith press and read everything I could find relating to the life and work of William Morris. Much to my delight, one evening Mr. Hubbard told me that William Morris's daughter, Miss May Morris, was presently to speak before the Woman's Club in Buffalo and that he wanted me to meet the charming young lady. I was thrilled, and when the much anticipated day arrived Mr. Hubbard gave me a letter addressed to the daughter of the man whose work I had so long admired. I left on the morning train for Buffalo, seventeen miles distant. When I arrived at the Woman's Club where the lecture was to be given, I was embarrassed to find that I was the only man present; when I saw Miss May Morris, I knew that Mr. Hubbard had been teasing me about the youth and beauty of the lady. She was not very attractive, and was at least twice my age. In her lecture Miss Morris was sarcastic and critical of America and spoke of the lack of culture in this country. Although I was disturbed and resentful, I was determined to present Mr. Hubbard's letter with its kindly invitation for her to come to East Aurora and the Roycroft Shop.

After the long lecture was finished, I summoned courage

and approached Miss Morris. When she unfolded the letter and saw the signature her eyes flashed. Looking up at me, she said: "I most certainly will not go to East Aurora, nor do I have any desire to see that obnoxious imitator of my dear father." With an air of disdain she crumpled the note in her hand and gave it back to me. Never before had I been treated with such discourtesy. I did not tell Mr. Hubbard about my experience, but whenever I see a Kelmscott book my thoughts go back to that little incident with Miss May Morris.

At frequent intervals noted visitors made the little journey to East Aurora, and it was my privilege to greet many of them. Often a well-known person would be placed at the large round oak dining-table over which I presided, family style, at the inn. These visitors were from varied walks and ways of life, and I recall meeting such personages as Eugene Debs, socialist; Carrie Jacobs Bond, composer of American songs; Gutzon Borglum, sculptor; Harry Lauder, of the English stage; Margaret Sanger, pioneer in birth-control; Horace Fletcher, originator of "fletcherism"; W. W. Denslow, creator of the illustrations for *The Wizard of Oz*; David Bispham, operatic baritone; Marshall P. Wilder, diminutive humorist; Brand Whitlock, reformer and diplomat; John Burroughs, Hudson River naturalist; and Paul Bartlett, American sculptor, who came to East Aurora to supervise the erection of his heroic bronze statue of Michelangelo in the Roycroft grounds. Clarence Darrow, Judge Ben Lindsey, of juvenile-court fame, and William Marion Reedy, editor and author, were frequent guests at the hospitable Roycroft Inn. The English essayist and poet Richard Le Gallienne would remain at the inn for months at a time, and he and I often walked through the woods and lanes of Erie County. This was before automobiles, when it was a pleasure to tramp undisturbed over the narrow dirt roads without fear of being run down at any moment. Richard had a small cabin in the dense woods, and on an oak slab over the door of this rustic retreat I crudely carved a Latin verse at his request. At Mr. Hubbard's invitation, Booker T. Washington, the famous educator, came to East Aurora to talk about the work of the Tuskegee Institute. Mr. and Mrs. Hubbard requested that I lunch with them and their guest, and with humility I accepted. This was not the first time I had dined with a Negro, nor was it to be the last. A half-century later Elmer Adler and I were guests at the Dorothy Hall, Tuskegee Institute, and for three weeks we were closely associated with the professors, librarians, and students of this renowned Negro institution.

At infrequent intervals young people came to East Aurora, and they were usually asked to join the small group of the younger Roycroft workers. One of the most intellectual young men who came to vacation at the Roycroft Inn was eighteen-year-old Victor Robinson, who had been born in the Ukraine. Aside from my brother Phil, Victor was the most brilliant companion I had during my early years. He was interested in subjects entirely foreign to me, and for the first time I was told about the work of Sigmund Freud and Baron Richard von Krafft-Ebing, the eminent neurologist. Although still in his teens, Victor was of a serious nature, and he resented any levity or jocularity on my part; nevertheless, we remained stanch friends during our youthful years. On Sundays we would go on long walks, and occasionally on weekdays I would shirk my work and we would go to the country for an entire day. This gave him an opportunity to expound his theories, most of which were well beyond my comprehension. One sunny working-day we were resting under the shade of a haystack along an unfrequented lane, and Victor was reading to me from one of the volumes of *Studies in the Psychology of Sex,* by Havelock Ellis. My mind was far removed from anything Victor was reading, although he thought I was giving strict attention. I suddenly looked toward the lane and was startled—the soft dirt road had given no warning that Elbert Hubbard was riding by on Garnet, his brindle mare. I tried to keep from being seen. In the tower studio at the shop I had left undone the disagreeable task of lettering a series of soap-wrappers for a well-paying customer. I knew that Mr. Hubbard would be displeased if he saw me idle, and I was almost certain that he had passed without seeing me. When my weekly wage came, however, I found a yellow slip rolled among the dollar bills. On this slip Mr. Hubbard had scrawled: "Resting in the shade of a haystack when there is work to be done will never fatten a pay envelope."

After our final separation in East Aurora, about 1906, contact between Victor Robinson and me was completely lost. I had long forgotten my youthful companion and his scientific teachings, but he remembered me, for in June 1944 I received a copy of his scholarly six-hundred-page book *The History of Medicine,* the flyleaf of which bore the terse inscription: "For Dard Hunter in memory of East Aurora more than forty years ago, from the Author." Victor Robinson died in 1947 after compiling a dozen works on the science of medicine and editing the monumental thirty-volume treatise *Historia Medicinae.* Other Roycroft companions of mine were Sterling Lord and Peter Franck, bookbinders; Karl Kipp, craftsman in metal; Raymond Knott, decorative designer; and Jules Maurice Gaspard, who drew the portraits for Elbert Hubbard's *Little Journeys.* Mr. Gaspard, a French gentleman of mature years and wisdom, was my studio companion, and from him I was constantly seeking advice and instruction.

A short time after the second set of windows for the Roycroft Inn had been installed, I had word from Chillicothe that my father was seriously ill. He died three days after I reached home. My brother Phil's illness was constantly growing more distressing, and my mother decided that we should go to a warm, dry climate in the hope that the change would be beneficial. Within a few weeks we left for Mexico, taking up our residence in Cuernavaca, a small town about fifty-five miles south of Mexico City. We acquired an old house that had formerly been used as the granary of Hernán Cortés, the Spanish conqueror of Mexico. The building had been constructed during the sixteenth century, with walls six and eight feet thick. The great patio was protected by huge swinging gates with massive iron barriers and hinges. Cuernavaca was a delightful town at that time, with the beautiful Borda Gardens, where Maximilian and Charlotte had played at king and queen, at the top of the cobbled road from our house. I used to walk through the moss-covered, tile-lined paths undisturbed; flowers grew wild, rare trees and shrubs were overgrown with vines, and the lichen-encrusted statuary had toppled to the ground; multicolored birds were everywhere. These oldest formal gardens in the Western Hemisphere had been neglected for a hundred years, but to me they were beautiful in their melancholy desolation.

My sojourn in Cuernavaca was marred by only one unpleasant incident. The little railway station that served the town was a mile or more distant, and was reached by horse-drawn carriages or stagecoaches over a narrow, stony road. For hauling heavy freight from the station to the town a narrow-gauge track had been laid, over which four mules pulled unwieldy flatcars coupled together. One evening, after dark, when the cars heavily laden with oatcake were coming around the curve in the track not far from our house, I heard an unusual commotion and hurried to find the cause. At the steep, winding bend the brakes had failed and the overloaded cars had run down the mules, mangling one of them terribly. Three legs of the poor animal had been almost severed. Running to the house for a pistol, I immediately put the dumb creature out of his misery. Before the smoke from the shot had cleared, two policemen hurried me to the jail, over behind the cathedral. There I was told that the animal should have been permitted to die a natural death; I was guilty of a punishable crime. My plea that a lingering death was cruelty to animals had no weight with the hard-hearted Mexicans, whom I had more than once seen burn and beat their horses and strangle kittens with cord and throw their limp bodies into the streets. I was sentenced to jail for three days.

After more than a year in Mexico, I returned to East Aurora. During our magic-show days I had designed much of our advertising—programs, booklets, posters—and, having been practically born in a newspaper and job-printing plant, I knew the rudiments of printing. On my return, Mr. Hubbard wanted me to try my hand at book-designing, and with all confidence I made drawings for title pages and initial letters. He seemed pleased with my work, but he had no more knowledge of design than I. The head printer, Cy Rosen, also apparently took kindly to my attempts. There was one dissenter, however: Mr. Hawthorne, a thin, auburn-haired individual known locally as "Rupert the Red." This gentleman was one of the most influential workers in the shop, being the chief of the business office. I recall being present when a set of my drawings which had been approved by Mr. Hubbard was shown to him. He took one glance, screwed up his wrinkled red face, and, looking at me seriously, said: "Dard, I could chew brown paper and spit better designs than you could ever draw."

## AN AUTOBIOGRAPHY

One of my first commissions at the Roycroft Shop was a hand-lettered memorial book. Mr. Hubbard brought the manuscript to me and explained that the fifteen hundred words must be completed within a week. The calligraphy was to be executed in my most flourishing style on heavy Japanese vellum. The client, a widow of tender age, was staying at the Roycroft Inn, and the book was to be a memorial to the lady's late husband, who had passed away not long before, leaving a tidy sum of insurance to our fair client. I soon grew tired of doing the lettering and illumination; the touching eulogies to the deceased husband bored me and I was eager to complete the task. Apparently the young woman had been very devoted to her mate, and nothing was too good for him; she wanted the best, little realizing what a novice I was in lettering and design. I had the pages all lettered, with a title page bordered by funereal urns and drooping festoons, and, as I was also to design the binding, I procured a complete assortment of all the materials in the bindery—pigskin, calf, morocco, parchment, and one or two other kinds of leather. With these samples and the hand-illuminated text I went to the bereaved widow's room at the inn so that she might select the leather most suitable for the memorial book. She looked over the specimens, but appeared uninterested, saying they were not appropriate. I was gratified, however, that she thought well of my lettering and designing; she complimented me upon my work. The attractive widow said that she would supply the binding material herself, and, going to her trunk, she took out a rolled parcel. The book, she announced, was to be bound in the leather contained in the package. I unrolled the parcel, but was unable to determine the kind of leather it might be. I did not like to show my ignorance, but I finally asked what sort of animal had produced leather of such delicate grain. She told me that the material was the tanned skin from the back of her late husband; she wanted the book to be a true and fitting memorial to him. We bound the book in her husband's hide, and the young woman departed, a satisfied and contented customer. A few years later I read that she had again married. It has often occurred to me what a strange feeling the second husband must have had when he saw the memorial book lying on the drawing-room table and perhaps thought of himself as Volume II.

There were about four hundred employees in the Roycroft Shop, and the payroll was a real consideration. To retain this number of workers, it was essential that a large volume of sales be maintained. This led to the development of commercial printing of all types, and, with Mr. Hubbard's connections and wide acquaintance, the shop was kept humming. We did considerable work for one of the large oil companies, a corporation in bad repute at the time because it was regarded as a "trust." Hostile newspapers in editorial comment called the rich company an "octopus," implying that the corporation reached out and grasped smaller and weaker organizations, to the detriment of the common people. We were doing a serious booklet for this corporation, a "preachment" written by Elbert Hubbard at the expense of the wealthy oil concern in an attempt to soften any ill-will that the public might hold against the company. Mr. Hubbard asked me to design a two-color cover for this booklet.

Personally, I held no grudge against the huge oil company, but perhaps it was only natural that I had absorbed a little of the mass feeling of animosity toward the so-called "trust." I could not restrain myself, and when I made the design for the cover of the brochure I used a conventionalized octopus as the motif. After the lettering had been added I submitted the drawing to Mr. Hubbard, not fully realizing the gravity of the situation in which a big, well-paying order was at stake. Mr. Hubbard studied the design for fully a minute, and then he looked up at me with a dim suggestion of a smile. I thought I detected a slight twinkle in his brown eyes. I expected to be sent back to my studio to make another, and less pointed, design. But, instead, his only comment was: "That's great, the officials of the oil company are so imbued with their own righteousness they'll never recognize themselves." Thousands of copies of the booklet, with the disguised conventionalized octopus cover in brown and black, were printed and distributed, but the officials of the "trust" never knew what quiet satisfaction we had at their expense. Mr. Hubbard never again mentioned the cover to me, but I had a feeling that he felt my little joke was fully justified.

Elbert Hubbard would be out of place in the present-day world, although he no doubt had a marked influence upon his own time. Even though the books produced at the Roycroft Shop were bizarre and lacked taste and refinement, they were, nevertheless, a step in the right direction. These books were better made than most of the work done in this country at the time, and people who had never before thought of collecting books began assembling the Roycroft issues. Mr. Hubbard probably had more influence in the development of book-collecting than any other person of his generation. In later years, to be sure, the Roycroft books were cast aside as of no further value, but the collecting habit had been formed.

Each month at the Roycroft Shop we received a number of European art magazines, notably *Dekorative Kunst, Deutsches Kunst und Dekoration,* and *Dekorative Vorbilder,* and through these publications I became interested in the "modern" tendency in design. These magazines were a monthly inspiration, and many of the commercial designs I made during my early years at the shop show this influence. Through a study of the German and Austrian art publications I developed a strong desire to go to Vienna, where most of the secession movement had its origin. I wanted to study under the men whose work was shown in these publications.

My brother, Philip Courtney Hunter, passed away in Chillicothe, Ohio, early in the year 1908, at the age of twenty-seven. We had been closely associated, and I had long depended upon him for guidance. During the years when he was a magician and necromancer, Phil had become a student of spiritualism, and although he was thoroughly acquainted with the frauds practiced by professional exponents of this cult, he felt, nevertheless, that perhaps it was possible for the dead to communicate with the living. Phil was aware that he did not have a great while to live, and with considerable ceremony we entered into a secret agreement that whichever of us passed away first would make every effort to communicate with the other. Phil drew up an elaborate code involving mystic symbols and devices so that no practicing spiritualist could possibly deceive. After my brother's death, spiritualistic mediums were given every opportunity to act as mediators between us. At Lily Dale, the New York State spiritualist colony, and elsewhere I was more than once summoned to appear for "talks" with my deceased brother; also "spirit messages" on slates supposedly written by him were shown to me. But in every instance I was disappointed. The secret symbols devised by him for direct communication between us never appeared. After nearly fifty years I have given up all thought of after-death communication.

# ⊹ IV ⊹

E VERY summer well-known musicians and speakers came to East Aurora to take part in the educational programs sponsored by Elbert Hubbard and his Roycroft Shop. Each evening during the season, concerts were given in the Roycroft Chapel or in the salon of the inn, and there was constant difficulty in procuring a local pianist capable of accompanying the noted and temperamental singers. In New York City the Hubbards were fortunate in securing Helen Edith Cornell, a petite young lady who was not only a brilliant pianist and accompanist but also a person of much charm and intellect. Each summer Miss Cornell performed her duties at the Roycroft musicales with abundant talent; she continued to carry on her musical career in New York during the winter months.

In March 1908, when I was twenty-four, Miss Cornell and I were married, and we left immediately for Vienna, although we did not reach the Austrian capital for more than two months. We chose a roundabout route, going first to Italy, then on to Morocco and Algeria, and finally to Egypt, as I thought we might find papyrus growing along the Nile. In this we were disappointed, but later in Sicily we did find the *Cyperus papyrus* plant in a semi-wild state. We eventually reached Vienna. Mrs. Hunter wanted to continue her work with the famous teachers Fräulein Marie Prentner and Dr. Theodor Leschetizky. We found a comfortable old vine-covered stone house with a pleasant garden at 31 Chimanistrasse. For years it had been my ambition to enter the Imperial-Royal Austrian printing-school—K. K. Graphische Lehr- und Versuchsanstalt—operated in conjunction with the Royal Printing House of the Austrian government. Before I left East Aurora, I had been told that it would be impossible for an American to study in this renowned institute, as it was under the direct sponsorship of Emperor Franz Josef and the regulations were that only students who had been granted diplomas from industrial schools under their own governments were eligible. Inasmuch as the United States government operated no schools of art or industry, it was almost certain that I could not be admitted to the Viennese school of printing. Not to be dismayed, however, I had an interview with the Herr Direktor, Dr. Eder, K. K. Hofrat. The austere Direktor explained the requirements of the institute and said emphatically that my entrance was out of the question because I did not have a diploma from a school under the direct jurisdiction of my own government. Although it was not my privilege to enter the institute, many other opportunities for study and observation were open to me.

During the summer months we lived in Gmunden in the Salzkammergut, where with friends we rented the Schloss Ort, a castle built in the early sixteenth century, on the lake at the foot of the Traunstein. We occupied the apartments that had been used by Maria Theresa, wife of Emperor Francis I. The castle, like so many of the older buildings of Austria, was in the Turkish style, with great bulbous towers covered with copper that through the years had assumed a beautiful green tone. The thick walls, the heavily barred windows, and the massive entrance gates gave the structure a mediaeval appearance. On the walls of the great inner court were hung carvings of coatsof-arms and crests, and a balcony extended around the inner walls of the second floor approached by a wide stairway. In the nineteenth century the castle had been the home of Prince Johann Ort, nephew of Franz Josef. This frail young Prince of the ancient house of the hapless Hapsburgs had fled his castle to marry a commoner. At the time of his sudden departure from Gmunden it was thought he had made his way to South America, but he never returned to Schloss Ort.

During our stay one of the servants of the young Prince remained in the castle. This feeble gentleman, tall and angular, shuffled about the hallowed rooms in loose-fitting slippers; he opened closets to show us the tarnished medals and faded uniforms of his princely master, whom he always expected to return. One vaulted basement room of the schloss was cluttered with armor and ancient weapons; chests of rusting guns and swords lined the room; moulding saddles and harness hung from brackets around the walls. An underground arched passageway led from the castle to the old chapel built in the middle of the lake. Prince Johann Ort has long since departed this earth, and during the First World War the castle was stripped of its knightly paraphernalia and the decaying personal belongings of the unhappy Prince. In later years the castle was renovated and the old buildings were used for educational purposes.

After more than a year in Austria we returned to the Roycroft Shop, where I made many designs in the modern Viennese manner. My inability to enter the Austrian royal school of printing was a genuine disappointment, and I was downcast over the defeat I had encountered. I felt that the rule of the institute in insisting upon a diploma from a government school of one's own country was a discrimination against me as an American. I was determined to enter the Austrian school, even though there were no industrial schools under the United

States government. I would create an imaginary school and make my own diploma! With a large sheet of genuine parchment and an assortment of gold seals and silk ribbons, I made a false diploma purporting to be from an American government-sponsored school. The completed diploma had a genuinely official appearance, and I hoped that when I eventually showed the counterfeit masterpiece to the gloomy old Herr Direktor he would give in and permit me to enroll.

After about six months in East Aurora we returned to Vienna. The old vine-covered house in Chimanistrasse had been demolished, so we leased an apartment over a fresh-smelling bakery at 16 Gymnasiumstrasse, not far from our previous house. I was eager to go to the Graphische Lehr- und Versuchs-anstalt and present my forged diploma. I was hoping that the austere Herr Direktor, Dr. Eder, was no longer there, but my hope was not fulfilled. As I entered the dismal office in Bahnhofstrasse, there sat the same Herr Direktor with the same flowing red beard, ponderous mustaches, and heavy eyebrows. He gave no intimation as to whether or not he remembered me. I unrolled the spurious diploma before him. I knew he could not decipher the wording, for I had learned by my previous interview that this pompous Direktor knew no English, but I was well aware that to an Austrian the gold seals and ribbons would be impressive. Dr. Eder evidently wished to convince me that he understood the contents of the document, so he studied it for a few minutes, then reached for his pen and filled out a blank qualifying me for entrance.

My days in the Viennese school were both pleasant and profitable. The professors did all they could to help with my work, as my knowledge of the German language was limited. It was my privilege to study with Dr. Rudolph von Larisch, the renowned calligrapher, probably the most scholarly professor

48

of the art of lettering in Europe. Also I studied with men whose work appeared in the art magazines I had long admired and imitated. I was graduated from the institute in 1911, my diploma being signed by the old Herr Direktor himself.

At the time of our two sojourns in Vienna, the city was the most beautiful and romantic in all Europe, and we were delighted with the many museums, art exhibitions, and concerts. Our house was not a great distance from the modest home of Katharina Schratt, the plump elderly actress, formerly of Vienna's Burgtheater, whom Franz Josef visited almost every morning for breakfast. I have often seen the rigid old Emperor, in immaculate gray uniform, enter the house of this erstwhile dancer who for so many years was his companion, confidante, and adviser. She died in Vienna a number of years ago at the age of eighty-seven. My real thrill at being near royalty came, however, at the sixtieth jubilee of Franz Josef's reign in 1908, when I sauntered alongside the horse-drawn carriage in which Franz Josef, Emperor of Austria and King of Hungary; Edward VII, King of England; Albert, King of the Belgians; and Wilhelm II, Kaiser of Germany, were riding in unconventional fashion.

After completing our work in Vienna, we left for London, where I was to seek my fortune as a commercial designer. I had not only specimens of the work I had executed for Elbert Hubbard but also several books that I had designed for a Vienna publisher. Perhaps the most original was an overelaborate edition of *Salome*. Reproductions of its title page later appeared in German and Italian graphic-arts magazines. In Vienna I had also made several designs for permanent mosaic and stained-glass work which had been put to use, the former in a rathskeller. Photographs of the large objects and reproductions of the printed material were classified and mounted, and the collection was put in a large portfolio that was so bulky I could scarcely carry it.

In London we were fortunate in finding a single house at 32 Lexham Gardens, Kensington, adjacent to the Cromwell Road. The location was especially desirable, as we were close to the Victoria and Albert Museum and the old Science Museum, institutions that were materially to influence my future. The London of 1911–12 was a vastly different city from postwar London; I was fascinated by the bookshops with their pleasant disorder, by the museums, the secluded courts and alleyways, and the ancient smoke-covered buildings, many of which have since given way to so-called "developments." We had been settled in peaceful Lexham Gardens only a few days when, seized with ambition, I gathered together the bulging portfolio and went to the City in quest of a job. At that time there were no restrictions on aliens working in England; in fact, not even a passport was required.

In London it was the custom for designers of commercial printing and advertising to work together in a central studio, a manager employing the artists and giving each worker a weekly salary. A number of studios were in the City, each employing from three to four dozen men, every worker a specialist in his particular field—newspaper and magazine advertising, department-store catalogues, book-illustration, perfumery, wine, beer, and cigar lists and labels. My first call was the Carlton Studio, 195 Strand.[1] I unfolded the portfolio of my designs before the dignified manager, and it was obvious that he was surprised by the variety of material. He said a place could be found for me, as they were in need of a designer who would work in the modern Viennese manner. I

[1] The building at 195 Strand was later acquired by the publishers of *The Illustrated London News,* and is now known as Ingram House.

was to receive five guineas a week. I had expected to be paid in pounds, but I was told that artists and professional workers always received their wages in guineas. The extra five shillings were welcome, as they would pay my fare to and from Lexham Gardens. A small corner room with one window was assigned to me, and I began work, my first commission being a catalogue cover for the London department store of Robinson and Cleaver. My studio was heated by a shell-shaped soft-coal grate. The light from the lone window was shut off by a huge column that formed part of the architectual façade of the building. The grate smoked so badly and emitted such dense sulphur fumes that I could scarcely breathe, and with the stone column shutting out the light I had to draw by artificial light throughout the day. Practically all of my designing was for catalogues for London shops and their branches in the colonies. My pay came regularly each Saturday, five shiny gold sovereigns and the extra five shilling pieces.

While working in the Carlton Studio I had little opportunity for any other study, and I needed time to visit museums and exhibitions. After about three months I gave up my work in the studio in the Strand; I could endure the smoky fireplace and the lack of air no longer, although the work was to my liking and the studio companions were agreeable. My dismal room was between the studios of Garth Jones and Harold Nelson, well-known English book-designers of that day. The guineas saved from my wages were sufficient to pay our way in London for some time to come, so I gave up thought of further studio work. My time was now almost wholly devoted to the old Science Museum, then housed in a temporary wooden building. There I saw for the first time a pair of moulds for forming handmade paper; and also was able for the first time to examine the punches, matrices, and hand moulds that in previous centuries had been used in making type. These appliances interested me profoundly. The paper-making moulds had been made by T. J. Marshall and Company, Stoke Newington, North London, a firm established in 1792. The type-punches and type-making appliances had been presented to the museum by the firm of H. W. Caslon, established in 1723. Day after day I returned to the Science Museum to study the papermaking moulds and the type-making appliances, methods of making paper and type which had long been obsolete in America. My research in the Science Museum and in the Library of the British Museum gave me a deep interest in old papermaking, watermarking, and type-founding.

The gold sovereigns that I had earned at the Carlton Studio were running low, even though our total living expense in Lexham Gardens was only two pounds, ten shillings a week. I again gathered together my portfolio and went to the City in search of employment. I did not wish to resume work in the Carlton Studio, as the fogs were still enveloping London and I could not bear to return to the small lightless room with the smoky fire-pot. I went to the Norfolk Studio in Arundel Street, between the Strand and Temple underground stations. Again I was taken on as a designer. Here I continued work in designing advertising for newspapers, magazines, and billboards, as well as booklets and catalogues for London and provincial business houses. Summer was approaching, and I wanted to go to the country, but Messrs. Taylor and Smith, the proprietors of the Norfolk Studio, kept me diligently at my tasks. They paid an additional guinea each week above the wage I had received from the studio-manager in the Strand.

King Edward VII had died in 1910, and the coronation of George V was to be celebrated. My friend Sterling Lord, whom I had known at the Roycroft Shop, was working in a London bookbindery, and as we both dreaded vast crowds we decided to walk through Wales during the coronation ceremonies and escape the congestion of London. Early one rainy morning, with luggage swung upon our backs, we started out through the fresh green countryside, walking to Bath, Somerset, and then into Wales, passing through Stroud, Gloucester, Hereford, Radnor, Oswestry, Wrexham, and on to Chester. Along the route we took part in the prolonged village coronation ceremonies. After several weeks, the coronation over, we returned to London and resumed our regular work, my companion in the old Zaehnsdorf bookbindery and I back at my drawing-board in the Norfolk Studio.

During my term of employment the Norfolk Studio moved to larger quarters in an eighteenth-century building in ancient Racquet Court, Fleet Street, near Ludgate Hill. The studio was entered through a narrow stone-flagged court from bustling Fleet Street. To the right of the entranceway were old wine cellars, and to the left, three steps down, was a moneylender's shop with the ominous sign on the door "Watch Your Step." To reach the studio we walked up a curved wooden stairway, then went through a narrow passage to the third-floor drafting-room. Autumn came on with fogs more dense than I had experienced, and I continued to be tormented by soft-coal smoke, as the only heat in the low-ceilinged studio was from a small center fireplace. For days at a time the thick yellow fog penetrated through the closed windows so that I could barely see the drawing-board before me. I arranged my work hours from nine in the morning until two in the afternoon to permit more time for study. I visited the shop in Stoke Newington, North London, where the moulds for making paper by hand which I had seen exhibited in the Science Museum had been made. In the musty office of this eighteenth-century concern I met Dudley Marshall, the grandson of the original founder of the firm. It was in this building, known as Campbell House, that the first "dandy-roll" for watermarking machine-made paper had been conceived in 1828 by Mr. Marshall's ancestor. Dudley Marshall, a portly old gentleman, was interested in my desire to learn about the making of paper by hand and did everything he could to assist me. Each afternoon, my work finished at the studio, found me at the mould-making shop, where I received instruction in the construction of papermaking moulds and in watermarking from elderly Mr. Thompson, a talented mechanic whose life had been devoted to making equipment for papermakers. A small vat, beater, and other appliances for testing hand moulds were fixtures in the vaulted basement of the old building, and in this dark, damp cellar I had my first experience in making paper by hand.

After the death of King Edward, the "dandy-roll" that had been used for watermarking the British stamps was adapted to the reign of the new sovereign, George V. In the watermarking of postage stamps the "dandy-roll" was almost completely covered with small letters formed in wire, each individual mark impressing the paper in the location where the stamp would eventually be printed. The stamps during the period of Edward VII had been watermarked especially for his reign, and these wires had to be removed and the wire lettering "G R" substituted. The long brass roll was transferred from the government paper mill to the workshop in Stoke Newington, and as I was a part-time apprentice I assisted with the work of making the necessary changes on the roll. I was proud that I was having at least a minor part in the making of the stamps for the new reign.

My work continued in the Norfolk Studio in the mornings and in the mould-maker's shop in the afternoons. At night I attended classes in the now demolished Finsbury Technical College. In this institute I studied toolmaking with Alexander Fisher, who was known for his superb work in cloisonné enamel. On Saturdays I went to the bookshops—the cheap stalls in Charing Cross Road and Shaftesbury Avenue, the book barrows in Farrington Road, and the old-established antiquarian stores throughout the City. Here my real zest for book-collecting began, and I purchased many old and rare items relating to papermaking, typefounding, and printing.

My work at the Norfolk Studio increased in scope, but I had no illusions regarding the importance of the work I was doing. In 1912 I designed the catalogues for the Napier and Siddley-Deasey automobiles, both elaborate brochures printed in several colors. This same year the designs for *Penrose's Pictorial Annual* were made by Norfolk Studio employees, and I drew the cover, title page, initials, and ornaments for this graphic-arts annual. During this period I had many conferences with William Gamble, the editor of this yearly publication, whose unceasing labors in the field of British typography have long been recognized.

There were more than thirty commercial artists working in the Norfolk Studio, and never before had I heard so many schemes for remodeling the world. There were men from England, Scotland, Ireland, South Africa, New Zealand, Australia, and Canada. I was the only American.

Although my work at the studio was essentially ephemeral,

I was not unmindful of the fine work of the private presses in and near London. On one of my trips to Hammersmith I became confused in the direction and stepped into a real-estate office to inquire the way to Kelmscott House. I was only a few blocks from the house where the most famous modern edition of Chaucer had been printed, but the irregular streets had misled me. Upon inquiring the way to the old workshop of William Morris, I was surprised to be told by the young real-estate agent that he did not know where William Morris had lived. He had never heard of Morris, and asked me if he had previously been the proprietor of a low roominghouse for mendicants.

The Essex House Press, Mile End Road, had closed a year before my coming, but I was welcomed in the small two-story house at 15 Upper Mall occupied by T. J. Cobden-Sanderson's Doves Press. During my several calls, two men and a woman were at work printing a bibliography of the Doves Press books. Cobden-Sanderson himself was always away from London, usually basking in the Italian sun, far from types, paper, ink, and press. I went often to the Eragny Press and was delighted with the delicately colored illustrations used in the books printed by Lucien Pissarro, the son of Camille Pissarro, the French impressionist. Lucien Pissarro and his plump wife Ester were then printing *La Charrue d'Erable,* by Emile Moselly, in an edition of 118 copies. Lucien Pissarro died in 1944 at the age of eighty-one.

The work of the English private presses was of keen interest to me, and I felt I should like to attempt something of the kind myself. I was convinced, however, that simply purchasing type from a commercial foundry and buying paper from a paper mill left too many of the vital steps of making books in the hands of disinterested workmen. It was my desire to have my own private press, but I wanted my work to be individual and personal, without reliance upon outside help from the typefounder or papermaker. I would return to America and attempt to make books by hand completely by my own labor—paper, type, printing.

# V

I N 1913 we were back in America. Our one thought was to find a property in the country where I could carry on the work in contemplation—the making of paper by hand, the cutting and casting of type by the early hand methods, and the hand printing of books. After no little search we found an old fruit farm near Marlborough-on-Hudson, Ulster County, New York. This farm consisted of about forty acres of rolling land, many fine trees, a small brook with an eight-foot stone dam, and a picturesque old stone-and-brick house. The property had considerable historical interest, having been an early Indian trading-post, and as this phase of its history has been dealt with authoritatively by Leon Huhner in his work *Daniel Gómez, A Pioneer Merchant of Early New York* (published by the American Jewish Historical Society, Vol. XLI, No. 2, December 1951), I can do no better than quote Mr. Huhner:

> In the records of Ulster County there appear a number of tax lists as well as a census of freeholders between 1717 and 1729. In the list for 1717–1718, mention is made of a "Mr. Gómez" while on subsequent lists of freeholders between 1724 and 1729, appears the name of "Gómez the Jew." The first name is not given in either case, and it does not appear whether the reference is to Lewis Gómez or Daniel Gómez. The main object of

Lewis Gómez, and probably his son Daniel, in acquiring the lands in Ulster County was primarily to develop an extensive trade with the Indians. . . . Between 1717 and 1720, "Gómez the Jew" built a massive stone house in the hollow, close to the main Indian trail leading across the mountains to the *Dans Kammer,* an Indian ceremonial ground. Near the house was a spring, which from time immemorial, was a favorite stopping place for the Indians. . . . In planning the structure Gómez naturally recognized the fact that his house must not be a station for barter merely, but it must be of such strength as to possess all the characteristics of a fort. He realized that the walls might have to defy attacks of enemies, and that the building must be commodious enough to form a huge vault for the merchandise he would bring hither, and for the furs for which it would be exchanged. The house, when finally completed, was therefore a veritable stronghold, the real type of stone blockhouse of the period. The house faces south, and in the time of Gómez, was probably invisible from almost any point of the hills surrounding. We need not use our imagination, however, to picture the fort which "Gómez the Jew" had constructed. Curiously enough it has been preserved to our own day, and now, after almost two and a half centuries, it still stands as strong and as massive as the day it was completed. The walls are about two feet thick in the front and about three feet thick in the back. To this lonely fort, known in colonial times as "the Jew's house," Gómez and his assistants would come and meet the groups of Indians on their way to the *Dans Kammer.* Here they bartered and obtained furs in exchange for hatchets, knives, and trinkets they had brought. Past the old house there runs a stream which continues its course for a short distance through the township of Newburgh, and joins the Hudson in the town of Marlborough. This brook is still known as "Jew's Creek."

In 1772 the Gómez stone blockhouse became the property of Wolfert Acker, a descendant of that Wolfert whom Washington Irving immortalized in "Wolfert's Roost." Acker added a second story, using bricks made on the estate. This property, which I purchased in the summer of 1913, was situated about sixty-five miles north of New York on the west bank of the Hudson River. In earlier years there had been a flour mill on the stream, but of this building nothing remained. Below the dam in Jew's Creek I constructed a small, half-timbered paper mill resembling a Devonshire cottage, using old oak beams and the handmade brick that had been discarded when the second story was added to the stone blockhouse by Acker's slaves. The straw used in thatching the mill was grown on our own land; we sowed the rye seed and brought in the harvest. The thatching of the paper mill was done by the Ward brothers, two Kentish men who worked on our Marlborough fruit farm during part of our nine-year residence.

Although we carried on fruit farming along with the publishing venture, only a few records of our farming activities remain: a notebook dated July 1915 lists that we grew and shipped to New York City: 1,230 quarts of currants, 2,678 pints of red raspberries, and 1,780 quarts of gooseberries, a goodly number of units to be picked in the early morning hours before the departure of the daily fruit train bound for the New York markets. There, if the health inspectors found a few wilted berries in any of the individual boxes, the entire crate was thrown into the river as being unfit for use. Several times we made shipments of fruit to New York and received nothing in return save a bill for the transportation. Our fruit-growing venture was not monetarily successful, although what we produced was the finest.

The power for the paper mill was furnished by Jew's Creek. The water wheel was constructed of cypress and pine by Joseph Kniffin, a local millwright, who met his death a few years later in the iron cogs of the great water wheel in the near-by Marlborough grist mill. The building of a water wheel required unusual skill, and although Mr. Kniffin was unschooled in mathematics he was able to construct the eight-foot wheel so that it was perfectly balanced. The wheel made for my paper mill developed about five horsepower, which was sufficient to actuate the small beater or "Hollander" used in macerating the rags to be made into paper. Aside from the beater, which held about twenty pounds of dry linen and cotton rags, all other appliances had been made in the mill —dipping-vat, rag-duster and -cutter, rag-boiler, and pressure press; I had also lined the iron tub of the beater with sheet copper to prevent rust from discoloring the paper. This equipment made up a complete handmade paper mill, the various utensils approximating the experimental appliances I had used in the mould-maker's shop in Stoke Newington, London, where I first made paper by hand.

The process of making paper, like that of weaving, is extremely simple and natural. In many ways these two crafts are closely allied. The most elementary type of weaving consists of intertwining at right angles two sets of threads spun from plant fibers, thus forming a fabric suitable for clothing or other domestic purposes. In making paper the same sort of plant fibers are macerated and then matted or felted together in thin sheets to form a lightweight flexible substance suitable for writing and printing. The principal implement of the weaver is the loom; the chief tool of the papermaker is the mould.

The material from which paper is made may be almost any form of fibrous vegetation: flax, cotton, hemp, jute, bamboo, straw, grass, and the bark and wood of plants, shrubs, and trees, all of which contain cellulose. For papermaking these fibers may be used separately or in combination, but each individual substance or combination produces paper with distinguishable characteristics.

The fundamental principle of forming sheets of paper is elementary: vegetable matter is beaten in water until the particles of cellulose are freed and separated into individual units or fibers. The next step is to place great masses of the minute fibers in a quantity of water in a vat. When the water is agitated, the fibers naturally rise to the water's surface, like filmy milkweed seeds floating on a brook. Then a layer of the fibers must be lifted from the water. This is accomplished by dipping a porous screen, called a mould, into the vat. The mould is brought up under the floating fibers, which mat in a tangled formation upon the flat face of the mould. The surplus water naturally drains through the interstices of the mould. After the thin layer of matted fiber dries, it is a sheet of paper.

During the warm months, after the fruit had been picked, I ran the mill and made numerous experiments in papermaking and watermarking, but with the limited amount of water in the millpond it was difficult to beat the new rags sufficiently to assure evenly felted sheets of paper. After a heavy summer rain, I would take advantage of the abundant water, which rose in Williams Falls a mile or more distant, flowing down the brook through the pasture and fruit-growing lands of our neighbors, each little spring and tributary adding its trickle to the stream, and at last flowed over my wooden water wheel and turned the small beater that macerated the rags. When there was a goodly supply of water, the capacity of the mill was about 150 sheets of paper a day, each sheet being formed upon moulds made while I was working in the eighteenth-century shop in Stoke Newington.

The paper-moulds measured 16 by 23 inches, a convenient size for book-printing, making pleasing proportions for both folio and quarto pages. I had no helpers in the paper mill. The cutting, dusting, and boiling of the rags was my task, and the beating of the boiled rags also fell to me, and when the stock was finally ready, after days of maceration, I formed the individual sheets of paper in the moulds. Each moist sheet was couched upon woolen felting, and lastly the pile of paper and felts, called a "post," was pressed in the cumbersome oak-and-iron press. The screw of the press was turned by a heavy steel bar that reached halfway across the mill. The expelling of the water from the newly formed paper was real labor, and often I had to call upon Jim Gallagher, who cultivated the rows of fruit bushes, to assist in screwing down the press. After much of the water had been pressed from the "post," the paper was removed sheet by sheet from the felts. We would press the sheets again, one upon another, and finally hang the paper to dry in the attic of the main house across the road.

Now that I had the equipment for making paper, I wanted to try a forbidden experiment. I had long been fascinated by the work of counterfeiters, especially in the forging of paper money. I wondered if I could make paper in imitation of that used in printing the United States currency so that I could at least deceive myself. This was during the time of large bills, and I took a few genuine uncirculated notes over to the mill and proceeded to try to duplicate the paper. This I found quite easily accomplished, and from all outward appearance the legitimate paper and my imitation were identical, even to the red and blue silk threads used in the government paper at that time. I made a full sheet of the spurious paper and cut the sheet into regulation banknote size. I then placed a few pieces of my paper with several genuine bills in my pocket. I wanted to test the "feel" of the paper with my hand without seeing it. I found myself at a loss to distinguish one piece from the other; I was entirely confused as to which paper was genuine and which I had made. I carried the paper around for a few hours as I attended the daily chores, and then burned all that I had made. It would have been embarrassing had a government inspector arrived that day; one had visited me previously. When I told my wife about the "experiment," she was alarmed and I promised never again to attempt anything so foolhardy. This was my first and last endeavor at the duplication of money paper, although I believe I could have counterfeited the currency of any government.

In dry weather when there was insufficient water to turn the mill wheel, and during the winter months when the paper mill was covered with ice and snow, I continued to work on the fount of type commenced in 1912. My type-foundry was in a room over the kitchen of the old brick-and-stone house; from the windows I could look across the dirt lane to the millpond and the half-timbered, thatched paper mill. In making type by hand in the manner of the early centuries of printing, each letter had to be cut, backward, in the end of a steel bar. The steel letter-punch, after being tempered, or hardened, by gradual heating and cooling, was driven into a bar of copper by a few blows of a heavy hammer. This indentation in the copper formed a matrix. After the matrix had been filed for correct levelness and depth, it was placed in a hand mould and the type was cast, each piece an individual unit.

The most comprehensive textbook on early type-founding was Joseph Moxon's *Mechanick Exercises: Or, the Doctrine of Handy-Works, Applied to the Art of Printing,* issued in London in 1683. From a study of this first English treatise on letter-founding, I was able to make many of the tools used in cutting the punches and in striking and justifying the matrices. The 18-point mould used in casting the types was made in my own shop, and was patterned after an eighteenth-century hand mould of different size that had been given to me by the Caslon firm during my studio days in London. The metal for the type—lead, tin, antimony, copper, and iron, Moxon's formula—was melted in a coal stove that also supplied the heat for the workroom. These methods of making type were obsolete, but I wished to emulate the fifteenth- and sixteenth-century type-founders, just as I was using the early methods of making paper.

In 1915, after working several years on the type and two years in the paper mill, I was ready to print a book. An old Washington hand press had been purchased and set up in the workshop along with the type-foundry. This press, ornamented with gilt medallions of Washington and Franklin, was never satisfactory, and I printed only two small books upon it. These books, made for the Chicago Society of Etchers, were issued in 1915 and 1917, respectively, and the handmade type was used for the first time, along with the paper that had been made in the water-power mill across the lane. I had no end of difficulty in printing these books; the entire experiment was one that had never before been tried, and it was little wonder that the result was not encouraging. I was deeply disappointed in these embryo attempts, and I thought seriously of abandoning the whole plan of making books entirely unassisted.

About this time I received a letter from Ruel P. Tolman, Curator of Graphic Arts at the Smithsonian Institution, inquiring about the making of type by hand. Mr. Tolman's interest in my struggles as a type-founder eventually led the institution in Washington to acquire the letter-punches, matrices, mould, and tools that had been used in making the type. Before relinquishing the equipment, however, I cast sufficient type for any printing I thought might be undertaken in the future.

I was constantly under the influence of William Morris and his Kelmscott Press, although his problems and procedures were far removed from my own. William Morris had had the best talent of England at his command. The firm of Joseph Batchelor, of Little Chart, Kent, an old mill with a hundred years of papermaking traditions, had manufactured the paper for the Kelmscott books. Edward Prince, an experienced letter-cutter, had made the punches for the Morris type, and it had been cast in a commercial foundry. The typesetting and presswork had been done by the most talented artisans to be found in Britain. The entire production of the Kelmscott Press was under the direction of Emery Walker, a craftsman of unusual ability. If I made my own paper and type with inadequate equipment and limited talent, how could I expect to produce fine books?

While working in the water-power mill near Marlborough-on-Hudson I developed an intense interest in the history and technique of early papermaking, an interest to which my life would be devoted. I resolved that should I print books in the future the subjects would be on some phase of papermaking, and I have never deviated from this resolution.

In May 1915, during our residence in Marlborough, we were shocked to read in the New York newspapers of the sinking of the *Lusitania* in the Irish Sea, with the loss of our former employers and associates, Elbert and Alice Hubbard. On the 12th of May, five days after the ship had been torpedoed by a German submarine, I received a letter from Edward J. Shay, business manager of the Roycroft Shop. He preferred to be known as "Felix Shay," and under this name he later wrote the well-circulated book *Elbert Hubbard of East Aurora,* published in 1926. The letter from Felix read:

> Hubbard and Alice are dead. I assume that you can't believe it any more than I can believe. Always there was so much by-play that I think the whole business is only a trick, and that Hubbard will be coming down the street presently with an epigram on his lips to explain away a part of it. There will be a memorial service here on July fourth and I hope you can come; I would like to have a talk with you along a good many lines. Today the wills are to be opened and nothing is definite until they are opened. But, I know it is the desire of everyone here to go on with the work. . . . By July fourth we can say whether the Roycroft Shop will go on and grow, whether it will be torn apart by litigation, or whether it is to be drooled out to the suffragettes. What you see in the New York papers is all that we know; there is nothing that I can say further about Elbert and Alice.

In the old stone-and-brick house across the road from the thatched paper mill, our first child was born in 1917. His mother insisted that he be named Dard, although I wished him to bear the name Cornell, after his mother's family. We compromised, and he was called Dard. In 1919 our second son was born, and on this occasion my wishes were fulfilled, for this boy was given the name Cornell Choate, after Alonzo Cornell and Amanda Choate, his mother's grandparents.

Owing to the insurmountable living problems connected with the old stone blockhouse, the beginning of the First World War, and, incidentally, the arrival of Dard Junior, we thought it best to dispose of the Hudson River property. In 1917 the fruit farm was unknowingly sold to a representative of the Russian government and used as a school for children of all races. The educational experiment was apparently unsuccessful, for within a short time the property was again offered for sale. In the meantime we moved to Chillicothe, Ohio, where our long-established family newspaper and printing-business was situated. Here we acquired the deserted "Mountain House," a castle-like stone-and-brick structure that had been built by a German political refugee in 1851. In this secluded hilltop building of mongrel Gothic architecture I planned to carry on my work.

It was our Marlborough fruit farm that first attracted Frederic W. Goudy, the noted type-designer, to the Hudson River Valley. Eight years after our departure from the old Gómez blockhouse I received a letter from Goudy which gave an intimate insight into his search for a country place that finally resulted in his purchase of the Mercy Buckley property, which he named "Deepdeen." The letter, dated July 8, 1923, reads:

. . . Last fall my wife and I decided that Forest Hills was becoming too "snobbish" for mere working people and we began casting about for a place that would combine working facilities and picturesqueness if possible. We became interested in the description of a property offered by a woman living in Greenwich Village. As I surmised from the reading of the advertisement it was the place where you carried on your work, and I arranged to go up and look it over. We found it delightful, but decided that the mill itself would hardly be large enough for the things we planned and the house too hard to heat since we must have an all-year place. We were on our way to Kingston where a former neighbor in Forest Hills lived and while there talked of what we had been seeing. His foreman suggested that we might get the Mercy Buckley place. We stopped there on our way back and were so charmed with the grounds and the old mill that we made overtures, not at first successful, but to make the story short we took title January second and expected to get up there in April or May, but a double abdominal operation in February changed our plans somewhat and we didn't sell our Forest Hills property as quickly as we had hoped, so didn't get up until June first—our 26th wedding anniversary was the second and we were sentimental enough to want to start on that day. In the meantime weeds had grown up and we are having all we can do to get the place into presentable shape. Workmen are fixing up the old mill—the sill and studding had rotted away badly on the north side, but when we get a stove installed and some skylights it is going to make a delightful place in which to work. We are trying to make as few changes as possible—none except in interest of comfort and to prevent further decay. The fine flavor of romance that hangs about your old place made it hard for us to give up the thought of acquiring it, but as the Mercy Buckley property is a part also of the original tract to which that belonged, any historical facts relating to your old place belong, indirectly, in a way to this. . . . I hope yet to produce a good type, not so much for myself as for the craft. I wish I could feel that I have still years to attempt punches, etc. as you did, but at 58— At least my intentions are good and sincere. Bruce Rogers was quite interested in your old "Mill House"; it can be purchased, I think, for little more than you sold it for.

The house and old textile mill that were purchased by Fred and Bertha Goudy were situated about a quarter-mile down the country road from our old fruit farm, on Jew's Creek, the brook that had turned the water wheel for my little paper mill.

In 1920, shortly after the close of the First World War, I again went to Europe, where I visited the handmade-paper mills. The making of paper by hand continued to fascinate me, and as time went on I became more and more absorbed in the old methods and in the history of the mills. While in London, I was told of a two-vat handmade-paper mill near Salisbury which was being dismantled to make room for a modern tannery. But no one could give the exact location of the mill. I immediately left for Salisbury, and after inquiry I found that the abandoned paper mill was in the village of Downton, directly south of Salisbury, on the road leading through Britford and Dodenham, about ten miles from the cathedral city. I walked to Downton and found elderly Mark Palmer, who had recently sold his paper mill to the tannery concern. The old handmade-paper equipment was being dismembered; I had reached the scene just in time to prevent the destruction of the vats, lifting-boxes, and knotters, all necessary appliances for making paper by hand and not easily acquired. I arranged with Mr. Palmer to purchase the equipment that had been in use in the Downton mill for over a hundred years, and the numerous pieces were packed and carted to Southampton, where the eighteen or twenty tons of antique machinery were put on board the *Berengaria* for shipment to America. It was my intention to make use of this equipment upon my return, but as a suitable property for the establishment of a commercial handmade-paper mill could not then be found, the old appliances were stored away for future use.

In the meantime my "Mountain House Press," Chillicothe, printed and published a quarto-size book entitled *Old Paper-making,* issued in 1923 in an edition of 200 copies. This book had a frontispiece by Ralph M. Pearson of the Marlborough mill; 112 pages; 57 illustrations in black and white and 25 in color; 9 specimens of paper. The books were bound by Charles Youngers, and sold for twenty-five dollars a copy. This was my first venture in printing one of my own compilations on the subject of papermaking. The demand for copies of the book astonished me. The edition was too small to fill the orders that came from many parts of the world; articles about the book appeared in a number of languages in publications from a dozen countries. The reception of *Old Paper-making* encouraged me to compile another book, and in 1925 *The Literature of Papermaking—1390–1800* was issued in an edition of 180 copies. This book was in folio with 48 pages; 22 illustrations and 24 reproductions of old title pages. The price was thirty dollars a copy.

When halfway through the printing of this edition, I had a distressing experience. Years before, when I was building the small paper mill in Marlborough, I had been struck in the left eye by a flying spike, but little was thought of the incident at the time. The shock had apparently been more severe than I realized, although it was not until ten years after the accident that a hemorrhage in the eye reduced it to total blindness. Since 1925, therefore, I have done my work with less than half normal vision. I have found, however, that being able to see with but one eye may be an advantage, as I am convinced that my sight is more acute than that of many of my friends blessed with two normal eyes.

In producing the first two papermaking books, I regarded the compilation of the text as the easiest step in the entire procedure. The real labor was the physical making of the books. The punch-cutting, matrix-adjusting, and hand casting of the type had required several years of work, and I had to overcome hardships in presswork which would not be encountered in using type from the commercial foundry. The printing was done on handmade paper, which had to be printed damp to assure the results that I hoped to attain. Only a worker who has been through the complete process of book-production by the old hand methods and without the proper tools could have a genuine appreciation of the tedious and arduous work involved. The writing of the text was pleasant diversion, and many times I envied authors who simply had to write their books without any thought of having to make the volumes.

# ⚜ VI ⚜

THE books issued in 1923 and 1925 had dealt with early European papermaking, the material having been gathered in England and on the Continent and from my own library. These books had been reasonably successful—at least each edition was sold at substantial prices without effort. I was encouraged. It was my desire to continue the writing and printing of books dealing with handmade paper. But, if I was to continue to write only on such an obscure subject, where could original material be found? I decided that I would go to out-of-the-way places seeking firsthand information: I would never be satisfied to write of any phase of papermaking without first having seen the work being done in the locality of its origin. After gathering the material for writing and illustrating a book, I would return to America and print each edition myself, as with the first two papermaking volumes.

For years I had been interested in the primitive bark papers of the South Sea Islands, and a few foreign-language articles dealing with mulberry-bark *tapa* were in my library. My enthusiasm for the subject became almost an obsession, and I looked forward to compiling a book about these little-known bark papers. I wanted to include in each volume actual specimens of the *tapas* from the various islands where the making of this material had been practiced from time immemorial. I

73

would visit the islands and bring back the necessary information, photographs, and examples of the paper-like material, all to be incorporated in a folio volume.

When I began arranging for my South Sea Island journey, I was apprehensive regarding the long voyage. My wife and I had lived and studied in Europe, but going alone to the Pacific islands was more of an adventure. My itinerary could not be planned in advance, as much of the travel was to be on local ships that did not have regular schedules.

The ship that sailed from San Francisco early in the spring of 1926, bound for Tahiti, was small and none too clean; a strong odor of disinfectant brought on a feeling of seasickness even while the ship was solidly moored alongside the dock. My shipmates were a mixture of New Zealanders, Australians, South Sea Islanders, three or four French Catholic priests, and several dubious Americans. Some of the more talkative passengers gave me considerable amusement: Sid and Goldie Bounce, Australian jugglers, were on their way home after touring Italy with a small circus. Goldie, who had a figure of sixteen and a face of sixty, told me that in their heyday they had played before royalty, and she proudly showed a pressed pink rose that she said had been tossed to her by King Edward VII. Another traveling companion was Battling Solomon, a Negro prizefighter from Panama, on his way to Tahiti for a series of bouts. This muscular gentleman entertained us by appearing in bright green trunks on the ship's narrow deck and going into all manner of contortions while striking at a suspended punching-bag. Another voyager with interesting tales was Captain McCurrie, also on his way to Papeete to join a three-mastered, square-rigged trading-ship. The Captain had visited dozens of the more remote islands, trading Manchester printed cotton cloth for copra, and he told me where the craft of *tapa*-making might still be practiced. Perhaps the most articulate person on the ship was Georges Pitard, a middle-aged Frenchman who, with his attractive Tahitian wife, was on the way home to Moorea. Mr. Pitard had been in San Francisco for an operation, for in the warm, humid climate of the South Pacific islands the blood of a European becomes thin, and incisions are slow to heal. The varicolored portion of his anatomy that had been removed by the San Francisco surgeon was preserved in a bottle of alcohol that Mr. Pitard kept on the dresser in his cabin. One rainy evening he invited some of the passengers to his room, where he gave a detailed talk about his operation and used the bottled display to illustrate the lecture.

After fourteen days of plowing through the Pacific we finally sighted land, first the Marquesas and then the low-lying Tuamotu Islands, where years later the raft *Kon-Tiki* was wrecked. I shall long remember my first glimpse of the island of Tahiti. After so many days on the water, it was an unforgettable sight to watch the island come closer and closer in the gray mist of early morning, the soft emerald-green mountain rising from the dense blue ocean. From the ship, lying outside the coral reef, I could distinguish low white buildings almost hidden in clumps of verdant vines, overgrown with scarlet bougainvillaea, a mass of color extending from the edge of the deep-indigo ocean to the double peaks of Orohena Mountain more than seven thousand feet above the sea.

I was eager to leave the ship, and it seemed hours before old Dr. Cassio, the medical examiner, finally came aboard, accompanied by a disheveled French soldier in a faded uniform. The island had lately undergone a siege of smallpox. After Dr. Cassio was satisfied that we were not bringing in more disease than was already there, he directed the ship to proceed through the narrow passage in the coral reef to the port of Papeete. This passage was barely sixty feet wide, and the entrance required careful seamanship. As we drew close to the shore, I could see Tahitians walking slowly along the water's edge; there were numerous bicycles, many pushcarts, and a few small French automobiles. The wharf was crowded with well-built Polynesians of all shades, clothed in scanty cotton breechcloths, their shiny bodies glistening in the sun. The women wore loose-fitting wrappers of English and Japanese cotton calico printed in vulgar imitation of the old-time *tapa*. A hundred years earlier, the Tahitian women had made wearing-apparel beaten from the inner bark of the mulberry tree, with beautiful decorations applied by fiber printing-mats and pigment made from tree bark and nut shells. I was aware that I would find no *tapa* being made in the Society group, but I was able to purchase several specimens of finely decorated local *tapa* that had been made before the coming of trading-ships and missionaries. These foreigners failed to foster the old Tahitian crafts, and hand work was abandoned soon after the island was opened to commerce and salvation.

Tahiti is about twenty-two miles in length, and I walked and rode many dirt paths and roads that no doubt had been familiar to Paul Gauguin only twenty-five or thirty years earlier. The town of Papeete was an interesting mixture of the primitive and the sophisticated, but although I was intrigued by the dilatory life of the island people, I wanted to be on my way to more remote places, where I hoped to find *tapa* being made and used. Tahiti had become too modernized, and I left the island with little desire to return.

With the spectacular natural beauty of Tahiti embedded in my mind and the idle life of the Tahitians well impressed upon me, I embarked for the Cook Islands, which lie about six hundred miles to the southwest. There also I found that the old craft of *tapa*-making had long since given way to the use of European and Japanese machine-made woven cloth, although a few sections of the fine old bark material remained as cherished island possessions. These soft, well-worn pieces were used at the birth of a child or in rare religious ceremonies. A British protectorate had been established in the Cook, or Hervey, Islands in 1888, and since that time the native royal family had enjoyed only limited power. In Rarotonga, the chief island of the group, I called on the New Zealand official in charge, and he suggested that we first pay our respects at the "palace."

The former queen had been informed of our coming, and she was waiting in the doorway when we arrived. A stately, pleasant-faced old lady well into her seventies, she welcomed us into the palace, where we sat on grass mats under a fiber-woven canopy. The house was large for the South Seas, and one of the few coral-built structures on the island. In the room where we were entertained there were three native-made chairs and an ugly golden-oak bureau that had been brought from New Zealand. Pictures from French and English magazines were pasted on the walls. The queen apologized for the absence of the king, and explained that he was down the lane milking the royal cow. She sent a young girl to fetch him, and he came at once, bringing two half coconut shells filled with warm milk and a basket of ripe bananas. Upon his coming, the queen retired to another room, leaving the New Zealand official, the king, and me alone while we drank the milk and ate the bananas. She re-entered the room only after we had been refreshed. Although I could not understand the conversation between the king and the queen,

I could sense that we were welcome, and I was at ease in the presence of those old remnants of South Sea Island royalty. When we left the palace, the dignified queen, with regal ceremony, presented me with a hymnbook in the Cook Island language and wrote her name—Tinomara Vaine—on the flyleaf.

Rarotonga, the largest of the Cook group, is thirty miles around, and at the time of my visit only two thousand natives survived. I also went to Aitutaki, Mangaia, and Atiu of this group, but even though these small atolls were more removed from ships and commerce, the making of bark paper had long since ceased. Coconuts, oranges, and bananas were the staple products, many other fruits being too perishable for shipment. The bananas were cut from the stalk individually and sent to New Zealand in boxes, packed like sardines in a can. I had never before seen them shipped in this manner. No foreigner could own land in the Cook Islands; it belonged wholly to the island people and their descendants. In front of each home was a family burial ground, each grave covered with a thick stone slab. On these flat tombs much of the family life took place, especially in the cool evenings. Then the children played upon the ancestral gravestones, and the parents and grandparents used them as low tables for games and for resting.

My visits to the Society and Cook Islands were disappointing insofar as gathering material for my proposed book was concerned. While in Rarotonga, I was told that if I wanted to see the actual making and decorating of *tapa* I would have to go to the Tonga, or Friendly, Islands, about six hundred miles west of the Cook group. My informant was also certain that a small ship made a monthly sailing from Auckland, New Zealand, to the Fiji, Tonga, and Samoa Islands, but first I would have to go to Wellington, and from there travel by train to Auckland.

When the ship finally reached Wellington in the late evening of a dark, rainy day, I was lonely and disconsolate. A dismal room was available in the Royal Oak Hotel, and after a dreary dinner I went to sleep with the disconcerting thought that I was almost eight thousand miles from home and that in all New Zealand I did not have a single friend. The following morning I was up at daybreak. The rain continued to fall, the skies were a dull gray, and the entire scene was one of discouragement. A feeling of homesickness overcame me.

As I was interested in the handcrafts of the Maoris, the highly developed aboriginal people of New Zealand, I inquired the way to the Wellington Museum. But after walking to the museum in the splashing downpour, I found that the doors of the institution would not be opened for another hour. I stood under the museum entrance seeking protection from the drenching rain. A few pedestrians and vehicles splashed through the puddles of water lying in the uneven street. A man, soaked through, came running up the museum steps and stood beside me under the meager protection of the doorway. He nodded casually, but said nothing about the weather, which I thought showed considerable restraint. He appeared to be a New Zealander. Finally he spoke.

"Stranger here?" he said.

I replied with a polite nod.

"Come recently?"

Arrived last night, I told him.

"From the United States?"

Yes, was my reply.

"I spent a day in the United States twenty years ago," he said with an air of having been around.

His short stay in the United States aroused my curiosity, and I asked how he could remain but one brief day in a country so large as the United States.

"I'll tell you" he said. "It was in 1906. I was a member of the Royal New Zealand Band. I played bass horn. We played in a number of Canadian cities, including Toronto and Hamilton. While in Hamilton, the band was invited to visit a small town in New York State, a short distance beyond the Canadian border. The name of the village was East Aurora, and an eccentric old man with long hair, flowing black tie, and a broad-brimmed hat had a socialistic community there. They printed books and made furniture and did all the work themselves. The old gentleman looked like a Quaker; his name was Fra Elbertus. It was a strange sort of place, different from anything in New Zealand."

I remained strangely silent regarding my early connection with Elbert Hubbard and the Roycroft Shop. The bandsman was telling me about a man and a place as familiar to me as my own name, yet I could not bring myself to offer a single word of explanation.

The stranger went on talking, the rain was gradually clearing, and I knew he would be gone in another moment. He continued in his low voice: "After our band concert was over in the village, the elderly gentleman with the long hair gave us each an inscribed book as a personal favor. My book was a story about a man who went for a nap in the Catskill Mountains and remained asleep for twenty years. I believe the writer was Irving Washington. I always liked that little book, bound in soft leather. In my untrained way I admired the peculiar decorations. On the last page of the book it was printed that the designs had been made by a person named Dard Hunter. Odd name, that. The rain's about over and I must be off. Hope you have a good look at our museum. Good-by, good luck."

I stood dazed and bewildered. Again I could not bring myself to call after the stranger and tell him what was in my mind. I never saw him again.

In Wellington I ascertained that my acquaintance in the Cook Islands had been well informed. I could get a ship at Auckland bound for the Fiji, Tonga, and Samoa Islands. Also I learned, much to my gratification, that in several of the less frequented islands of these groups the old-time methods of beating and decorating *tapa* were still practiced. My stay in Wellington was terminated within a few days, as I was desirous of moving on to Auckland, where I hoped to procure a berth for the sailing of the *Ufano*, bound for the islands I wished to visit. Auckland lies about three hundred miles north of Wellington. When I bought a sleeping-car ticket the agent told me that there would be three other men in the same compartment. After a short wait in the Wellington station the train was ready, and upon entering the compartment I found but one occupant; the two other gentlemen joined the train a station beyond.

They all talked freely, the most loquacious of the three being a member of the New Zealand Parliament. The second stranger was an Auckland physician, the third a "jackaroo" from Australia. He explained that a jackaroo was the first assistant to the manager of a sheep station. He had been in New Zealand looking for a job on a ranch, but as he had not found work he was on his way back to Australia. These three men, knowing that I was from America, plied me with questions: the member of Parliament wanted me to explain the functions of our Senate and House of Representatives; the physician asked about the Mayo brothers; and the young jackaroo wanted to know the wages of a "shepherd" in America. Then came questions about Prohibition and whether the forty-eight states would remain together or eventually divide into separate countries. The three gentlemen on the Wellington-Auckland express had ludicrous ideas about life in the United States, and no wonder, for in the Wellington newspaper they had brought with them there were just two items of news from my country. One heading read: "Chicago Bridegroom Murders Three at His Own Wedding," and the other headline, in still larger type, outlined another bit of worthy American news: "New York Actress Takes Bath in Champagne to Entertain Breakfast Guests."

Our sleeping-compartment appeared strange to me, and I was at a loss to understand how four berths could be made up in such cramped quarters. The train stopped at a station for dinner, and we all sat down together in the commodious dining-room. When we were again aboard, the steward came to prepare the berths for the night, and I was all attention. The backs of the seats swung up on hinges and were secured by heavy belts with buckles. These formed the upper berths. Railings were placed around the outside edges of the bunks, and the bedclothing was made tight by wide leather straps. There were no curtains to enclose the berths, and I felt timid about preparing for bed in the presence of a member of the Parliament of New Zealand. After the doctor, the member of Parliament, the jackaroo, and I had retired, the train came to a sudden sliding stop and my three companions sprang from their bunks. Nothing was wrong, they told me; we had only arrived at another restaurant station, and we must have cold mutton and tea. My sleeping-car mates were surprised that I would not leave my berth, but only two hours earlier I had consumed a four-course dinner.

When my companions returned to the compartment I was asleep, but I was awakened by having a generous cold-mutton sandwich thrust into my face by the hospitable member of Parliament. In the morning we made our way to the tiny washroom of the sleeping-car, where we pumped the water and dried our faces and hands on the long red roller towel so thoughtfully provided by the government-owned railways of New Zealand.

The small ship *Ufano* was to arrive in Auckland on Sunday, and was to sail for the Fiji, Tonga, and Samoa Islands the following Friday. I wanted to see the ship upon which I was to spend several weeks, and on Sunday morning I went to the dock and watched the vessel come slowly into port. I stood in the rain, my attention focused upon the unloading of oranges and bananas by Fijians brought on the ship for the purpose. A great crane swung around and placed the boxes of fruit on the wharf. I heard the Fijian language for the first time and was fascinated by the voices of these scantily clothed brown men. Suddenly the supports of the huge wooden crane gave way and the heavy beam crashed to the wharf. Two Fijian laborers were in the path of the falling timber. Their bodies were crushed. Fijians carried the warm corpses to the storage house and placed them on crates of fruit. Work continued without the aid of the crane.

Early Friday morning I was on the Queen's Wharf ready to go aboard the *Ufano*. The day was bright and sunny, a decided change in the weather, and everyone was singing; a gay mood prevailed. There were half-caste Tongans and Samoans going to their island homes after visiting friends and relatives in New Zealand; Chinese and Indian merchants on their way to Suva; and several Catholic missionaries bound for the small island of Vavau. The ship appeared clean in the bright sunlight, and the gaiety and merriment of the native passengers had a soothing influence, although I could not help recalling the two Fijians who had been killed only a few days before. I looked over at the platform where they had been crushed; the spot was covered with sawdust.

My cabin was small, with a short, narrow bunk; the room was numbered 12-A. There was no number 13, but had there been it would have been mine, as the 12-A label over the door had been used to avoid the unlucky number. My place at table was between a lovely Samoan widow and a Chinese Episcopalian minister. They both spoke English. The food was nourishing: mutton, mashed taro, breadfruit, with a plentiful supply of oranges, bananas, passion fruit, watermelon, and mummy and custard apples.

The six-day voyage to Fiji was uneventful save for the death of a Fijian fireman, whose burial at sea was conducted by the Chinese minister of the Church of England. It was at dusk that we first sighted Fiji, although we did not reach the island of Viti Levu, upon which Suva was situated, until early the following morning. Fiji was not as colorful as Tahiti, but the climate was less warm and humid, and the evenings were pleasantly cool and balmy. Suva was the most important port in the South Pacific, with accommodation for large ships. A short walk through an open field and over a narrow bridge brought us to the heart of the town. Most of the commerce of Suva was carried on by merchants from India, who appeared to outnumber even the Fijians. The shops were low wooden buildings scattered along the river's edge, where old broken and decayed boats were lying derelict in the mire along with the odoriferous refuse of the town. I went from shop to shop seeking mulberry-bark paper, which in the Fijian language was called *masi*. I was ever mindful that I had made the long voyage to gather material for a book dealing with the primitive bark papers of the South Sea Islands.

During part of my sojourn in Suva I was entertained in the home of Captain Strong, a retired officer of the British army who had lived in Fiji for more than fifty-five years. The Captain's wife was a charming half-caste Maori, her father having been a British sailor and her mother the daughter of a Maori chief. Captain Strong was present at the last attempted cannibal feast, and he had retrieved a man from being consumed at a native repast. He explained that the cooked flesh of a human had the flavor of roast pork and that the fat was yellow like that of a turkey. Of Captain Strong's many stories of old Fiji, one in particular stands out in my memory. In the late seventies, while walking in the woods, he came upon a little Fijian boy about ten years old, sitting on a log. He was amusing himself by casually shooting bone-pointed arrows into the naked body of a hopelessly sick old man lying in a heap on the ground. The spirited lad had five arrows in his quiver, and when all five had been shot and were protruding from the torn flesh of the impotent creature, the lively youngster would jump down from tht log, extract the arrows, and continue his play all over again.

Aside from gruesome stories of Fijian life of three quarters of a century ago, Captain Strong was familiar with the fine old crafts of the Fijians, and he told me where the making of *masi* was still carried on and how to reach these outlying settlements. No bark paper was being made in or near Suva. The finest work in *masi,* or *tapa,* was done on the island of Taveuni, where I was fortunate enough to see the entire process of both beating and decorating. At the time of my inspection, the plain bark paper was being ornamented by the use of banana-leaf stencils, which were placed on the upper surface of the newly beaten white bark material in the same general manner as European metal stencils. The incised geometric design was rubbed over with a bark-paper swab that had been dipped in native-rendered dye. The colors were black and a pleasing dull red. The black was made from burned candlenut shell, *tiri,* and the leaves of the *tavola* (*Terminalia catappa*), the red from the bark of the *kura* (*Morinda citrifolio*).

One evening, while staying in a remote settlement along the Rewa River, I was invited to the home of a chief, who sent a weathered octogenarian to guide me to his habitation. I walked with him through a wooded path for a mile or more, and finally came to the chief's house. The grass hut was lighted by two oil lanterns. Several men were lounging in the single room, and in one corner a woman was cooking over an open fire. I was delighted with the prospect of a native dinner, which proved to be different from any food I had ever had. After the repast the chief brought out several beautiful old pieces of *masi* and said that I might have the one I liked best. I selected an elaborate *masi kesa* that had originally been used as a bed-covering. While I was in Fiji, many examples of old and modern *masi* were presented to me, along with the tools used in making this material so essential to Pacific Island life before the introduction of prosaic woven cotton cloth from Japan, India, and Europe.

After completing my investigations in the Fiji Islands, I continued on to the Tonga, or Friendly, Islands. In every locality I visited I was told that in this group the old customs and crafts had been less disturbed than in any other part of the South Seas. The ship was to sail in the evening, and I was aboard early. Many lean pigs, scrawny chickens, and sheep on their way to the islands were already roaming along the narrow deck. Two dignified Fijian chiefs attired in cotton breechcloths, stiff hats, and European-style jackets came up the gangplank amid vigorous singing and clapping by their own people, who had come to see them off. Just as the ship was drawing away from the wharf, a lingering native passenger came running through the storage house, waving his arms and shouting that he wanted to go aboard. The gangplank was hurriedly run up for him in the nick of time. The few passengers were leaning over the ship's rail, and as the vessel gave a sudden lurch we saw the heavy gangplank fall, pinning a frail Fijian lad underneath, killing him instantly. His supple brown body was carried to a near-by shed. This was the fourth death, all Fijians, I had seen since coming to the South Pacific islands.

Early one morning after a few days of sailing we reached the island of Tongatabu, Tonga, lying five or six hundred miles southeast of the Fiji group. The first European to land in the Tonga Islands was Jacob Lemaire, in 1616. He was followed by Abel Janszoon Tasman, the Dutch navigator, in 1643, and Samuel Wallis in 1767; later came Captain James Cook, who remained seven weeks. There are about 150 islands in the group, many of them not surveyed.

I was ashore in the village of Nukualofa on the main island of Tongatabu even before many of the inhabitants were astir. The morning was cool, with a gentle ocean breeze that made the tall coconut trees wave and sway. It was like an Indian-summer day in New England. In the evening the hushed stillness, the soft air, and the constant lapping of the sea made me feel that perhaps the islands of the South Pacific really had the elusive charm so engagingly described by romantic writers.

A letter of introduction is usually useful, and as I had one addressed to Dr. Payne, the Wesleyan missionary in Tonga, I started at once for his house. I was put on the right path by a young medical man from New Zealand who was in the islands temporarily, investigating hookworm and elephantiasis. Two Catholic priests spoke to me and asked for the latest news. After about a half-mile walk through a grassy lane under coconut trees, with slow-moving giant land crabs at almost every footstep, I came to the Wesleyan church and Dr. Payne's parsonage. The church had been built by skilled Tongans following the ancient custom of making every building of oblong shape. The interior was remarkable, as not a nail or bolt had been used; the roofing timbers and supporting pillars had been lashed together with thin, varicolored coconut-fiber ropes, the different colors of the twines forming beautiful geometric patterns at every juncture. Never before had I been in a church where the construction and decoration expressed such abundant religious devotion.

Dr. Payne was an Australian who had lived with the Tongan people for nineteen years. When I arrived at the parsonage he was entertaining two handsome middle-aged chiefs, both attired only in breechcloths. In Fiji and other islands, these simple loin-coverings had been made of European cotton cloth, but the two Tongan chiefs were wearing breechcloths made of *tapa*. As I had come to the South Pacific islands especially to see this material being made, to find it in actual use was indeed heartening. Dr. Payne was a sensible missionary in his desire to foster and preserve the old island crafts. He said that I had arrived at precisely the right time, as *tapa* was being made for the centennial of the church. This festival was called *Koe Senituli*, and was in celebration of the coming of the first missionary to the Tonga Islands in 1826. Dr. Payne gave me a native-drawn portrait of the Reverend Mr. Thomas, the founder of the Christian religion in the Tonga Islands, whom the natives devotedly called *Ko Misa Tomasi,* a corruption of his name.

Dr. Payne assured me that I could see the making of *tapa* anywhere in the island, and if I would listen for the hollow sound of the constant beating I would soon discover the women at work. Following this suggestion, I located any number of old crones sitting cross-legged in front of their grass huts and beating the inner bark of the mulberry tree into strips of course paper. Later Dr. Payne took me to a community house where twenty-eight women were uniting the small pieces of beaten bark into a great sheet of *tapa* which was eventually to assume the tremendous proportions of 24 by 90 feet. The decoration was applied to the bark paper as the strips were put together with glutinous arrowroot paste. The great sheet of *tapa* was to be presented to the church at the centennial festival.

The *tapa*-making party was presided over by the wife of a chief, who directed every phase of the work. The entire procedure suggested a Methodist quilting party in a small American town. The workers wore skirts made of grass, with strips of *tapa* tied around their middles, the costume giving them a bulging, although not inartistic, appearance. As they worked, they rolled leaves into long brown cigarettes, which they smoked incessantly. At the same time they ate watermelon and used the discarded rinds to hold slow-burning punk, from which the cigarettes were lighted. At intervals the women would rise and dance and clap their hands in a relaxing fashion. Attractive young girls, also dressed in grass skirts with *tapa* sashes, were engaged in making *kava,* the native drink, and it was in this community house that I first tasted this universal South Sea island concoction. In former and more natural years the root of the *kava* plant was masticated by young women selected for their fine teeth. After thorough chewing, the saliva was expectorated into a large wooden bowl filled with water; after straining of sediment, the liquid formed the much cherished native drink. When I watched the girls make *kava*, a stone was used to grind the root, but the same style of native-made round wooden bowl was used as the receptacle. The sediment was removed from the bowl in the ancient manner, a girl drawing her hair through the liquid mass in the manner of a sieve. The hair was finally wrung out over the bowl so that none of the precious juice was lost.

This drink was served with considerable ceremony, the person of highest rank drinking first, then passing the half coconut shell of liquid to the seated guests, all drinking from the same cup. After the shell had been emptied, it was rinsed thoroughly in the *kava* bowl before being refilled. I did not at first like the taste of the beverage, but it was best for me to drink every time the cup was passed; I could not risk offending these hospitable people. Although *kava* was mildly unpleasant at the time of drinking, the aftertaste was refreshing and stimulating.

Upon my final visit to the community house I was given many presents, with the request that they all be taken back to America. There were watermelons, baskets of mangoes, homemade cigarettes, two or three grass skirts, strings of seed beads, mummy apples, *kava* root, and bunches of *taro*, but I was most pleased with several large pieces of *tapa*, as well as hand beaters and other tools used in its making. The presents were wrapped in sections of bark paper, and several Tongan boys were summoned to carry the gifts to the Mission House.

The Tonga, or Friendly, Islands retained their royal family, and the Queen presided in the palace on the main island of

Tongatabu. I was invited to the palace, but upon my first visit the Queen was indisposed. At that time, however, I had a profitable talk with the Prince Consort, who was acting as Premier. He told of his work in ridding the islands of disease, and of his desire to introduce new vegetation. The Premier later took me on an inspection tour of Tongatabu in his 1920 Ford, license number eleven.

Of the recent ruling family of Tonga, King George Tubou died in 1893 at the age of ninety-six. He was succeeded by his great-grandson, King George II, who died in 1918. After his death came Queen Salote, the ruling monarch at the time of my visit. The Queen was a fine-appearing woman of about thirty-five or perhaps less. She was large and well developed, and I may have been deceived in her years. She was most regal. I was impressed by her smooth bronze face, dark glossy hair, stately figure, and fine carriage.

The Queen's palace was a square wooden building with an ornamental cupola. A low wall enclosed the palace grounds, and within the garden lived a large tortoise, its gnarled and broken shell indicating great age; indeed, I was informed that the tortoise had been presented to King Tubou in 1773 by Captain Cook when he first visited the islands. Captain Cook had captured the tortoise in the Galápagos Islands, and he had explained to the Tongans that his original intention had been to carry it on to Britain as a gift to King George III, but he and his men had been so royally received by the Tongans that he wanted King Tubou to have the fine creature for the palace grounds. It was given the title of *Tui*, or chieftain of the tribe called *Malila*, with all the privileges and rights of a noble. Since Captain Cook's visit in 1773 the tortoise had survived two forest fires and a broken shell from having been struck by the wheel of a cart; a horse's kick had caused the loss of one eye. When I stroked the head of this crusty old palace pet it seemed to answer to the name *Tui-Malila*. The outline rendering of this tortoise appeared as a watermark in the paper of Tongan postage stamps, many of which bore the portrait of Queen Salote.

When I told my friends in Nukualofa that I wanted to go to the Haapai group, they tried to dissuade me, saying that nothing there would be of the slightest interest. I was eager to go, as *tapa*-making might also be found there, perhaps by a different technique from that of Tongatabu. Haapai was about a day's voyage to the northeast, and when we reached the island, the ship anchored outside the coral reef. As a few tins of New Zealand biscuit, some tinned fish, and a Singer sewing-machine were to be landed, I got into the rowboat that was to carry the freight to shore. After energetic work by the oarsmen, we pulled up on the beach of the scant settlement of Lifuka. There were a few half-naked men to receive the freight, but they had not expected a visitor. The island was desolate: a few scattered grass houses, an old derelict sailing-ship cast upon the sands, some straggly coconut trees, and an old gray horse, nothing more.

It was early morning when we arrived in Lifuka, and there was little to do but walk. The day was warm, although not oppressive, and I tramped from one end of the island to the other, a distance of about a mile. When I saw how the women and girls were dressed I wondered why a sewing-machine, or even a needle, was brought to the island. Their clothing was scant and did little to conceal their velvety brown bodies. The hours dragged heavily in Lifuka. Not a trace of *tapa*-making could be found, and I soon became tired of walking and sat in the shade of a small grove of shaggy coconut trees. I had not been resting long when three or four barefoot girls approached, each smoking a thin brown native cigarette. When they saw me, they were neither embarrassed nor afraid, but came over to where I was sitting and reclined near by. Their modesty was natural, free from affectation; I was impressed by their dignity and lack of bashfulness. One of the girls wore a beautifully patterned strip of Tongan *tapa* over her filmy grass skirt. I touched the beaten-bark material and tried to express my appreciation of the design in the manner one would admire a becoming dress worn by an American girl. With befitting modesty the young Polynesian unwound the *tapa* from her slim, well-modeled body and handed it to me. This narrow section of bark paper, decorated with a pattern in sepia, is one of the most exquisite and certainly one of the most intimately associated examples of *tapa* in my collection.

When I returned to the ship, the ceiling and walls of my cabin were literally black with mosquitoes. The insects had come from the island, and the only way to rid my room of them was to scrape down the walls with a yardstick and stomp upon the agitated mass as it reached the floor. After so many hours on the little island, I was glad to go to bed between damp, mildewed sheets in the narrow bunk; as I went to sleep I watched two giant cockroaches running a race up the slippery cabin wall toward the porthole.

Two more days brought the ship near Vavau, first visited by the Spanish navigator Maurelle in 1781. Small atolls were scattered everywhere, and to reach the landing-place the ship wound in and out around great green mounds of earth rising abruptly from the sea. We approached Vavau after dark, and the natives built brush fires to show the way. The ship crept along silently and cautiously, and finally moored beside a row of low-built houses, each dimly lighted by candles and oil lanterns. I walked in the darkness up the winding path to the house where I was to stay, and except for the far-off beating of a native drum the night was serenely still. I passed scores of candle-lit huts, interspersed with small open shops where melons and bananas were sold under the dim light of hanging lanterns that threw weird shadows on the faces of the brown merchants.

Before arising the following morning I could hear the rhythmical pounding of the *tapa*-beaters, a sound distinguishable from all others. This was a welcome sound, for it assured me that I would see the ancient craft of *tapa*-making in Vavau as I had in Tongatabu. The first woman I found beating bark was seated in front of her small thatched cabin among naked children, mangy dogs, and lean pigs. I watched her for two or three hours, and during this time she did not cease the constant beating. A strip of the inner bark of the mulberry tree, soaked in water, was laid upon a long log and struck at right angles, the beating-mallet falling squarely on the wet bark. As the woman beat, the fresh, clean bark was pushed over the wooden anvil, falling in folds on banana leaves spread upon the ground. At each stroke of the heavy wooden mallet, the bark would become slightly wider, and when twice its original width, the material was doubled, then tripled, and again beaten, being sprinkled with fresh water during the constant pounding. I tried the work, and found the beating hard on my wrist owing to the vibration of the wooden anvil, both ends of which rested on large stones. One old man told me he enjoyed the hollow resonant tap-tap-tap of the beating, but he could not endure the work himself—it was too fatiguing. He had, however, shaped and carved many of the wooden mallets used in the beating. As I went from worker to worker, I asked if I might purchase the tools, but in every instance the grooved wooden

94

beaters, the printing-mats, and other appliances employed in making and decorating *tapa* were given to me.

The two Fijian chiefs whom I had met in Suva had arrived in Vavau, and a native dance was arranged for them. For this colorful celebration the Tongan men brought huge wicker baskets of fruit from the country, including many kinds I had never before tasted. They roasted whole pigs in stone pits and carried the meat in fiber nets swung from bamboo poles. Everyone shared in the festivities, and I was fortunate to be present to partake of such primitive splendor.

My next island stop in search of information and specimens for my proposed book was Upolu in the Samoan group. Here again I was entertained in royal manner, on this occasion by the Chief Laumuina of Lepea, Faleata, a man of magnificent physique with the classical features of a Roman gladiator. Knowing of my intense interest in the making of *tapa*, he arranged for several women to come to his house and perform the various processes in the Samoan manner; each island group, had its own distinctive technique in both beating and decorating. The aristocratic old chief and I sat upon folded pieces of *tapa*, piled high, which made up the Samoan bed, while we drank *kava* and he smoked island cigarettes. The women brought the carved wooden beaters, the fiber printing-mats, and pots of native-made dye. In turn they went through the various steps of their centuries-old craft while I made photographs, drew rough sketches, and filled pages of my notebook. At the conclusion of this command performance I was ceremoniously presented with the tools they had used and the pieces of *tapa* they had made, along with a number of sections of antique bark paper that had been made years earlier by their ancestors.

# MY LIFE WITH PAPER

While in Apia, the chief settlement in Upolu, I did not fail to walk the steep winding path "under the dark and starry sky" to the peak of Vaea where Robert Louis Stevenson lies buried on his Vailima estate.

From British Samoa I returned to Vanua Levu of the Fiji Islands, a distance of over six hundred miles. Lying midway between Samoa and Fiji was the small volcanic atoll of Niuafoou, which was discovered in 1791 by Captain Edwards of the ship *Pandora*. The island was in eruption in 1853 and in later years, but at the time of my visit in 1926 everything was tranquil, with three Europeans living on the island: two Scotchmen and a French Catholic priest. About fifteen hundred natives survived. Owing to the way that the island rose abruptly from the sea, a ship could not land, and it was a dangerous undertaking for a small boat even to cast away. Our ship carried mail for Niuafoou, long known to philatelists as the "Tin-can Mail." We approached the island as closely as safety permitted, about a half-mile from the steep, rugged cliffs, and there cast anchor. In the distance a half-dozen natives could be seen swimming toward the ship, each man astride a heavy bamboo pole, his outstretched hand holding upright a short stick to which a small bundle of letters was tied. When the men reached the ship's side, a bucket was lowered, and the swimmers threw the letters into it and the bucket was drawn up to the deck. The mail for delivery to the island had previously been sealed in two large biscuit tins, which were thrown overboard to the swimmers. These cans were secured to the bamboo poles, and the naked men returned to their lonely island. Owing to the many man-eating sharks, the natives swam back and forth in close formation. In good weather the islanders had mail every five weeks, but when the sea was

96

rough, mail communication with the outside world was often delayed for two or three months.

After another week in Fiji, I returned to the United States by way of the prosaic Hawaiian Islands, and with the specimens of *tapa* I had collected and my photographs and notes I began the production of the folio book *Primitive Papermaking*, which was completed during the last month of 1927. This book had a frontispiece of the Mountain House, reproduced from a lithograph of 1852; 48 pages of text; 35 line illustrations with one in color; 10 photographs; 31 specimens of bark paper and 2 examples of mulberry bark. The books were issued in sheets held in portfolios made by Peter Franck. For this edition of 200 copies I used the hand-cut and hand-cast type with which the first two papermaking books had been printed. As these two books had sold readily at twenty-five and thirty dollars, respectively, I arbitrarily set the price of *Primitive Papermaking* at seventy-five dollars a copy, with the thought that no book of mine would sell for such an exorbitant figure. As with the first two books, I was happily mistaken. Orders came in almost faster than I could pack the books and carry them to the express office. For the most part they were sold to American libraries and private collectors, but orders also come from England, France, Germany, and Holland. Maggs Brothers, the renowned booksellers of London, cabled for a dozen copies and did not even expect a discount. The edition was exhausted within one month. I was still further encouraged.

# ✣ VII ✣

AFTER *Primitive Papermaking* was printed in 1927, my enthusiasm for making paper by hand took a dubious turning: the establishment of a commercial handmade-paper mill, the only one in the Western Hemisphere.

In 1920, as I mentioned previously, the equipment for the operation of a full-size handmade-paper mill had been purchased in England, and the many tons of appliances carted to Southampton and shipped to America. Upon arrival in the New York Custom House, I was greeted with an enormous bill for freight and storage, a total that amounted to ten times what had been paid for the antique equipment.

While in England I had visited several of the localities where the making of paper by hand remained a lively trade, and as the workers in this craft have always lived within a little world of their own, they were soon aware that I had bought the old mill. They naturally supposed that a handmade-paper mill was to be established across the sea. Shortly after my return to America I received a letter from Robert Perry Robertson of Maidstone, Kent, where the making of paper by hand had been carried on for more than two hundred years. Mr. Robertson wrote of his desire to emigrate to the United States and explained that for generations his family had been papermakers. At that time I had no plan for importing skilled work-

*98*

ers and I hastened to tell him so. A year later I received another letter, dated June 23, 1921, in which he again expressed his wish to leave England and take up his home in the United States. He hoped that I might help him consummate this move.

It was my plan to set up the equipment I had purchased in England and try to revive in America a craft that had all but died since 1817, when the first papermaking machine in this country was put in motion near Wilmington, Delaware. I wanted to find an old water-power mill in New England, install the English appliances, and produce genuine handmade paper, which, I hoped, would be purchased by printers, publishers, artists, and the appreciative public in general.

From my experience in the little mill near Marlborough it was evident that singlehanded I could not even satisfy the most limited market. Trained help would be needed, and there were no makers of handmade paper in America. Also, I lacked business ability and salesmanship. My plan for the establishment of a mill, therefore, did not materialize until early in 1926, when I received a lengthy letter from an enthusiastic young Michigan businessman who was totally unknown to me. He was certain that a commercial handmade-paper mill in America would be a pronounced success. He was an experienced perfumery salesman, he wrote, and suggested that we should go into the papermaking venture together. He assured me that he was capable of selling every ream of paper that could be made. Although his plan appeared to have merit, I had theretofore worked entirely alone, and I was reluctant to enter into an association with another person, even though he might be a businessman of ability.

After several visits to my home, however, the handsome young perfumery-salesman convinced me that a handmade-paper mill in prosperous America had every chance of success. I told him of the search that would be required to find a suitable location for a mill; also I tried to impress upon him the difficulty of procuring handmade-paper workers. The apprenticeship in England for training a vatman was seven years, and the Original Society of Papermakers, established in 1800, would not consent to their expert artisans leaving England. I further outlined the importance of highly skilled workers, explaining that any novice could mould a few sheets of paper of indifferent thickness and formation, but that when the worker was required to make ream after ream, day after day, with every sheet of paper the same weight and thickness, genuine skill was essential. The young salesman from Michigan continued to assure me that every obstacle could be overcome, and we finally launched a definite plan to set up the only handmade-paper mill in America, to be incorporated with the name Dard Hunter Associates. It should be remembered that this was in the period after the First World War, when the country was in the middle of a post-war boom; conditions appeared bright for any unusual undertaking.

Although I was familiar with a number of old water-power mills in New England, none was entirely suitable for our purpose: some lacked the necessary water power, one or two did not have an ample supply of fresh water, and several other properties would have been too costly to renovate. In a roundabout manner I learned of an abandoned mill in Lime Rock, Salisbury, Litchfield County, Connecticut, which was for sale at a reasonable price. After investigation regarding the purity of the water and other essential requirements, the long, rambling mill buildings, two and one-half acres of land, dam, millpond, and riparian rights were purchased on April 16, 1928.

Most of the mill structure was of wood, with a smaller end

section of brick and stone, all lying precariously along the Salmon Fells Kill, a trout brook that flowed to the Housatonic River about a mile away. The oldest part of the building, dating from about 1760, had been a flour mill, and the old buhrstones for grinding grain, driven by a water turbine, remained in their original position. The main section of the building, dating from about 1845, had been a woodworking-shop for making patterns to be used in casting ironwork for railway cars and engines. The casting was done across the brook in a dilapidated one-story building, the entire earthen floor of which was ankle deep in black sand. The cupola of the foundry, looking like the turret of a ruined castle, stood in a leaning position close to the millpond. The dam had been solidly constructed of cut granite blocks brought to Lime Rock by oxcart from the quarries of Vermont.

After I acquired the mill property, I was proudly told by old Salisbury residents that during the Revolutionary War part of the huge chain that had been stretched across the Hudson River to prevent British ships from entering had been forged near Lime Rock. Also, the wheels of the railway carriage that carried Abraham Lincoln's funeral cortège from Washington to Springfield, Illinois, in April 1865 had been cast in this secluded Connecticut foundry.

After the purchase of the mill, we wished to provide space to set up the antique papermaking equipment I had brought from Downton, England. This involved removing thousands of wooden patterns for casting parts of early American railway cars and engines. These patterns, of all shapes and sizes, were moved to a shed across the road from the mill, there to await classification and final disposal. The old wooden patterns had historical interest, but within a few weeks the small storage building mysteriously caught fire and every pattern was destroyed. In the attic of the mill we found a number of dust-covered boxes and trunks filled with records, correspondence, invoices, and drawings that had collected during the long industrial life of the foundry. This manuscript material was eventually given to the business school of Harvard University.

After the mill buildings had been renovated and put in fair structural order, the English handmade-paper appliances, two hydraulic presses, and the heating-plant were installed on the ground floor of the central building. The rag-cutting tables, beater, stuff-pump, stuff-chest, and plater occupied the second floor, while the entire third floor was devoted to the drying of the paper. A stubborn elevator connected the three levels.

In the meantime, remembering Robert Robertson's letters in which he had so strongly expressed his desire to move to America, we wrote him again and found that his eagerness to leave England had not diminished. The arrangements for the entry of the English family to the United States involved writing to government officials, both in this country and in England; trips were made to Washington in an effort to speed the coming of the craftsmen. We informed the government officials that there was not a single handmade-paper mill in the United States and that therefore we were inaugurating a totally new industry. All members of the Robertson family were to make the journey to America: first Robert Robertson and his son Thomas were to come, to be followed later by Mrs. Robertson and another son, Reginald, the daughter Gladys, and her husband, who had been a greengrocer's assistant in Maidstone, not a papermaker.

Early in the spring of 1931, Robert Robertson, vatman, and Thomas Robertson, coucher, arrived in the port of New York, the Lime Rock handmade-paper corporation having borne all the expense of the move. After a day at dreary Ellis Island, we drove to Lime Rock, arriving late at night; the two new arrivals were delighted with their adopted country, although it was densely dark and nothing could be seen. The Robertsons, father and son, worked diligently and conscientiously in the mill, as much still remained to be done in arranging and installing the equipment. Additional papermaking-moulds had to be procured in England, and the woolen felting used in couching the paper was also purchased there. When the felting, which had cost more than two thousand dollars, finally arrived, we were fined ten per cent by the United States Customs because the Yorkshire weaving-firm had shipped the huge burlap-wrapped bundle without the required "origin of country" marking. We also paid duty on moulds, although no papermaking-moulds had been made in America since the early nineteenth century. The payment of duty worked both ways, however, as there was a high tariff on European-made paper and this was decidedly to our advantage. Otherwise there would have been no chance of competing in price with foreign handmade-paper mills.

At the time of the Lime Rock enterprise there was probably more interest in the use of handmade paper than in later years. A few of the machinemade-paper mills even tried to capitalize on the appreciation of genuine handmade paper by advertising their machine product with such catch-phrases as "hand-fashioned," "hand-fabricated," and "hand-finished." One machine mill boldly used the term "handmade" in its advertising. Aside from any thought of unjust competition, I was displeased with this deception, and gave a detailed explanation to the Federal Trade Commission, outlining the methods used in producing genuine handmade paper. I tried to convince the commission that the wording of the machinemade-paper advertising was false and deceptive and that the advertisers should be forced to withdraw the misleading propaganda. This brought a Federal Trade Commission agent to Lime Rock, where he saw for himself how each sheet of paper was formed individually in a hand mould, the careful manner in which every separate sheet was couched upon the felting, and the slow methods used in drying, sizing, and finishing the paper. He went away with a fairly clear conception of the vast difference in quality between handmade paper and that made in an endless web on a paper machine. The firms that had been using the misleading advertising were required to desist, and since that time there has been no encroachment upon the just heritage of the makers of paper by the ancient hand process.

Manufacturers also tried to imitate handmade paper by cutting false deckle edges on machinemade paper. One day a young man from New York came bouncing into our small office, his briefcase bulging with samples. He presented his card, which gave his occupation as "expert deckler." With an air of superiority the salesman told us he had invented a machine for cutting deckle edges on any sort of paper, no matter how inferior. While at the mill this young prodigy was shown that a genuine deckle on a sheet of handmade paper was caused by the four-sided wooden frame that was placed upon the hand mould to hold the beaten-rag fibers within bounds. We explained that the deckle edges on handmade paper were necessary imperfections, like a selvage on a piece of cloth. We also pointed out to the youthful inventor that he was trying to duplicate something that could not possibly be imitated and that his invention did nothing more than attempt to imitate an imperfection.

My partner, the perfumery-salesman, had long since moved his family, consisting of his wife, her mother, and nine children, to Lime Rock village. The salesman's three brothers-in-

*A specimen of handmade paper from Dard Hunter's mill on the Salmon Fells Kill, Lime Rock, Connecticut. This example, termed "antique laid" was made to emulate European paper of the fourteenth century. The sheet of paper from which this sample was cut was made in 1930 and measured 26 by 20 inches. The Lime Rock mill was completely demolished in the flood of 1955.*

law had been at work in the mill since the beginning. The Robertson family of six was comfortably housed near by. It seemed as though the population of a small town had descended upon me. By now the Great American Depression had overtaken us, and there were twelve adults, nine children, and three dogs all depending for support upon the revival of the craft of making paper by hand!

After endless tribulations and discouragements, we were producing about three reams of paper a day, equal in quality to most of the handmade paper imported from Europe. The Robertson family worked day and night to make the venture a success, and the erstwhile perfumery-salesman struggled with sales and collections. Our most important customer went into bankruptcy. Of the thousands of pounds of paper that were shipped from the mill to all parts of the country, we received payment for only a small number of reams. The natural result was that the list of worthy creditors began to outnumber even our salesman's children and relatives. The enterprise was eventually forced into receivership, with the brisk young salesman appointed as one of the two receivers. The revival of the craft of making paper by hand had cost more than sixty thousand dollars. All I received from the venture was experience, not all of it in the field of papermaking.

Before the beginning of months of litigation and disagreement I had paid my share of the indebtedness, and on December 9, 1931, I received a release from the Court, by order of Mr. Justice Edward S. Thomas of the United States District Court of the District of Connecticut. My connection with the revival of making paper by hand in America had extended over a period of three years and nine months.

After the failure of the mill, the members of the Robertson family gradually went into other work in near-by towns, and the salesman's brothers-in-law also left Lime Rock village. Only the receiver-salesman remained to the very last hour of the very last day, which was 2.30 p.m. on November 4, 1933, when the mill, the old English equipment, and a large stock of paper were all offered at receivers' sale. On that bleak, rainy November afternoon I stood in the millyard along with a small group of curious onlookers who had also come to witness the last sad rites of a "noble experiment." The property was put up at auction to satisfy the remaining creditors, but not a bid was forthcoming. The representative of the Court asked me to advance an offer, but on that dark, gloomy afternoon I was doubly certain that I never again wanted to try my hand at the revival of a dying craft. The shivering little group in front of the mill stood cold and silent. No bids were heard. Without warning a little old man drove along the road in a dilapidated car and stopped in the mill driveway. He did not leave his seat, but shouted an offer for the mill property which was tentatively accepted by the representative of the Court. No one at the sale knew the old man who had just purchased the only handmade-paper mill in America, but later it appeared that he was an obscure New York printer. Why he wanted the property always remained a mystery, for he never made use of the mill. In the eventual settlement of his estate, it was again offered for sale. In the interim I had lost much of my antipathy toward the property, so I purchased it for about twice the price the stranger had given at the November 1933 auction. I had no wish to put the mill in operation again, but we did renovate the buildings and make numerous repairs and changes, including the demolition of the eighteenth-century flour mill, which had become so ruinous that one entire side of the wooden structure had collapsed into the brook.

During the period that I was active in the Lime Rock venture we had many visitors: Childe Hassam came to buy our paper for his prints, and said he could find none other that answered so well; James McBey, the Scotch etcher, also purchased Lime Rock paper for his printing, as did Troy Kinney, Ernest D. Roth, and Bernhart Wall. The book-printers who came to the mill included James Guthrie of the Pear Tree Press, Flansham, Bognor, Sussex; Spencer Kellogg of the Aries Press; Elmer Adler, Pynson Printers; Frederic Goudy and Bruce Rogers, typographical designers; and Peter Franck, bookbinder. Ernest Elmo Calkins, writer and advertising executive from near-by Lakeville, was a regular visitor, and Harry Miller Lydenberg, librarian of the New York Public Library and Harrison Elliott of the old Japan Paper Company made the little journey to Lime Rock. Walter Prichard Eaton came to write an article about the mill for the New York *Herald Tribune*.

William Edwin Rudge, Senior, New York printer and publisher, came often to the village. He insisted that I compile a book on the subject of papermaking for his firm to print and publish. At last I had the novel experience of having only to write the text and assemble the illustrations for a book—I would not be required to set the type and print the edition myself! Mr. Rudge's request resulted in the edition of *Papermaking through Eighteen Centuries*, designed by Frederic Warde, with 375 pages of text and 214 illustrations, issued in 1930.

Two years before the demise of the Lime Rock mill I had purchased from the receivers sufficient paper for the printing of a folio book of about 200 copies. Although made of superior rags, this paper was not the finest that was produced in the mill, but it had been formed on my own moulds with a personal watermark, and I felt obliged to accept the thirty or more reams. This paper was used in printing the book *Old Paper-making in China and Japan,* with 72 pages; 19 illustrations in black and white; 11 in color; 5 photogravures; woodcuts by J. J. Lankes; 15 specimens of old paper and 3 examples of bark. The edition was ready for the subscribers late in 1932 at seventy-five dollars a copy. My own hand-cut and hand-cast type was used for the fourth and last time. As the typesetting for this book progressed, I found that I lacked certain eighteen-point letters, and to supplement my type-case it was necessary to borrow my matrices and mould from the Smithsonian Institution, a favor that was graciously granted.

An appropriate and fitting ending for the Lime Rock hand-made-paper mill came when, in 1948, the property was purchased by my friend David Clark Everest, President of the Marathon Corporation, Rothschild, Wisconsin. Through Dr. Everest's thoughtfulness, the old English equipment was removed from the mill and presented to The Institute of Paper Chemistry at Appleton, Wisconsin, for exhibit in one of the display rooms of that renowned research organization.

# ⚜ VIII ⚜

THE assembling of ancient Oriental material for *Old Paper-making in China and Japan* had aroused my interest in present-day Asiatic papermaking, and I wanted to visit the small family paper mills of the Far East. Although I was acquainted with the Japanese handmade papers that were sold in the United States and Europe, the methods of the Orient were not entirely clear to me; there was a decided difference between the techniques of the East and the West. I had read everything available on the subject of Asiatic papermaking, but most of the writers had not been papermakers, and their descriptions failed to give lucid explanations of the various procedures. If I was to acquire a comprehensive understanding, I would have to visit the small mills myself.

In the spring of 1933, after more than three weeks on the Pacific Ocean plowing through the roughest of seas, my ship reached Yokohama and I was ready to go ashore and once more have a firm footing. I was met by my friends Yasunosuke Fukukita of the Oji Paper Company, Dr. T. Seki, octogenarian paper historian, and Shigeo Nakane of the research department of the Department of Commerce, United States Embassy. The Oji Paper Company was one of the huge corporations of Japan, manufacturing by machine great quantities of paper for export and supplying about one third of the paper used in the empire. The company had thirteen mills with about fifty machines. They also owned forests, power plants, railroads, and steamships.

After luncheon at the Imperial Hotel in Tokyo with a group of gentlemen interested in papermaking and printing, we drove to the Oji Paper Company, where we were greeted by Mr. Takashima, manager-director and an ardent bibliophile. He and Mr. Fukukita had already arranged for my visits to many of the small handmade-paper mills throughout Japan. Mr. Yamada, a graduate of Miami (Ohio) University, had been selected to accompany me.

Dr. Seki, Mr. Yamada, and I left Tokyo the following evening, traveling north to the village of Takefu, in the province of Echizen, prefecture of Fukui. This journey required the entire night. My diminutive Japanese friends found the sleeping-accommodations comfortable, but the berth was too short for my six feet, and, owing to its outward slant, I was constantly sliding toward the floor of the car. I was amused by a half-dozen funnel-shaped holes that opened through the floor of the aisle to the railroad track. Every superfluous object was cast into the aisle, and if it did not at once find its way into one of the floor openings, it was soon kicked to the goal by some passenger who was passing through the car. In the dining-car a five-course dinner cost one and a half yen, or about thirty-two cents. Just before I went to Japan one of the young men employed as a dining-car waiter had placed poison in a patron's wine and had then set about to rob him. All male waiters had been discharged forthwith, and comely young women had been hired to take their places. The change required employing two thousand girls between sixteen and twenty-two. They were paid thirty to forty yen a month.

After changing cars at Takada and Toyama, we continued

to Takefu, where we remained several days. At Okamoto-Mura, a short distance from Takefu, we visited the first hand-made-paper mill I was to see in Japan. This mill, with a history of several hundred years, was owned by Ichibei Nishino, a mild-mannered little gentleman with the graciousness of ancient Nippon. Before taking us to see the actual making of paper, he insisted that we have hot tea, and after a thorough inspection of his mill we were again served tea with little chocolate confections. In Japan the preparation and drinking of tea was a study in itself. My friend Yasunosuke Fukukita was an authority on the Japanese tea ceremony and had written a monograph on the subject, a copy of which he inscribed for me.

Mr. Nishino lived in an ancient weather-beaten wooden house with paper doors and windows; a dozen fire buckets made of sections of bamboo hung above the doorway. The house was heated by a *hibachi,* a large earthenware bowl in which nestled sticks of glowing charcoal, brought to a red heat by constant fanning. I found it difficult to keep warm during the early days of spring and, like the native people, I was constantly rubbing my hands over the *hibachi.*

In Takefu I had my first experience in a rural inn, as there was no hotel in so small a settlement. Toward evening we were approached by a sworded policeman who was concerned about my presence in the village, as I was the first foreigner to remain overnight. We were politely told that each night a policeman would stay by the door of my room, so that I might be under constant surveillance. Perhaps I was a spy, and they were taking no chances.

While in Takefu we also visited a machine-paper mill. This method of making paper did not particularly interest me, although never before had I seen paper being made that was to be used exclusively for wrapping incense for burning at religious ceremonies. As we walked slowly through the large modern plant, the workmen, huddled over bowls of glowing charcoal, bowed low, touching their shaved heads to the damp stone floor. Such old-world manners had not appeared out of place in the rambling cottages where we had seen paper made by hand, but such reverence in a modern machine mill was an anachronism hard to understand.

The manager of the machine-paper mill arranged a dinner for us at the local restaurant, and this was my introduction to evening social life in Japan. In general the inns and restaurants were extremely clean, although damp and chilly, with low doorways that constantly caused me to stoop. The entrance to the dining-room of this particular restaurant was through a charming garden with bent and gnarled evergreen trees and low-growing shrubs. It was penetratingly cold in Takefu, and the paper windows and doors of the frail wooden buildings did little to keep out the drafts. Nor did the *hibachi* make much cheer. The large private dining room was dimly lighted and without ornamentation. A polished wood table stood no more than eight inches above the floor. I was given a cushion at one end of the table, while our host sat in the opposite position, with Dr. Seki and Mr. Yamada occupying one side. Also very much in evidence were four beautifully dressed *geisha*. These young ladies appeared to be cultivated and refined, and I was not embarrassed when the most dignified one sat on the cushion beside me. She was a graceful girl with faultless manners. Through Dr. Seki's interpretation I was told that the young woman wished to entertain me with some photographs she had recently made, and I expected to be shown views of the beautiful Echizen landscape. She withdrew a small brocaded album from her bodice and with the utmost decorum began turning the pages of the little volume. I was astonished by the photographs, as all were of the most lurid pornographic character. My embarrassment was somewhat relieved when two of the girls, Kikue Yamada and Fukueyu Matsunoya, began singing an old papermaking song they had learned for my benefit. The verse was sung over and over in high-pitched rasping voices to the accompaniment of the samisen. I could not learn the history of the song, but it related to Echizen papermaking.

The dinner continued hour after hour, and sitting cross-legged in my stocking feet upon the cold floor did not add to my pleasure. Each dish was brought separately, and most of the food was palatable, but the red and white raw fish, so much relished by the Japanese, did not appeal to me. At another repast in a more remote district the native guests ate the fresh palpitating flesh cut from a large living fish. The cutting was continued until only the head, tail, and vital inner parts remained. The disfigured fish swam around and around in a great bowl of water, apparently undisturbed. After this gruesome sight I lost appetite for any sort of fish.

After our dinner and entertainment at the Takefu restaurant, we walked by lantern light to the inn where we were to spend the few hours remaining before morning. After we had removed our shoes and placed them on the cold, moist stones of the outer court, we were shown our rooms. Every bedroom floor was covered with straw mats, each mat measuring three by six feet. The size of a Japanese room was designated by the number of mats, and an ordinary sleeping-room had eight to twelve. Before we had arrived in Takefu, considerable snow had fallen, and in the courtyard there were great drifts where the sun had not penetrated. The windows of the rooms were covered with mulberry-bark paper (shōji), the only shield from the cold and dampness without. My bed was made up on the floor with a *hibachi* at the foot, all wrapped in heavy blankets. As sleeping-garments were provided in country inns, I was given a *kimono* that was much too small. After lying down in the charcoal-heated bed with a hard hair-stuffed cylinder as a pillow, I was served a cup of tea, pink coconut balls, and a green-paste concoction done up in leaves. I slept well, and in the morning the charcoal bowl at the foot of my bed was still warm.

Making one's toilet in a Japanese rural inn required patience and no little ingenuity. The washing was done in brass bowls filled with hot water by the maids and placed on a highly polished brass grating supported over a long wooden box resembling an old-fashioned horse trough. There was steaming hot water for bathing in a stone-floored common bathhouse fitted with large wooden vats. The men and women sat upright in the vats and enjoyed the intensely hot water, but the heat was too great for my comfort.

After inspecting dozens of handmade-paper mills in Takefu and in the papermaking center of Gifu, we went to the cosmopolitan city of Osaka, where in the Miyakojima mill of the Oji Company I examined the most comprehensive library of papermaking in the empire. This collection had been assembled by Mr. J. Horikoshi, one of the mill directors. I was especially interested in his important collection of Empress Shōtoku's *dhāranī*. In A.D. 770 this Empress caused a million charms to be printed upon paper and one hundred thousand distributed to each of ten temples. Each rolled-paper charm was contained in a turned wooden pagoda about eight inches in height. The hemp paper had probably been made by Japanese workmen, but the Empress imported Chinese artisans to execute the actual printing of the prayers. This was the world's first text-printing upon paper.

The next place of papermaking interest at which we stopped was Kōchi, on the island of Shikoku, which lies south of Honshū in the Inland Sea. We left Kobe in the evening and traveled through the Kii Channel into the Bay of Tosa, arriving at our destination the following morning after fourteen hours on the small ship *Tenyumaru*. This Inland Sea ship had been built for local passenger service, without consideration for the comforts of Occidental travelers. This made for complications, and although I slept well in the narrow coffin-like bunk, the morning toilet facilities were somewhat inadequate: nothing more than ten or twelve round holes cut in the floor of the exposed deck. The holes were in a row about eighteen inches apart and entirely devoid of railings or supports. It does not require a very vivid imagination to picture the problems posed by such a simple arrangement in a rough, choppy sea. The sight of a half-dozen serious, seasick Japanese men and women trying to arrange themselves over these conveniently shaped openings while the ship was rolling will always remain in that niche of my memory reserved for humorous situations.

When the ship docked at Kōchi, we were met by one of the ever present sworded policemen, and also by the manager of the Nippon Shigyo Kaisha, the largest handmade-paper mill on the island. We walked to the Shironishi Kan, a low, rambling inn, where the paper-covered windows of my room overlooked almost tropical vegetation. In the evening we were given a delectable dinner attended by men connected with the town's paper industry. The feast was held at the Tokugetsu-Ro— "The House of Catching Moon"—where more than five hundred *geisha* were in attendance. As in the restaurant at Takefu, the girls had practiced an ancient papermaking song for me, and it was sung to the customary samisen accompaniment. I could not learn the origin of the verses, but I was assured that they had been sung in Kōchi for hundreds of years, possibly from the time of the introduction of papermaking into Shikoku. The translated verses read:

*The famous products for which Tosa is renowned*
*are artistic coral and whale,*
*Paper, raw silk, and dried fish,*
*Come, come and visit our province.*

*In the town of Kōchi in Tosa Province*
*when I was walking through Harimaya-bridge*
*I saw a Buddhist priest with a shaved head*
*purchase an ornamental red coral hairpin.*

*Throwing aside all of her tangled love affairs,*
*as if she were discharging the pulp from her mould,*
*Miss Kōchi, prettiest of all papermaking girls,*
*is happy when she can see her reflection in the water of her*
*vat.*
*But from whom did she receive the ornamental red coral hair-*
*pin?*
*We are longing for Kōchi and red coral!*

In Japanese verse the sentiment is never fully expressed: the words or phrases merely suggest a certain thought or emotion. As a Japanese poem is really only a framework, or skeleton, into which the poetic reader must put his own thought, a translation does not convey to the Western mind the full meaning of the writer. In Japan an ornamental red coral hairpin is a token of love, but a Buddhist priest does not marry, and he is not supposed even to look upon anything of a feminine nature. The inference is made, however, that the priest gave the coral ornament to the girl papermaker and she was contented when she saw the reflection of it in the water of the vat from which she dipped the sheets of paper.

Our days and nights in Shikoku were filled with pleasant social diversion, and through the co-operation of the mill-owners and workers I gleaned a most gratifying insight into the making of Japanese paper. It was with regret that we left Kōchi, but we wished to visit the Kamafu mill, in the village of Kawanoye, at the extreme north of the island. The railroad was under construction, so we drove the hundred miles over a most dangerous mountain roadway without walls or protective fencing anywhere along the route. The small automobile jolted along scarcely eight inches from the edge of the narrow road, with a perpendicular drop of hundreds of feet to the bottom of the deep, rocky valley.

Although there was a possibility that at any moment the car might be dashed to the stony depths below, there was so much of interest along the way that danger was almost forgotten. The scenery was spectacular. As we rode along, at no great speed, we passed all manner of carts drawn by men, women, children, horses, dogs, and goats. The crude wheeled vehicles were laden with all sorts of produce of the island: logs, bales of papermaking barks, fruits, melons, vegetables, and flowers. In every village along the route there were workers in front of open shops: men making and decorating paper umbrellas, women and children husking rice and grinding the grain in primitive hand mills, workmen, almost naked, forming gray clay roof tiles, peasants stripping mulberry, mitsumata, and gampi bark for the papermakers. Carpenters with odd-shaped handmade tools sat at the edge of the roadway fashioning cabinets of soft white wood, the aroma of which scented the air. Workers were everywhere doing their tasks in the exhilarating mountain air, apparently unaware of the scenery around them and entirely oblivious to their own quaintness and charm. Only after seeing the out-of-the-way parts of Japan could an Occidental visitor truly appreciate the outdoor scenes of Japanese life so graphically depicted in the woodblock prints of Utagawa Toyokuni, Kitagawa Utamaro, Hiroshige, and Hokusai. Everywhere the composition of an old print showed itself in real life, with all the distorted positions and the soft coloring of costumes and buildings; peasants in their water-soaked rice fields, craftsmen at their various chores along the lanes and in the doorways—everywhere pictures, everywhere workers. There was no place for idleness on the lovely island of Shikoku.

After visiting the Kamafu mill, we left Kawanoye for the town of Takamatsu, where there was a newly built European-type hotel, and I was glad to sit on a chair again. The proprietor proudly gave me a room that appeared to have every modern convenience, although the Japanese maid had arranged the bedclothes in such a complicated manner that it became a veritable puzzle to retire. The bathroom was lined with exquisite green and white ceramic tiles, and the floor was of Italian marble, as were the door and window casings. It was the most sumptuous bathroom I had ever seen. After bathing, however, I opened the outlet in the magnificent porcelain tub and, to my astonishment, the floor of the room was soon flooded. No provision whatever had been made for the water to drain away. The architect and builder had evidently devoted so much thought to the bathroom ornamentation that they had neglected this minor necessity.

While on the subject of Japanese hotels planned in the Western manner, I cannot omit a brief observation on the famed Imperial Hotel in Tokyo. This hotel, planned by the renowned American architect Frank Lloyd Wright, may have withstood earthquakes, tornadoes, and fires, but from the standpoint of comfort it was noticeably deficient. The upper hallways were dark, tunnel-like passages with hidden steps and turnings. In going to and coming from my room I had to exercise constant vigilance to avoid tripping and falling. After reaching my room, fortunately without breaking my neck, I had to be content with a dimly lighted, poorly ventilated cramped cell, devoid of comfort or attractiveness.

To reach the mainland of Honshū again from Takamatsu we ferried across the narrow channel, and within an hour arrived in Okayama, where we visited more handmade-paper mills, and then continued on to Osaka, where a dinner had been arranged for us. At this elaborate banquet we were served raw oysters, each dyed a different color. Never before had I tried to devour red, green, yellow, and purple oysters. For dessert we had the largest strawberries I had ever seen, two or three being sufficient for a serving. The berries were delicious if the method of fertilization with human excrement could be overlooked.

Traveling to Nagoya the following day, we were entertained by a group of paper merchants, who later in the evening insisted that we attend the annual performance of the Cherry Dance, for which Nagoya was noted. Before entering the large hall where the dance was to be given, we removed our shoes. Each pair was tied together and hung on a long rope stretched from one low post to another. The hundreds of pairs of shoes were checked by attendants, and every shoe-owner was given a small wooden shingle with a number so that he could claim his shoes after the performance.

Before the entertainment began, I was introduced to many of the girls who were to take part in the dances. Some of them did not appear to be more than fourteen years old; others were considerably more mature. Every face was painted with thick calcimine, which cracked at the corners of the mouth and eyes like whitewash peeling on a smooth plaster wall. The dancers' thick black hair was done in elaborate fashion, high on the head, with jewels and artificial flowers intertwined. The hair was not curled, but held in curves the way horses' tails are arranged at a horse show. In all parts of Japan the girls seemed to have an identical odor, not of perfume, but the aroma of mixed spices with a dash of delicate feminine perspiration.

After two hours of tedious dancing and monotone singing, during which I was uncomfortable in my stocking feet, the performance was over. I was afraid that there would not be sufficient shoes to go around, but as we drove away from the hall I looked back at the long rope where so many pairs of shoes had been hanging: there was but one lone slipper remaining.

In Osaka, several days later, we were invited to attend an afternoon performance of the Osaka marionettes, a traditional entertainment of the city. I was remotely familiar with the European type of puppets controlled by strings from above, but the Japanese version of this age-old form of Oriental amusement was totally unknown to me. We were given seats well toward the front of the theater where every detail was visible. Each wooden figure in the play was four or five feet in height, with movable mouth and eyes, and a body fitted with loosely hung arms and legs. These ornately dressed images were carried around the brilliantly lighted stage by men dressed in black cloaks and wearing black masks. It required the efforts of four or five men to operate each dummy figure: one man held the marionette, another opened and closed its eyes and mouth, other blacked-robed men agitated the legs and arms. When there were four or five of the wooden actors taking part in a play, there were at least twenty black-clad men putting them through their various contortions, a most ludicrous and incongruous spectacle to Western eyes. At the side of the stage sat two men: one recited the lines of the play as each figure was put through its part, the other extracted weird tones from the samisen.

Much to my relief, when the long-drawn-out play was about half finished, an attendant came to us with the request that we go behind the scenes. After we had tea with the director, he showed us the hundreds of marionettes that were suspended upon railings in the storage room. The limp wooden figures were dressed in silk, velvet, and brocade, and decorated with gold and silver braid. The director explained how the mouth of each figure could be opened and shut, and how easily the eyebrows could be lifted. I held several of the puppets and found them extremely heavy. After tea was again served, we went to the hotel, where I was glad to rest. Visiting in Japan with hosts of hospitable friends often required more social endurance than I could command.

After completing the investigations relative to the making of paper by hand in Japan, I wished to see some of the Korean establishments. While I was in Tokyo, Mr. Takashima, the bibliophile, had invited me to his home, where I examined many specimens of old Korean paper. I found it difficult, however, to determine either from him or from others just where such paper was being fabricated in Korea. Unlike modern Chinese and Japanese handmade paper, the product of Korea was practically unknown in Europe and America, for little of it had ever been exported. Determined to see Korean paper being made, I started out from Tokyo alone, as Mr.

Yamada, who had been with me during our visits to the Japanese mills, could not make the tedious journey. I was well supplied with introductions, although no one knew where the mills were located.

After a rough crossing from Shimonoseki through the Tsushima Channel, the ship arrived in Fusan, Korea, the following morning. Before I left Tokyo, Dr. Seki, the paper historian, gave me a document written in Japanese in which my mission in Korea was set forth. At the time of my visit the new Japanese state of Manchukuo was under "development" and the authorities were apprehensive regarding spies. Immediately upon landing in Fusan, I was approached by U. Nakamura of the Japanese secret service. He had been informed that my mission in Korea was to investigate the *kami* of the country, and that I wanted to collect specimens of every variety, both old and modern. The secret agent could not believe that the collecting of *kami* was my real reason for coming to Korea. But although he had misgivings regarding my visit, I was permitted to proceed on my northern journey, the kindly official wishing me success in my quest.

Sometime later, when I was in Fusan, I met Mr. Nakamura again, and he was profuse in his apologies for having previously treated me with suspicion. It seems that on my first arrival in Fusan, the officer of the secret service had been informed that I was in Korea to investigate *kami*, which meant both paper and hair. He explained that when I originally arrived he thought I had come to examine human hair, both old and new, and he had visions of me going from person to person clipping specimens for my collection. A story appeared in the Fusan newspaper about the eccentric American who had journeyed halfway around the world to collect ancient and modern Korean hair. It was little wonder that the courteous officer had apprehensions when he first met me in Fusan, but on our second meeting we had tea together and he could not forgive himself for having confused the meaning of the word *kami*.

After reaching Korea, I learned that paper was being made by hand in several places that I was able to visit without going far into the interior. But upon learning of the papermaking center of Ompei, Keiki Dō, in central Korea, I wanted to go there, as I was told that every person in the settlement was engaged in some branch of papermaking and that the methods had remained unchanged from ancient times.

I proceeded by train to Seoul, through mountainous country almost barren of trees although beautiful in its severity; the air was fresher and more invigorating than that of Japan. It was springtime, and all along the route the peasants were breaking the earth with ox-drawn plows made of heavy pointed sticks, a method unchanged from that used in these same fields hundreds of years earlier. Along the way I was constantly hoping that I would see paper being dried upon boards or upon the ground, and through my own observation discover an additional papermaking center, but nothing that even suggested papermaking was seen after I left Taikyū, near Fusan. The quiet countryside, with low, closely built straw-roofed mud houses, was more suggestive of China than of Japan. The men and women were clothed entirely in white, while the children's dresses of bright yellow and red gave touches of color to the somber landscape. It required no imagination to understand why Korea was called "The Land of Morning Calm." Serenity was felt everywhere. Never was a country more truly named.

As I looked from the car window upon the still countryside of that ancient, peaceful peninsula, I felt a sense of satisfaction, for here, I thought, was one small portion of the world which would never be disturbed. Korea would remain unchanged. Within the train, however, there was a totally different atmosphere, a feeling that change was certain to come. Connected to the regular train were several cars filled with Japanese troops on the way to the "front" in Manchuria. The "Manchukuo incident" was at its height. The young soldiers appeared rugged in their green-brown uniforms with red trimmings and their high yellow leather boots. They were strongly reminiscent of the German and Austrian soldiers I had seen in Berlin and Vienna before the First World War.

The dining-car of the Seoul train provided an excellent five-course dinner served by doll-like Japanese girls who wore tiny blue jackets and short white skirts. Later in Tokyo I noticed an advertisement in a newspaper for dining-car waitresses in which it was stated that only very tall girls would be considered: no girl should apply who was not at least five feet tall.

Upon arriving in Seoul I was surprised to be met by three Japanese gentlemen who had been advised of my coming by my friends in Tokyo. They arranged for my visit to the central Korean papermaking village. It was a typically calm morning when we set out from Seoul to make our way to Ompei over rocky roads along winding streams swollen by the spring rains. On the last stretch of the road we passed the only remaining section of the crenelated stone wall that in ancient times made its eleven-mile course around the city of Seoul. The wall had originally been pierced by eight massive gateways. After arriving at the Great White Buddha at the base of the mountain, we walked the remaining distance to the treeless village of Ompei.

Although a few days earlier I had visited other Korean handmade-paper mills, I was not prepared to see such a primitive setting as we encountered in Ompei. Out in the open, alongside a clear, gushing river, were several crude stone rolls for macerating pulp, with dipping-vats half sheltered under thatched roofs supported by wooden posts. The entire paper-making village represented a unique and picturesque industrial scene such as might have been seen on the same spot hundreds of years before. The paper made in Ompei was of an unusually large size, measuring 28 by 46 inches, and was used on the floors of Korean houses in the same way that the Japanese used straw mats.

In contrast to the use of the *hibachi* for heating in Japan, the houses of Korea were heated by oven fires located under the floors, and the smoke issued through chimneys that pro-truded from the foundations of the cottages. In the larger houses the flues ran underground, the smoke making its exit through chimneys built in a garden wall twenty or thirty feet from the house. The Korean climate was cold, and the thick handmade-paper floor mats provided necessary insulation, as the Koreans, like the Japanese, lived close to the floor.

In Ompei we made dozens of photographs, and I carried away quantities of paper as well as various moulds and tools employed in the ancient craft of Korean papermaking, a trade that came to Korea from China in the seventh century of our era.

In Seoul, across the broad road from the European-type hotel where I was staying, a pretentious antique emporium sold Korean chests studded with ornamental brass bosses and fitted with incised corner plates and complicated locks and hinges. After passing the shop on numerous occasions, I finally de-cided to go in and examine the antiques more closely. I was greeted by three elderly, thin-whiskered Korean gentlemen dressed in shiny white cotton costumes and white slippers. I expressed a mild interest in purchasing an old Korean chest. The three owners, all gleaming in anticipation of a sale, led me to a row of chests that were obviously so new that the finish was hardly dry. One of the Korean proprietors said that the chests were exceedingly old, and his two companions declared that all the chests in the shop were the most ancient to be found in Korea. It required no knowledge of cabinet-making to see that not a single chest in the entire establishment was more than two or three years old. The shop-owners continued to insist that all the chests had been made hundreds of years earlier, and they said they would give me a certificate signed by each of them vouching for the great age of any piece I would purchase. This certificate, they explained, could be shown to the United States Customs officer and the chest would be permitted to enter free of duty as a genuine antique. Angered at such arrogance and effrontery, I told them so in no uncertain manner and started to leave the shop. One of the old men followed me and, grasping my arm, said that perhaps they had made a mistake. I asked him to explain their deliberate deceit, and especially their willingness to sign a declaration that they knew to be absolutely false. They were profuse in apologies and said they had meant no harm and hoped I was not offended. After they realized that I could not be too easily duped, the yellow-skinned charlatans urged me to accompany them to their small factory, where I was not surprised to see in the process of construction the same sort of Korean chests, with the identical new brass ornaments, that were offered in the shop as authentic antiques.

When my Asiatic journey was completed, I became acquainted with two young American women on the ship that was taking us to San Francisco. They too had been to Seoul, and each had purchased a Korean chest from the three elderly owners of the "antique" shop across the road from the hotel. The young ladies were certain that their brass-entrusted chests were more than two hundred years old, and to prove the age of the pieces they proudly showed me two certificates duly signed by the three Korean shopkeepers. I did not mention my own experience, but upon our arrival at the port of San Francisco, I was amused to see that the Customs officials were well acquainted with the false certificates. The examining officer told the young ladies that their "old" Korean chests were newly made and added that the regular duty imposed on modern furniture would have to be paid.

While in Seoul, I visited the Technical Institute, where Japanese instructors were teaching Korean artisans the Japanese methods of making paper by hand. With the exception of several schools in India, this was the only academy in the world that included in the curriculum the teaching of paper-making by hand. In the seventh century the Koreans taught the art of papermaking to the Japanese, and in the twentieth century the Japanese were teaching the Koreans the present-day methods of Japan!

When I finally left Seoul to take the early-morning train to return to Fusan, I was surprised to see the usually quiet streets lined with Koreans, with a great number of police all along the way. The people were waving flags of old Korea, and the Japanese flag was noticeably absent. After arriving at the station I was told that Prince Yi, who had been in Korea for two weeks, was returning to his home in Tokyo. Prince Yi was the Crown Prince of Korea, but after the Japanese moved in and took over his country, he no longer held his princely position. He was thirty-five years old and married to a Japanese princess. This was his first visit to his native land in five years, and at every village along the railway clusters of Koreans had assembled to greet him with flags and banners. No one made a sound, only bowing low in respect as the train passed.

When we reached Fusan the following morning, the royal party was ceremoniously put aboard the ship bound for Shimonoseki. At breakfast I sat next to the rotund young Prince and saw that he consumed two tangerines, three hard-boiled eggs, and a pot of black tea. From Shimonoseki we proceeded to Tokyo by train. Although the Korean Crown Prince was given no end of quiet attention by his own native people all along the route from Seoul to Fusan, after leaving Shimonoseki no notice whatever was given the passing train.

Later in my Asiatic journeys I visited Chekiang and Kwangtung, but I was disappointed in the quality of the paper being made in China. In times past the Chinese had fabricated the finest paper produced in the world, but I had arrived a hundred or more years too late, and the paper I saw made was most inferior to either the Japanese or the Korean product.

The material I had gathered on the trip resulted in the edition of *A Papermaking Pilgrimage to Japan, Korea, and China,* printed and published by Elmer Adler's Pynson Printers, New York, 1935. The edition was printed on Japanese mulberry-bark handmade paper, with 150 pages; 68 photogravure illustrations; and 50 original specimens of handmade papers that had been collected in Japan, Korea, and China. It was bound by Gerhard Gerlach in three-quarters leather with paper sides printed from an old woodblock I had found in northern Korea. The edition was limited to 370 copies that were sold for thirty-six dollars each.

# ❖ IX ❖

AFTER the material for *A Papermaking Pilgrimage to Japan, Korea, and China* had been assembled and prepared for publication, I again felt the urge to be on my way, this time to other Asiatic countries where paper was being made by ancient hand methods. The papermakers of Siam had long interested me, and I wanted to visit the villages where the black-coated paper used by the yellow-robed priests for their religious manuscripts was made.

Although the definite object of my voyage was the paper-making districts of southern Siam, I arranged for around-the-world passage on the British freight ship *Penrith Castle* of the Dodwell-Castle Line of Liverpool. My plan was to leave the freighter temporarily at Singapore, journey overland to Siam, and join the same ship at Penang after a cargo of tin and rubber had been taken aboard. One of the advantages of traveling by freighter was the time required for unloading and loading at various ports. These intervals often extended to five or six days, and it was possible to take short trips into the interior and rejoin the ship at a later port of call.

Singapore was not an interesting city, and its commonplace qualities became even more pronounced while I awaited the departure of the semi-weekly train bound for Bangkok. I was aware that no paper was being made by hand in the Federated

Malay States, and therefore I was impatient to be on the way to Siam, where it was reasonably certain the ancient methods were still in use. The usual way to get from Singapore to Bangkok was to travel by ship through the China Sea into the Gulf of Siam, arriving after a week's comfortable voyage in Paknam, the entrance port for the Siamese capital. As I wished to see as much as possible of the country, however, I chose to go by the winding railway that penetrated the rubber plantations and jungles of the long, slender Malay Peninsula. This trip covered a distance of 1,188 miles in about sixty hours.

In the train that departed from the lofty Singapore station on Sunday morning, April 7, 1935, I was one of four Occidental passengers. The railway from Singapore to Bangkok was narrow-gauge, and the cars were correspondingly contracted; the seats were covered with slippery rattan, and as they inclined forward, the traveler had a feeling of insecurity, as if at any moment he might slide to the floor of the car. The narrow aisle was choked with bunches of bananas, wicker birdcages, and all manner of nondescript luggage. But with over one thousand miles of strange jungles and desert ahead, and the romantic city of Bangkok, with its promise of a primitive paper mill, as my destination, my spirit and enthusiasm were not to be daunted by minor discomforts. The train made its way slowly through the monotonous rubber plantations of the states of Johore and Pahang, stopping at the settlements of Jahore Bharu, Kluang, and Gemas, and finally in the sultry evening reaching the luxuriously tropical city of Kuala Lumpur, with its hundreds of impudent monkeys at every turn. After several hours in the ancient capital, a coach with permanent berths was made ready to continue the northern journey. Never before had I tried to find rest on such a hard, unyielding bed. Through the meshes of the mosquito netting that draped my berth, I could see, in the dimly lighted carriage, the dark-skinned Malays, Chinese, Siamese, Indians, and Japanese making preparations for the night. There was little sleep for me. Not only was the bed short, hard, and lumpy, but also my window could not be closed, and throughout the night I was kept busy extinguishing the sparks that fell on my bed-covering from the wood-burning locomotive.

Before daylight I was awakened by the Malay guard: we had reached the station where a change of trains had to be made. It was a relief to leave the uncomfortable berth, although anything but pleasant to be rudely shaken from even a fitful sleep and to stumble bag and baggage into the dark tropical morning of a strange place. With the help of a flickering match I read the station signboard and discovered that I was in the small Chinese settlement of Bukit Mertajam. There was to be a wait of several hours before the train for Bangkok would be ready. In the misty morning the station was dismal, but the hospitality of the Malayan stationmaster and his assistant more than compensated for the bleak surroundings. After break of day I walked through the streets of the settlement. Most of the inhabitants were asleep; only two or three old Chinese merchants who had slept on the counters of their shops were to be seen through the filmy windows, preparing for the day's trade. The few restaurants in the village, dingy hovels presided over by swarthy Celestials, did not appeal to me, at least not in the early hours of a Malayan morning. When I returned to the railway depot, the kindly stationmaster suggested that he brew a pot of tea. With a box of English biscuits from my luggage, and a few bananas, we had breakfast together.

The train for Bangkok was finally assembled, and with regret I left the drab Chinese village of Bukit Mertajam. Not only had the stationmaster been most considerate, but as the day drew on I had been kindly received by the Chinese residents, several of whom had suggested that I attend a near-by funeral. For the first time I saw the Buddhist ceremonial rite of burning "spirit-paper," an ancient custom not entirely unknown to me. This experience increased my desire to know more of the use of this weird paper and to gather specimens of the numerous types that could be found. Perhaps in the distant future a book about the use of this paper might be written and the original examples tipped in each volume as illustrations.

After two stops in the state of Kedah, the narrow-gauge train, late in the afternoon, reached Padang Besar on the border of Siam. Here the Malay trainmen gave way to dapper little Siamese. I thought the Siamese more capable and efficient, but even so, when we were approaching the settlement of Muang Lung, some five hundred miles south of Bangkok, the engine gave one last breath and doggedly refused to go farther. This caused a delay of several hours, as extra locomotives were not plentiful in the wilds of Siam.

The lower part of the peninsula was desolate, with dry alluvial clay capable of producing only the scantiest and scrubbiest vegetation. The few mean houses scattered along the railway were encircled by stout wooden stockades, suggesting the presence of marauding wild animals. During the day the heat was noticeable, although the nights were delightfully cool—a welcome surprise, as I had expected Malaysia and Siam to be oppressive and enervating. I had experienced more trying humidity and intense heat in the eastern United States.

During the following night the train made stops at many villages, and by the third morning we reached Bang Saphan Yai, only 235 miles south of Bangkok. As the train grew closer to the Siamese capital, the heat increased, and the floors of the railway carriages were covered to a depth of half an inch with the dry, hot dust of the desert. The towns and villages of the northern part of the peninsula began to appear more promising, with scattered green trees and a few wilting flowers. It was a little disconcerting, however, to watch the gaily dressed Asiatic passengers leave the train to lunch heartily on thick slices of coarse native bread spread heavily with unsavory condensed milk poured from individual cans. Late in the afternoon of the third day the weary train arrived at the great steel railway shed at Bangkok. My long and uncomfortable, although highly interesting, journey had ended, and the newly built Rajdhani Hotel in the rambling commercial center of Bangkok offered needed rest.

In this hotel I met the young gentleman who was to be my guide, Perm Kumpangtong, a representative of the government of Siam. According to previously acquired information, one of the mills I wished to visit was near Bangsue, the other in Bang Khen. The directions for visiting these two places had been given me about a year earlier, and my guide shared my belief that these cottage mills continued to function. Much to my disappointment, however, when Mr. Kumpangtong inquired along the canals about the mills, we were told that paper was no longer made in these two outlying districts of Bangkok.

We then made a tour of the capital's dingy paper shops and, after going from house to house, finally found an old parchment-faced Chinese paper merchant who told us that only one place remained where paper continued to be made by hand. This was a small mill near Bangsoom which had long been owned by an old papermaking family named Niltongkum. This information was heartening, and after further inquiries along the dusty roads that led to the waterfront we were directed to a dilapidated wharf on the Nênam Choa Bhraya and found the cadaverous owner of a river gondola who thought he might be able to take us to Bangsoom. The rounded roof of his boat was so low that I could not sit upright on the narrow wooden seat, and the heat of the equatorial sun upon the sheet-metal roofing, to say nothing of the swarms of flies and mosquitoes, did not add to the comforts of travel. We floated quietly along the river, passing slow-moving barges of all sizes laden with the colorful products of Siam. Finally our boatman, who seemed familiar with every twist and turn of Bangkok's vast canal system, left the busy river and turned up a narrow, overgrown passage scarcely wide enough for even his small gondola to slip through without scraping the muddy banks. We glided silently along past wooden houses and shops, all built upon stilts in the marsh, which was covered with tropical aquatic plants whose exotic odors permeated the close, still air.

Each house along the way had its own board steps leading down to the canal so that every member of a family could conveniently reach the filthy brown water. The men, women, and children who were bathing and washing their clothes in the sluggish stream scrambled cheerfully up the steps to permit our little craft to pass. The Siamese were extremely patient and, like the Chinese, had an abundance of humor which helped ease their endless hardships. It was difficult to pass the numerous skiffs, which carried pyramids of highly colored melons and fruits, folded palm leaves tied together like bundles of newspapers, and wooden bowls filled with the much loved betel nuts. I was especially entranced by an elaborate floating drugshop with gaily painted compartments piled high with many varieties of Oriental herbs, barks, and roots, the whole boat decorated with gilded wood-carvings and shiny metal and glass ornaments. Sitting upright in the center of this floating medical establishment was the old apothecary himself, suggesting an Eskimo paddling his hide-covered kayak. As we turned from one canal into another, each succeeding stream became narrower. The low-hung trees scraped the roof of our craft and formed an archway over the water. Snakes and lizards slithered up the slippery banks of the canals, and everywhere there were children playing in the stream. Mere babies placed their small hands together, cup-shape, and drank the dirty warm water with delight. Never before had I seen such disregard for sanitation.

Hour after hour we wound in and out through miles of waterways, under such wild vegetation as I had scarcely dreamed existed. I was pleased to discover along the canals a number of *khoi* trees (*Streblus asper*), whose bark for hundreds of years had supplied the material for Siamese paper-making. The branches and twigs were gathered and tied together in convenient bundles by the country people, who sold them to the papermakers. Our small gondola was dexterously guided from one leaf-hung canal to another, and as the tide was coming in, our progress was fairly rapid. All along the route I was looking for familiar signs that would suggest paper-making, and after seemingly endless travel we approached a rambling wooden house, well elevated on stilts above the level of the stream, from which came sounds of the dull rhythmical beating of bark. Through the thick vegetation that lined the banks of the waterway I could distinguish a number of tall papermaking-moulds leaning carelessly against the wooden posts that supported the house. It was obvious that we had reached our destination. Bangkok seemed far away, and only a boatman who had spent his life upon the vast network of canals could have found Bangsoom or could return to the Siamese capital without being lost in the maze of channels.

Our little craft was made fast to a mooring-post, and we entered the house, where I was ceremoniously introduced to the various members of the Niltongkum family. In my quest for information and appliances relative to handmade paper, I had in years past visited many remote mills, but seldom had I been so thoroughly captivated by a papermaking establishment. The thatched house was raised about seven feet above the ground on stout teakwood posts, like a huge bamboo bird-cage perched on stilts, with steep steps leading to the living-apartment. Under the house proper, on the well-packed earthen floor, many of the various stages of papermaking were performed, and here numerous moulds and other tools of the papermakers' craft were stored. The house, surrounded by dense trees, low vegetation, and thick climbing vines, made a haven for myriad gnats and mosquitoes that thrived in the moist, warm atmosphere.

The Niltongkum family consisted of Tym, the father, Piung, the mother, and two grown daughters, Luolin and Pyn, to say nothing of many chubby little grandchildren and innumerable dogs. In Siam no road or habitation was complete without its scores of diseased and crippled canines of every mongrel variety. Tym, the venerable grandfather, too old for the arduous work involved in making paper, occupied himself with rocking one of the brown babies in an ingenious hanging bamboo cradle, but his betel-chewing helpmate, Piung, although more than eighty years of age, continued to be the most active member of the family. I had never before seen the equal of Piung Niltongkum. Even at her advanced age she not only beat the *khoi* bark with hand mallets to reduce it to fiber, but also formed the sheets of paper and attended to the business of the family enterprise. Although the two shapely daughters, Luolin and Pyn, were capable and skillful in all branches of the craft, the withered and bent octogenarian, stripped to the waist, insisted that she alone show me the entire process of making paper. Her unbounded enthusiasm was incomprehensible; every nerve and muscle of her diminutive, dried-up bronze body quivered with energy and strength. When I asked that photographs be made while she was ambidextrously beating the *khoi* bark, she could not be induced to remain posed with beating-mallets in mid-air sufficiently long for a time exposure. She continued to beat the bark vigorously regardless of my overtures. Through my guide, acting as interpreter, the old woman told me that it was impossible for her to remain quiet; all her life she had beaten bark for making paper; she had never before had her picture taken; and she simply did not know how to be still and composed.

Piung Niltongkum could give but little information regarding the origin of her paper mill and its dim history. It was apparent that this particular phase of her family industry had never entered her mind, and she was noticeably surprised that I was interested. She did believe, however, that paper had been fabricated on the same hard earthen floor and in the same stream for more than two hundred years and that the original mill had been set up by one of her forefathers. She told of the great quantities of paper that had been made during her early life and complained of the slackening demand in recent times. She was critical of the Chinese merchants, who did not pay her regularly and were even given to cheating. But, regardless of these present-day trials, she stated emphatically that as long as she was able to grasp bark-beating mallets between her bony fingers and wade knee-deep into the stream to form sheets of paper, she would continue her beloved craft; it was her life work, and nothing could induce her to give way to the inroads of the paper machine.

At intervals during our stay, our venerable hostess would set aside her bark-beating for an instant, but without leaving her seat upon the floor she would reach for a coconut and with astonishing vigor break the shell with her mallet and pour the milky contents into a bowl that had been cooling in the stream. She insisted that I drink, and the coconut milk was refreshing, as the temperature was well over one hundred degrees. Piung Niltongkum was contented only when busily engaged in some branch of making paper so that I might see every detail of the process, or when performing some act of hospitality to make my visit agreeable. Even though this shriveled old woman was as primitive as a native of the jungle and had never been more than a few miles from her native plot of packed earth bordered by the muddy canals of Bangsoom, she possessed a graciousness that would have befitted a lady of more exalted birth and calling.

The actual forming of sheets of paper in the Siamese manner, as practiced by the Niltongkum family, was almost identical with the method conceived by the Chinese eunuch Ts'ai Lun when he invented paper during the second century of the Christian era. The books of Siam were long and narrow in shape, formed in accordion folds, and the manuscripts were read by turning the leaves or folds away from the reader. The sheets of Bangsoom paper were formed in long, narrow moulds to conform to this method of bookmaking, a practice that had its origin in the earlier use of oblong palm leaves for manuscripts. Many of the religious books of Siam were written in yellow pigment on handmade paper that had been stained black on the surface. Calligraphy transcribed in yellow upon a background of dense black had long been considered by oculists the most restful for reading, but it was unlikely that the Siamese ever attached any scientific importance to the use of their unusual color combination.

The paper was blackened at the mill where it was made, and I was fortunate to see this procedure during my stay with the Niltongkum family. The ground charcoal used in making the black pigment was rendered from the shells of betel nuts burned in an open stone oven. The betel palm (*Areca catechu*) was much prized in many parts of Asia, as the nuts, when mixed with the ovate leaves of the betel (*Piper betle*) and a little shell lime, formed a masticatory used by almost two thirds of the native people of Siam and Indo-China. The teeth of the habitual chewer assumed a rich, lustrous black.

We had been at the Bangsoom mill since early morning, and gentle old Tym and Piung Niltongkum and their two healthy daughters had been exceedingly helpful in explaining every step involved in making paper from *khoi* bark. Packages of paper, bundles of bark, papermaking-moulds, bark-beating mallets, and other equipment were made ready for me to take away to use in writing about Siamese papermaking. During the last hours of our stay the old boatman grew nervous about the outgoing tide and at last politely insisted that we leave without further delay, as otherwise we might be left high and dry. At low tide many of the canals became unnavigable even for a gondola of the most shallow draft.

The papermaking paraphernalia was hurriedly piled in the little boat and, after many salutations, in which all members of the Niltongkum family, including the plump brown babies, pressed the palms of their hands against their foreheads in the ancient Siamese custom, we again glided through the inter-winding canals, finally reaching the wide Mênan. A few more miles on the muddy river brought us once more to the astonishing city of Bangkok with its gaily colored temples, low-built shops, narrow streets, and winding canals. The long hot day had been fatiguing, although one of the most interesting and instructive that I had ever spent in pursuit of the craft of making paper by hand.

The journey to Siam in 1935 and the visit to the Niltongkum family mill in Bangsoom resulted in the fifth publication from my private press. The book *Papermaking in Southern Siam* was issued in the autumn of 1936. It was quarto in size, with 40 pages of text set in Caslon type and 17 photogravure illustrations from photographs taken in the Niltongkum mill with the temperature hovering around one hundred and twenty degrees. The paper used in printing the text and photogravures had been made in the Lime Rock mill on moulds that bore the watermark of my private press. The specimens of Siamese paper tipped in each book included examples of both plain paper and paper that had been coated with black pigment for bookmaking; all the specimens had been made by Piung Niltongkum from the beaten bark of the *khoi*. In the colophon of the book it was bluntly stated: "Due to my strong aversion to the monotony of press-work only 115 copies of this book have been made." This was the real reason for the small number of books, as sufficient specimens for additional copies were available had I chosen to print them. The actual printing on the hand press was always burdensome; this part of the work was never a pleasure. As with the earlier books from my press, this edition was bound by Peter Franck, my friend of many years. The price of this book was twenty-seven dollars and fifty cents a copy. The edition was exhausted within a short time.

# X

MY curiosity regarding the use of "spirit-paper" in Chinese rites and ceremonies had been awakened that morning I spent in the Chinese settlement of Bukit Mertajam. Although I was familiar with Marco Polo's observations regarding "spirit-paper" as set down in the thirteenth century, I had known little about its use in my own time until that visit.

After Marco Polo's long residence at the court of the famous Kublai Khan, the Tartar emperor of China, he returned to his native Genoa only to be confined in prison, where he dictated his adventures to Rustichello of Pisa, a fellow prisoner. His description of "spirit-paper" was probably written in A.D. 1275:

> And when they come to the burning-place, they take representations of things cut out of paper, such as caparisoned horses, male and female slaves, camels, armor, suits of cloth of gold, and money, in great quantities, and these things they put on the fire with the corpse. And they tell you that the dead man shall have all these slaves and animals of which the effigies are burned, alive in flesh and blood, and the money in gold, for use in the next world.

The use of paper, cut, pasted, and painted to represent various animals and objects, for burning at Chinese funeral ceremonies had long antedated even Marco Polo, and continued through the centuries to modern times. These ghostly paper objects included highly ornate chests fitted with shining gold and silver paper handles and locks, flowing robes embellished with golden dragons and intricate patterns, slippers, hats, and all other manner of wearing apparel. For the relatives of the rich the craftsmen in paper constructed full-size carts, horses, and, in later years, even automobiles, with the consolation that these fragile effigies which went up in flame and smoke would assume reality in the next world for the heavenly comfort of the deceased.

I was fascinated by the skill and patience displayed by the Chinese artisans as they diligently worked with paper, paste, and paint in their open-fronted shops along the narrow, dirty streets and in the dismal courts. The façade of each shop was decorated with rows of slanting mirrors painted over with the names of the establishments in ornate Chinese characters surrounded by borders, garlands, and festoons in gay colors. The interior of each cramped shop had the appearance of a veritable paper museum, with every variety of funereal paraphernalia hanging from the rafters; drawers, boxes, and shelves were literally bursting with every conceivable style of stained and decorated paper, all for use in making reproductions to be consumed by fire at mortuary ceremonies. The quality of the material and the workmanship varied to suit rich and poor.

In Bangkok, where the Chinese population predominated, I stood for hours in a busy street in front of a funeral-paper shop watching the making of a replica of a life-size dog with an open mouth that showed a curved tongue and tusk-like teeth, a realistic visage frightening to behold! The bent framework forming the body of the animal was made of thin strips of split bamboo rendered pliable by being soaked in salt water.

The bamboo skeleton was covered by pasting layer upon layer of handmade paper, and was finally painted with water-color pigment, so that it made a truly lifelike replica. When I asked the Chinese paper-sculptor how the imitation dog would be used, he told me that an opulent Chinese tea merchant had lately passed into the next world and the effigy was a reproduction of the dead man's beloved mastiff. The facsimile canine had been ordered by the well-to-do relatives of the deceased. It was a rush order, the artisan explained, and was to be burned at the funeral of the merchant so that he would have the companionship of his favorite dog when he arrived in the spirit world.

For centuries the Chinese had been making their homes in almost every village, town, and city of the Far East, and wherever the Chinese had settled, the paper images continued to be burned. More than any other people, the Chinese had preserved their traditional customs, no matter how far they might remove from the mother country.

The burning of elaborate and expensive images, however, was insignificant when compared with the tremendous quantities of mock paper money that were burned every year by the Chinese wherever they had taken up their homes. It was probably reasoned out by the thoughtful Celestials that if sufficient "money" was consumed by fire at a funeral, the essence of the money would rise to the spirit world and the deceased relative or friend would himself have the cash to purchase elaborate clothing, fine horses, and other luxuries for his heavenly life. In the large centers of population throughout China, the mock paper money, tied in compact packages with fiber twine, was sold in special shops that dealt in joss paper, candles, incense sticks, and other commodities used in sacrificial offerings. In the villages and outlying districts, the decorated money paper could be had in almost every provision shop, the bundles of paper being invariably stored on the uppermost shelves of the crowded stores, which were pungent with the aroma of incense, spices, nuts, herbs, and dried fish. The most important center for the wholesale disposal of these weird papers was the historic city of Hangchow. In one province of Chekiang, nearly 127,000 workers were engaged in the manufacture of paper by the old hand methods, a great part of it used for burning at funerals and in temples.

The first Chinese funeral I had the privilege of seeing in its entirety was in Kwangtung province near a remote village where the ancient customs and traditions had remained uncontaminated. The entire performance was carried on in a manner befitting the ancestors of the deceased, who had lived in this same district from time immemorial. A young Chinese teacher, Mr. Chao, who had taught for a short time in Canton and had acquired a disjointed knowledge of English, offered to take me to the house of death and remain with me throughout the funeral procession. Mr. Chao was a distant kin of the dead man; in isolated districts almost all the families seemed to be related. My young guide lived in a village near by, and he suggested that we meet at a certain path-crossing at a given hour and proceed together to the funeral. As I was staying closer to the home of the deceased than was Mr. Chao, I reached the place of meeting before he arrived. After waiting a few minutes I noticed a well-draped form approaching on a bicycle, its nickle-plated frame sparkling in the sun. I soon saw that the rider was Mr. Chao, splendidly dressed in a flowing white robe, with padded black silk slippers on his feet, which were energetically pedaling the cycle. I also noticed a neat bundle strapped to the handlebars, but for a moment I could not determine what the package might contain. As he came closer I could see that a

*An example of ceremonial "spirit-paper," the prototype of which Marco Polo found in China during his travels in the thirteenth century. These papers, made of bamboo fibre, were often printed in red from woodblocks. When tinfoil was applied to the paper it was usually brushed over with a liquid rendered from seaweed which imparted a gold lustre to the metal foil. There were hundreds of different patterns of these sacrificial papers. This specimen was found in South China about thirty years ago.*

small bale of "spirit-paper" was tied to the bicycle. Mr. Chao's thoroughly up-to-date mode of conveyance, his old-world dress, and the bundle of mock paper money, a remnant of archaic times, formed an anachronism ensemble that gave me considerable secret amusement.

Mr. Chao explained that his deceased relative, an opulent village merchant, had died of an undisclosed disease at the advanced age of fifty-three. Mr. Chao hesitatingly suggested that I also procure an assortment of "spirit-paper" to carry with us to the house of death. I readily acquiesced, and we stopped in a dried-fish shop to purchase a small bale of the bamboo-fiber paper, with the customary tinfoil decoration. It would not do for me to go to the funeral emptyhanded, Mr. Chao said. We then turned into an overgrown dirt path that led to the deceased merchant's home. My guide rode slowly on his shiny bicycle, and I followed through the dusty trail on foot; he talked and I listened as we made our way.

Mr. Chao was anxious to impress upon me that his relative had been given thorough medical attention: numerous herbs and roots had been steeped for him, and to increase the efficaciousness of the concoction, the dried skins and teeth of certain animals had been boiled along with the plant nostrum. Everything humanly possible had been done, but the termination of the "old man's" life had been predestined. Every remedy had failed, Mr. Chao explained, and the fleeting spirit could not be retained. The moment death had come, candles had been lighted before the ancestral shrine and the dead man made ready to appear before the various gods—the god of the local temple, the god of the village walls and moats, and the god of Hades. His head had been shaved, his body washed, and his finger- and toenails carefully trimmed, the parings being religiously wrapped in paper and preserved by the remaining members of the family. The shaving and washing of the warm corpse had been done by the local barber, who received a substantial fee for his service. The money paid the barber had been handed him wrapped in a square of thin red paper, the red being symbolic of good fortune and capable of dispelling any evil influence that might otherwise have arisen through the barber's contact with the dead. Naturally I was interested in the use of paper in so many different ways and the part it played in Chinese ceremonies. After the deceased had been shaved and washed, and his nails trimmed, the body had been lifted from the hard death-couch and placed in an upright position. This was desirable, Mr. Chao assured me, so that the spirit might depart from the upper, rather than the lower, part of the body. It was also important that the merchant's feet should not touch the ground after death, and they were there-fore supported during the entire preparation of the corpse by a female member of the immediate family, who held them within the folds of a linen cloth.

When we reached the house of mourning, the corpse had already been well settled in a paper-lined coffin that had been built locally from heavy oak planks held together with wooden pegs. Mr. Chao gave me to understand that his relative's coffin was of superior quality. He also told me that the most tuneful Chinese musical instruments were fashioned from well-seasoned slabs of coffins dug up from ancient graves: the wood long subjected to the action of the earth gave a more mellow tone than was possible to obtain with ordinary timber.

When we entered the room where the massive coffin and the corpse were displayed, a dozen or more men and women were grouped around a series of metal trays filled with small paper objects that they were burning; some of the papers were formed in the shape of ingots covered with tinfoil that had been stained to imitate gold by being brushed with a liquid rendered from seaweed. There were also strips of yellow and white paper cut in the form of coins with square holes, in imitation of genuine metal coins made for stringing in the ancient manner. Along with these there were the common forms of bamboo-fiber mock money paper printed from woodblocks. These papers were being burned close to the coffin, and at this stage of the ceremony both Mr. Chao's "spirit-paper" and the bundle I had procured at the fish shop were set afire, all adding to the heavy, smoky air of the death chamber.

A table with two bowls—one of rice and the other of green vegetables—appropriately provided with chopsticks, was set near the dead man's head. Mr. Chao said that hearty meals had been served to the corpse regularly since death. Everything had been done to make the rich merchant's passing into the nether world as comfortable and pleasant as possible. As time passed, the room became overcrowded with wailing humanity, each person eager to burn his own bundle of "spirit-paper" or small paper images. The house was so saturated with the fumes of burning incense and smoldering paper that I had to seek the outside air. A written record was kept of the visitors and the amount and quality of the "spirit-paper" each mourner had brought, in much the same fashion as the name and address of the donor of flowers might be written down for future acknowledgment during an Occidental funeral.

Mr. Chao and I arrived at the home of the dead tradesman in the morning of the day of the funeral procession and the actual burial. The people of the village and surrounding countryside had been awaiting the spectacle, as the shopkeeper's funeral was to be more elaborate than any that had been held for more than a year. The grotesque procession that was to accompany the coffin to the grave was formed like a circus parade, with much shuffling and commotion. It was led by a huge make-believe figure of an ancient Chinese god carried on the shoulders of paid attendants who had, no doubt, carried this same shopworn figure at many previous burials. The image was obviously one of the undertaker's stock properties that had been paraded in all kinds of weather and become the worse for wear. Mr. Chao told me that this giant figure was the "clear-the-way god," and that it was its duty to rid the funeral route of evil spirits, making a clear passage for the corpse. Next came several men carrying streamers and large papier-mâché effigies with clumsy wagging heads, also intended to frighten away any evil-minded goblins that might be lurking along the path. These brightly colored heads were followed by two robed men carrying newly made paper lanterns especially decorated for the occasion and inscribed with large brush-painted Chinese characters denoting the name of the family and the official title of the deceased. As the parade passed, my companion and I stood at the side of the dust-laden road amid throngs of men, women, and children, all talking and wailing. I could detect no real signs of bereavement among the adults; they appeared to be thoroughly enjoying the spectacle. Only the solemn, round-faced babies and children seemed silent and dejected.

At intervals, dismal-sounding gongs were beaten by attendants clothed in long, tattered robes, also obviously from the undertaker's warehouse. Toward the middle of the procession came the paper-scatterers, whose mission it was to strew quantities of small squares of decorated paper along the course of the *cortège*. They threw the papers with marked dexterity, sailing them into the air as a conjuror would fan out a deck of cards, the papers falling in a cascade. The paper "money" thrown out along the course of the procession was thought to appease the malevolent spirits who, according to general belief, infested the roads, lanes, and streams and could cause the corpse all sorts of misadventure.

Still another form of paper used by the scatterers was the ancient "nine-hole paper" cut in sheets about six inches square, each sheet being crudely pierced in nine places. It was thought that when the evil spirits had taken the time to pass through every one of the nine holes, they would be so retarded in flight that the corpse would have had a better chance to evade them. Myriad evil demons were always present at funerals, and the greater the quantities and varieties of "spirit-paper" cast into the air, the less was the danger that they would molest the corpse.

When the heavy coffin borne by eight robed men reached the burying-ground, a great pyramid of paper and wood was set afire, and various paper replicas and quantities of imitation money were thrown into it. After the coffin had been placed in the shallow opening dug in the dry ground, a large ornamental paper chest stuffed with mock money was cast onto the bonfire. The pile of paper made a dangerous flame, but as the burying-ground was a desolate tract of dull gray clay without vegetation, there was no cause for alarm.

After the paper had been consumed, the ashes were carefully scooped together and placed along each side of the coffin as it rested in the grave. The band of wailing mourners returned to the village, leaving the building of the circular mound over the grave to attendants. Mr. Chao and I followed the crowd, he slowly riding his bicycle and I walking behind him.

For many years I had been interested only in the actual making of paper, but after seeing it used in Chinese religious ceremonies I became interested in compiling a book that would deal with this subject. Such a volume required a comprehensive collection of the "spirit-papers" and an assemblage of the Chinese "paper-gods." When I began gathering these examples, I little realized the bulk that the collection would gradually assume. I procured "spirit-papers" in the great cities of China and in the muddy country hamlets; in the moist, mouldy shops of Indo-China; from the open counters in the Chinese district of old Manila; in the small sidewalk shops of the villages of Java and Sumatra; in the Chinese markets of Penang, Kuala Lumpur, and Singapore; and in the ornate paper shops of Bangkok's crooked lanes and winding canals. These bundles of paper were packed in wicker hampers and covered baskets purchased along the way.

When I arrived in New York with this collection, the Customs officials were baffled as well as amused, but no duty could be collected. During the transfer of the numerous wicker containers from the pier to the express office for shipment to my home, one of the reed trunks burst open and, as it was a windy October day, the route through the New York streets was strewn with Chinese "spirit-paper," much to the bewilderment of the sophisticated New Yorkers, who perhaps had thought they were familiar with every kind of "street literature" but now saw something different. Little did they realize that the small sheets of gold and silver paper with printed characters and woodcut decorations blowing in the wind were the counterparts of block-printed papers that Marco Polo had seen in China in the thirteenth century.

My interest in "spirit-paper" and the collection of this material culminated in the writing and printing of a book entitled *Chinese Ceremonial Paper,* which was issued in 1937 in an edition of 125 copies. I set the pages in Caslon type and printed the text on Asiatic handmade paper; the 9 photogravures showing Chinese papermaking were printed on paper that had been made in my Marlborough-on-Hudson mill, and the 9 additional illustrations were on paper made in the Lime Rock mill. Each book contained thirty-nine original specimens of Chinese ceremonial papers, with examples of the various "kitchen gods," "gate gods," and other unusual specimens. Two samples of old Chinese paper were included for comparison with the more modern papers. One of the old examples was from the period of K'ang Hsi and the other from the time of Ch'ien Lung. The books were bound in three-quarters Chinese-red leather with a paper covering that I printed from a woodblock procured in the Peking Palace, a block that had been used in printing the screen paper for the private apartment of Emperor Wen Tsung Hien about 1850. The edition was soon sold at thirty-seven dollars and fifty cents a copy, and evidently the price was not exorbitant, as copies were later sold by book-dealers at two and three times the amount I had received for them when the edition was issued.

## ✣ XI ✣

DURING a visit to Kwangtung, China, I had learned that a remote locality of Tonkin, Indo-China, had long been a papermaking center where the trade had been carried on by the Annamese and handed down from one generation to the next. This meager information aroused my curiosity, and I decided to go to Tonkin.

The voyage from Brooklyn to Hong Kong by way of the Panama Canal during the winter of 1934 was wearisome. More than forty-six days were required for the small freight ship to push her way through the fourteen thousand miles of ocean. My Indo-China pilgrimage was to have its real beginning in Hong Kong, for from this busy cosmopolitan crossroads of the Pacific I planned to embark for Haiphong, the entrance port to Tonkin. The freighter from Brooklyn arrived in Hong Kong on a dark, gloomy Tuesday morning during late February, and I wanted to set sail for Haiphong as soon as possible. Hong Kong had never held any fascination for me. I learned from a schedule posted at the pier that a ship bound for Haiphong left Hong Kong "irregularly on Saturdays." This irregularity proved to be my good fortune, as a small ship was to sail that very evening.

This coal-burning ship was anchored in the roadstead a mile or more from Hong Kong's crowded waterfront, and after boarding her in rain and fog by means of a lurching Chinese junk, I found that this vessel was even more dilapidated than the one I had just left. The crew was a nondescript group of Cambodians, Tonkinese, Annamese, and Chinese. I was the only Occidental passenger. The few cramped cabins were separated from the more utilitarian sections of the ship by rusted iron bars that had been reduced to about half their original size by the action of salt water; two or three obsolete iron cannon pointed seaward on the lower deck. The Chinese members of the crew were squatting on the foredeck burning oppressive-smelling joss before the carved rotund figure of a burnished gilt Buddha set in a lacquered shrine with ornamental folding doors. Other members of the superstitious crew were hurriedly setting up a small, newly cut tree, from whose branches streamers of bright-red paper fluttered wildly in the sharp evening breeze. The Asiatic mariners hoped that the entreaty to the Buddha and the flying of the paper would assure a safe passage through the Hainan Straits, a remote part of the world where the sea was in perpetual turmoil. They also hoped that the iron gratings and the rusty cannon would discourage attacks by pirates, for such bands of marauders were not uncommon along the ship lanes of the China Sea.

The Tonkinese steward of the ship was addicted to chewing betel nut, and his stout teeth had taken on the rich color of ebony. The habit also gave a brilliant red hue to his saliva. When I asked him about the length of our voyage, he replied with a grin that displayed his jet-black teeth, which made a startling contrast to his flaming-red tongue and lips. His smile was suggestive of a fiery "gate god," one of the gaudily colored posters that were pasted on Chinese houses and walls to frighten away impish spirits. The malevolent-appearing steward spoke only Tonkinese, but by running his lean finger around and around the dial of my watch he made me understand that I would be aboard the slow ship for a number of days and nights.

There was but one other voyager in the confined quarters euphemistically designated first-class—a handsome young Chinese gentleman who introduced himself as Wong Hsien-Chih, a merchant of Canton. He invited me into his cabin, which had the heavy, herby odor of a Chinese apothecary shop. He explained that he was applying the herb nostrums to his feet in an attempt to alleviate the suffering from a hideous disease that had developed in Hong Kong. This distressing infection was contracted by walking barefoot on filthy floors and pavements; the feet were attacked by myriad minute worms that penetrated to the base of the toes, causing them to disintegrate and, according to Mr. Wong, eventually drop off in the stocking, like peanuts in a paper bag.

Seven thirty was the evening dining-hour, and the steward led me to the dismal saloon by the easiest approach, which was past the coal bunkers. Two places were set at the ample table, one for me and the other for Mr. Wong. He soon shuffled painfully into the dimly lighted room attired in long wool underwear partially concealed by a lavish gray silk robe. His ailing feet were enveloped in padded red felt slippers that he removed while seated at the table, at once scenting the dining-room with the aroma of pungent herbs and narcotic lotions. There were six bottles of wine on the table, and the four-course dinner proved most appetizing. The *pièce de résistance* consisted of roasted birds—not completely devoid of feathers and entrails—which nestled in heavy metal bowls. The birds has been smothered in alcohol and were served while afire, the flickering blue flames throwing weird shadows on the walls and ceiling of the gloomy saloon. After the pyrotechnics had subsided, I could see that this gastronomic delight resembled a small stork or crane; the head remained erect, for the ship's chef had carefully twisted the neck around and around like the coils of a spring. Mr. Wong, with marked pleasure, crushed the bones of his bird between his stout teeth and, after he had completed his sumptuous meal, calmly broke the bird's head from its spiral neck and nonchalantly used the pointed bill as a toothpick.

During the second course of our first dinner I noticed a large black object dart noiselessly across the gray-white tablecloth. The alert Mr. Wong was not slow in plunging at it. For a moment I thought the intruder a small mouse or bat, but after my companion had pinned the poor creature to the wooden tabletop with the sharp point of his fruit knife, I was relieved to see that our interloper was nothing more than a corpulent Asiatic cockroach, the larger and bolder prototype of the American species.

Despite our lack of language communication, Mr. Wong and I were most congenial traveling companions, and I was genuinely sorry when he disembarked at the South China port of Kouang-Tcheou-Wan only two days after we had boarded the ship in the harbor of Hong Kong.

The ship rode at anchor about a mile from the waterfront of Kouang-Tcheou-Wan for an entire day. Passengers began coming aboard by all manner of craft—launches, junks, barges, and rowboats—but I looked in vain for another companion who might share with me the dismal and lonesome dining-saloon and in a measure fill the place of Mr. Wong. As each person came aboard, he was searched for weapons, so that pirates disguised as passengers might be apprehended. The new passengers were picturesque: dignified Chinese merchants in long robes, loose velvet slippers, and little round close-fitting brocaded hats; fair-skinned Annamese and Ton-kinese women and girls in straight loose trousers and long form-fitting dark jackets, their dense, glossy black hair artistically braided with strands of pure-white silk; elderly Chinese women in sleek glazed trousers, their tiny bound feet protruding from the pantaloon legs, hopelessly inadequate to support bodies that had grown too fat. One old lady, handsomely robed in vivid silks, was the proud possessor of feet no larger than those of a child, and her attendants had to give her support every time she rose from her wicker chair.

Every sort of baggage was hoisted aboard: painted metal strong-boxes with flimsy tin locks; carved teak furniture; mirrors painted with garlands of flowers; bales of "spirit-paper"; emaciated chickens; live pigs tied into palpitating bundles with stout rattan; caged birds; gilt Buddhas in ornamental shrines; carved figures of Kwan Yin, the goddess of mercy; fresh vegetables and exotic fruits; ornate artificial flowers of wax and paper—a conglomerate variety of impedimenta that littered the small deck in bulging piles. During the entire time that the steamer was anchored in the roadstead of Kouang-Tcheou-Wan, a score of Chinese women were unloading hundreds of bags of flour shipped from Hong Kong. Each robust young woman had a baby strapped to her back; the infants assumed all sorts of positions and went through fantastic contortions as the mothers bent their agile bodies to lift the heavy bags, but not a child cried or awoke from sleep; it was a hardship they and their mothers had learned to accept.

Amid a great commotion of shouting and gesturing, we at last departed from Kouang-Tcheou-Wan. Not until an Occidental traveler has visited out-of-the-way ports of the Orient can he realize the needless confusion that attends entering or leaving a port. There were singing, yelling, and screaming in a jumble of languages and dialects akin to bedlam; goatskin drums were beaten and hollow bamboo poles were tapped; there was noise everywhere. The ship was well out to sea before the passengers became reasonably composed, drifting one by one to the bowels of the vessel to await with Buddhistic stoicism the inevitable seasickess, a malady to which almost every Asiatic seemed subject. I peered through the half-open doors of the row of little cabins with the hope of finding a traveler who might share the sumptuous dinners with me. I missed Mr. Wong; he was endowed, as so many of his compatriots, with quiet humor and subtle understanding. It would have been gratifying to make friends with the humble Chinese and Indo-Chinese passengers, but I was aware that they would not have accepted me, "foreign devil" that I was.

The next port, I thought, would surely be Haiphong, my destination, but my expectation was not be be fulfilled. On the third day the ship again anchored and I was told that the foghung Chinese town that could be dimly seen in the distance was ancient Hoihow, the port for the perfectural town of Kiungchow, capital of the island of Hainan. The two towns were separated by three miles of low hills almost entirely covered with the cylindrical mounds of countless Chinese dead. The harbor of Hoihow was an open roadstead entirely unprotected from the northeast monsoons that might be expected with unrelenting rigor from September to April. From the distance at which we were anchored, the low-built harbor town of gray buildings clustered together suggested a drab stage-setting with a background of such smooth, rolling hills as Grant Wood took delight in painting. On the island of Hainan there were Presbyterian missions in the towns of Kiungchow, Hoihow, Kachek, and Nodoa, and numerous Catholic missions.

# MY LIFE WITH PAPER

As the steamer was leaving Hoihow, I was surprised to hear a few words of English, a most cheering sound. Two German tradesmen and a Filipino lad had come aboard unnoticed; the common language among the three was my own. The Germans had been on the island selling the medical products of the I. G. Farbenindustrie; the Filipino was an agent for a popular American automobile. The German traders were loud in their praise of the missionaries and told of the splendid work they had done in the leper colonies of Hainan. From the enthusiasm expressed by these salesmen I assumed that the missionaries had placed substantial orders for the products of the German company. In my travels in different parts of Asia I had come in contact with missionaries of many denominations, and it had been my privilege on several occasions to dwell within the mission compounds. I must confess a lack of enthusiasm for most of the solely religious missionaries, but those workers, both Catholic and Protestant, whose first consideration was the healing of disease accomplished no end of good.

Our next port of call was Pakhoi, a large Chinese town situated on Kuantao Head, a peninsula with low hills. Like Hoihow, this town was exposed to the terrific velocity of the winds of the northeast monsoon; for more than six months of the year shipping became a hazardous undertaking, and during long periods it was impossible for a vessel to anchor there. My salesmen shipmates disembarked at Pakhoi, no doubt hoping for trade as lucrative as in Hoihow. I found Pakhoi a most picturesque settlement, with irregular rows of low, close-built shops open to the roads. The merchants sold all sorts of commodities: green cabbages, crisp bits of roasted pork, and dried fish for the consumption of the living, and neatly tied bundles of gay "spirit-paper" and fragrant joss for the benefit of the dead. Each shop had its distinctive odors and aromas. The

most unusual feature of the town was the only means of transportation: a great number of heavy creaking carts drawn by
slow-moving oxen whose muscular bodies quivered at every
step. The carts were constructed of thick hand-sawed planks,
and the ponderous wheels were hewn from solid blocks of
timber. The swaying, irregular motion of the cartwheels cut
deep furrows in the roadway like the chariot ruts in the narrow
streets of ancient Pompeii. Carts of identical construction
could well have been seen along these same Kwangsi roads
even before the Chinese invented printing during the momen-
tous Tai Tsung period of the T'ang Dynasty.

Early the following morning the ship silently and cautiously
steamed through the grass-grown channel of Haiphong. As we
approached, the rice swamps came into view; the atmosphere
was charged with a cool, penetrating humidity that made
everything limp. Before 1884, when the French had at last
absorbed all of Indo-China, the original town of Haiphong had
been confined between the Cua-Cam and Song-Tam Bac
rivers, but during the last fifty or sixty years the settlement had
spread well beyond its ancient confines and had altogether
about eighty thousand inhabitants. Far distant toward the
north was the old rugged "Tooth of Nam Maû," a well-named
mountain rising to thirty-five hundred feet. The rice fields
stretched for miles over the low country. The weary workers
stood knee-deep in the soggy swamps, and with bent bodies
tended endless rows of tender plants in the wet, warm earth.

I was eager to be on my way to the *Villages du Papier* of
Tonkin, and was informed that the chief papermaking district
was not far from Hanoi, the capital. Although not shown on
most maps of Tonkin, the ancient papermaking centers were
known locally as Yên-Thai and Lang-Buoi. The distance from
Haiphong to Hanoi was about seventy-five miles by either rail-

way or narrow road. I chose the bus, which was waiting beneath a wide-spreading banyan tree; it was a French car with three seats, each seat for a specific class: first, second, and third. As I had a first-class ticket, the driver placed me on the front and most uncomfortable bench; the other two seats were filled with Tonkinese, Annamese, and Chinese; no other person shared the front seat with me. As I required only part of it, and as the other two seats were crowded with sweating humanity, the native passengers naturally placed their miscellaneous baggage beside me. Not only was I surrounded by bundles, bags, and boxes, but also an old wrinkled Tonkinese could find no safe place for his odoriferous pet monkey other than the bench designated as first-class.

The barefoot driver of the bus was a Eurasian, no doubt one of the numerous offspring of French government officials and affectionate Annamese ladies. Each native traveler had an ample supply of betel nut, the expectorated juice of which soon sprayed fresh red liquid over the floor of the automobile.

The natives were at last settled in the bus and full of anticipation of the trip to Hanoi. As we left the port city and approached the open country, the roadway gradually became narrower. It was literally choked with peasants carrying on their heads wide bamboo trays filled with handmade pottery and a variety of tropical fruits and vegetables. For the most part, these were women trudging along in sleek black pantaloons and long, close-fitting jackets. Many of them were burdened so heavily they could scarcely stand erect. As the bus rushed by at reckless speed, the frightened women would clear a passage for the car by sliding down the steep embankments at either side of the roadway, upsetting their baskets in haphazard confusion. After the thunderous vehicle had rolled by in a haze of dust, the women patiently gathered themselves and their wares together and diligently plodded on without even a whisper of protest. I tried to warn the driver about his carelessness, but his only concern was to reach Hanoi within the insufficient two hours and twenty minutes allotted for the journey.

On both sides of the road, at intervals of forty feet, beautiful silk flags hung from bamboo poles. Every flag was large and elaborately embroidered in soft colors with lions, dragons, elephants, and all sorts of symbolic designs. Each banner had a fringe of rich, heavy silk in tones that could only have been produced by permanent vegetable dyes such as were in use before the introduction of European synthetic pigments. I could not learn the occasion for the display of the flags, but they apparently extended for hundreds of miles along the roads and lanes throughout Tonkin. They may have been in honor of a notable event or for a special religious ceremony. They certainly had nothing in common with the gaudy, ephemeral decorations of banners and bunting used in America on memorial occasions. Each individual flag was a masterpiece of the embroiderer's art, representing years of tedious toil by the nimble fingers and weary eyes of artisans highly skilled in silk and damask craftsmanship.

The car continued at breakneck speed past the endless weary cavalcade of humanity. Rain began to fall in the usual drenching tropical shower, which added to the already humid atmosphere; in Tonkin one soon grew accustomed to dampness and humidity. Without reducing speed we would reach a village and the barefoot Eurasian driver would apply the brakes so suddenly that the car would slide along the wet highway, finally coming to a halt in front of a fragrant shop. Then everyone crawled from the cramped quarters of the bus to sample the exotic confections of the locality: balls of boiled rice smothered in grease and studded with bits of browned pork, all garnished with strips of red and green peppers; small birds roasted with heads and feet intact, their eyes and beaks giving them a most dejected and wistful appearance; tiny sparkling gold and silver fish, no larger than minnows, which were dipped in sweet sauce and devoured in a gulp by the hungry passengers; cubes of goose fat strung on cotton cords like beads; and garlands of fantastically colored sweets. I satisfied my hunger with rice balls held in shallow green leaves and by drinking tea brewed from the flowers of the chrysanthemum. Village after village welcomed the rushing bus, and I noted a number of the little communities where we stopped: Cho P. cái, Bán y nhan, Phô noi, My hào, and Quán goi. We had just left Quán goi on our way to Hai Duong when the driver looked at his watch and saw that we had tarried more than the allotted time in Quán goi and that we were behind schedule. This state of affairs called for still greater speed, and the wide brown Eurasian foot pressed the accelerator until it touched the dripping red floor of the automobile.

The never ending procession of heavily laden women and girls trudged along the road and continued to make way for the hurrying bus by throwing themselves down the embankments. They must have been relieved when the mechanical monster was well out of sight. I turned my eyes for a moment from the road, and in that instant there was a dull, nauseating thud—the inattentive driver had struck one of the pedestrians. The car was at last brought to a sliding stop. The peasants gathered at the side of the road, encircling the person who had been run down. I walked back to the group, somber in their black and brown clothing, and, thinking that I might be of help, they opened the circle so that I could reach the victim, a barefoot Annamese girl. She appeared to be mortally hurt;

only faint signs of life remained. She was dressed in the customary sleek black trousers; her thick hair was braided with white silk. She was perhaps twenty, well formed, and matured beyond her years, as were most Annamese women. With glazed eyes she stared at me appealingly, but she did not speak, nor did anyone in the group make a sound. I raised the girl's head from the road and thought I detected an expression of resignation pass quickly over her pale, round face. She died in my arms. The native people seemed reluctant to touch her, so I carried the limp, warm body down the embankment by the side of the road and laid her in the damp grass.

The Eurasian driver and his passengers had remained seated in the bus. The weary pedestrians gathered the baskets of fruit and vegetables and continued on their way to the markets. The malodorous monkey chattered as he was jostled to make room for me to sit on the crowded seat again. Once more we were on our way to Hanoi.

The next village was Pham xá, and the stage halted for more rice-flour sweet cakes and chrysanthemum tea. I was depressed; no one had spoken since we had left the dead girl. The rain had ceased as suddenly as it had begun, and the silk flags along the route hung damp and limp. As dusk came on, candles were lighted in the roadside shops and in the old temples, which made an eerie appearance in the flickering glow. The villages of Phu Thai and Vàt Cách were hurriedly passed, and the swaying bus arrived in the metropolitan capital city of Hanoi just as a group of French colonial officials and their elaborately dressed ladies were entering the magnificent *Théâtre Municipal* for the opening of the opera with a cast brought from Paris for the occasion. I could not turn my thoughts from the slain Annamese girl; the picture of the

patient peasants throwing themselves down the rough embankment to clear the way for the onrushing Haiphong-Hanoi bus
persisted in my mind.

There were several hotels in Hanoi owned and operated by
the French, and I chose the Métropole, of the Société Foncière
du Tonkin et de l'Annam. The French manager could give
little information about the near-by *Villages du Papier* which
I had traveled fifteen thousand miles to visit.

It was apparent that I would have to seek a native guide. I
made inquiries in the French section of Hanoi, and finally
succeeded, toward evening, in finding an interpreter who
knew the papermaking district. My guide was Le-Van-Binh, a
Tonkinese who said he knew many of the native papermakers
and could take me to their villages. My newly acquired courier
insisted that I visit his home in the native quarter of Hanoi,
where we could plan our little expedition for the following
day. We at once mounted jinrikishas, each two-wheeled vehicle
lighted by a Chinese paper lantern dangling at its side. The
barefoot jinrikimen in their mushroom-shaped hats topped with
small brass balls pattered through the spacious streets of
French Hanoi, which finally narrowed into the rambling lanes
of the native district with its tumbling shops and houses amid
squalid, disheveled surroundings.

After a half-hour's ride, my guide shouted to the jinrikimen
and we came to a sudden halt before the open front of a
dimly lighted shop where tea, spices, and sweet cakes were
sold. I was led through the fragrant shop up a flight of deeply
worn, winding stone steps to a commodious chamber above.
This apartment was the home of Le-Van-Binh and his fat
Annamese wife, who welcomed me with true Oriental grace.
The only light in the room filtered up the stairwell from the
flickering tallow candles in the shop below, but when my

guide's spouse lit her oil lamp I could see that the room was handsomely furnished. There were native-carved teakwood tables and chairs inlaid with mother-of-pearl. A teak bed with faded damask draperies stood in a corner of the apartment, and an elaborately carved divan served as a receptacle for charcoal; shining copper kettles of food and jugs of water stood under a three-legged bench used as a culinary work table. A half-dozen stalwart chickens scratched and pecked about the floor of the shadowy room; from a far corner came the cries of a baby in a swinging rattan hammock. The kindly housewife offered tea and balls of dough over which she poured a thin gruel of sweetened goose grease. Both my guide and his wife audibly showed their enjoyment of the early evening repast by much gurgling and smacking of lips, with a proud display of betel-stained teeth.

Tonkin, like all places in Asia, had its own individual odor —an aroma suggestive of overripe fruit and sweet tropical spices mingled with a dash of offal, opium, and joss. It was a fascinating, although oppressive, aroma, one that was always present in country and city, penetrating even the innermost rooms of the inns and houses. It is true that moving pictures often correctly depict the life of the people in foreign countries and realistically show the scenery and the architecture of every locality. Even the natural colors and sounds are present. But not until cinema technicians have mastered a method for recording smells and aromas will moving pictures provide the genuine atmosphere of a particular community in any part of the Orient.

With customary Oriental hospitality, Le-Van-Binh and his wife insisted that I remain for late dinner, and I gratefully accepted. Being tired, I lay down upon the carved teakwood bed and under the relaxing influence of the moist, tropical air immediately fell asleep. After an hour or more of rest, I was half aware of the sound of shuffling in the room, then of a muffled noise that gave way to loud and resonant squawking, but, try as I would, it was difficult to arouse myself from the heavy hypnotism of sleep. Finally I felt drops of warm liquid trickling upon my face, and with a renewed effort I forced the drowsiness from my eyes. The complete picture of what had taken place was at once apparent: nothing serious had happened during my deep sleep; my host had pursued one of the scrawny chickens around the room and after capturing it he had severed its head so close to the teakwood bed that the fowl's warm blood had spattered my face. For dinner we had the rawboned chicken, surrounded by the favorite delicacy of rice balls dipped in sweetened grease. There was also chrysanthemum tea with little pink and black cakes from the confectioner's shop below.

I returned to the hotel in the French quarter of Hanoi with the promise that Le-Van-Binh would call for me the following morning to visit the ancient paper villages. My diminutive guide, wearing a long black silk jacket, arrived at the French hostelry with no little dignity and pride; never before had an American come to see the paper centers of his native Tonkin. Rigidly seated in two jinrikishas, we wheeled silently through winding dirt roadways between low-built bamboo-and-grass dwellings and shops that stretched along the muddy road for several miles between Hanoi and the *Villages du Papier*. Congested masses of somber-clothed natives trudged along in the direction in which we were moving; other throngs of heavily laden men and women pushed and milled toward the markets in the native section of Hanoi. Unlike the automobile, the lightweight, man-drawn vehicles had no terror for the peasants, and they crowded into the road and literally forced the jinrikimen to come to a halt every few yards.

My previous Asiatic journeys had prepared me for hardships among the workers of Indo-China. Little had I realized, however, the squalor, poverty, disease, and distress that would be found in the paper villages of Tonkin. The narrow roadway, ankle deep in soft brown mud, swarmed with swarthy men, women, and children all bent upon converting vegetable fibers into sheets of finished paper. Vendors, beggars, and idlers thronged around the papermakers' huts. Half-naked peddlers covered with sores, scabs, and scars sold unsavory thick gruel and the ubiquitous balls of dough dipped in grease. The food was sold from wicker receptacles that hung from the hawkers' shoulders on swaying bamboo poles. Boiled entrails of animals dangled in limp shreds from the outstretched bony fingers of the vendors, who roughly thrust the food before the faces of the papermakers with the hope of tempting them to lay aside their moulds for a moment. I noticed several of the vat-women gulping these slimy, intestine-like objects as they leaned against their dipping-vats. Men shaken with palsy and others with faces and hands devoured by leprosy begged coppers from the workers and grew sullen and insolent if their demands were not met. Although the papermakers' huts were roofed with straw, the sides were open, which made it convenient for the hawkers, beggars, and drones to push their way from one shelter to another, chattering back and forth in a babble of tongues well beyond my comprehension.

Old Tonkinese women stood behind low wooden stalls selling the product of the locality: packages of coarse bamboo paper for common writing and for burning in the temples. Also displayed, but in smaller quantities, were neatly tied packages of the thin, absorbent bark papers to be written upon by Oriental scholars with firm, sure strokes of a camel's hair brush. These calligraphic papers, when made of superior fiber, were stronger and more durable than the produce of the paper machine that was eventually to replace the traditional hand-made papers in Indo-China.

My first day's visit in the paper villages was bewildering and disheartening. Being totally unprepared for the ungodly conditions that existed in Yên-Thai and Lang-Buoi, I had to become adjused to the turmoil, the jostling, and the nerve-racking noise before I could make even a few fragmentary notes and sketches. Photography called for perseverance and patience; the papermakers themselves were meagerly co-operative, but the hundreds of idlers and mendicants constantly clawing, begging, and haranguing were a hindrance. Many of my photographs were useless, as my camera was often jostled by the multitude. It was necessary to bring a photographer from Hanoi who had more control over the crowds than I was able to command.

Papermaking was no doubt introduced into Tonkin by the Chinese when Indo-China was under the direct influence of the mother country. The exact date of introduction, however, will always remain obscure, as no authentic records exist. The Annamese came originally from the highlands of Tibet, but the methods used in Indo-China differed from the Tibetan technique, which is now found only in Siam, Burma, and a small section of Kwangtung, China.

My journey to Indo-China furnished the material for a monograph on the subject of papermaking to be printed at my private press. Although my investigations in Tonkin were completed before the outbreak of the Second World War, the edition of *Papermaking in Indo-China* was not ready for sub-

# MY LIFE WITH PAPER

scribers until late in 1947. The handmade paper used in printing the edition of 182 copies was made in the Connecticut mill in 1932. I set the text in 18-point Caslon type with ornaments especially cut for the book by Dard, Junior, who also did the presswork. There were 110 pages and 19 reproductions from photographs made in Tonkin; the binding was red leather with paper sides printed in three colors from a woodblock I found in Indo-China. Each volume contained original specimens of the finest paper made in the *Villages du Papier,* Yên-Thai and Lang-Buoi. The books were sold for thirty-eight dollars and fifty cents a copy.

# ❧❧ XII ❧❧

MY journeys to Mexico, Europe, the South Pacific islands, Java, Sumatra, Malaysia, China, Korea, Japan, Siam,
and Indo-China had resulted in more than a half-dozen books,
all on the subject of making paper by hand. Fifteen years had
been spent in this work. I could scarcely believe that I was
fifty-four, an age I had never expected to attain. My father had
been fifty-four when he passed away only a few days after he
had personally accepted an honorary Master of Arts degree
from Marietta College.

I decided that my next book should deal with papermaking
in India. For a number of years I had been in correspondence
with Tekumalla Venkajee, a paper chemist of Rajahmundry,
Madras, and he agreed to supervise my journeys to the remote
districts of India where paper was made by hand. I arranged
for outward and homeward passage on the 5,500-ton freight
ship *Seminole*. This small freighter on its unscheduled voyage
took five weeks to reach Karachi, and seven weeks to return
to Boston from Calcutta.

In October 1937, after a five-day delay in New York, I
boarded the *Seminole,* which carried a miscellaneous cargo
well below the vessel's capacity. The delay had been caused by
urgent repairs in the engine room, and even as we left New

York the chief engineer said that further overhauling would be necessary when we reached Port Saïd.

After I had been more or less comfortably established in a compact, oddly shaped cabin with a built-in wall bunk draped with red calico curtains, I made a tour of the ship in the hope of meeting the six other passengers with whom I was to be so closely confined during the long voyage. They were all missionaries, of one religious faith or another, on their way to battle with sin and disease in India. I was the only "civilian." In this small group was kindly old Sidney Gamble, a medical missionary of the Church of Christ who had devoted his life to the destitute of Madras. He was not one of the propagandists who offer little except salvation. Another, a lone, middle-aged woman, also a medical worker, was going to a maternity hospital in the northern hills of Chittagong. Two others were a Methodist missionary and his wife. They were taking with them several American goats in order to introduce new blood into the Indian breed. They explained that each American goat would give six quarts of milk a day whereas the Indian breed produced little more than a cupful.

The remaining passengers, the Reverend Mr. Featherby and his wife, who were on their way back to India after a money-collecting expedition in the United States, were to me the most entertaining of the group, although they probably had no conception of the amusement they provided. They sat next to me at the table in the combination dining- and lounging-saloon, and they seldom ceased talking about their work of converting the lowly natives. They explained that they were both "open-air preachers" who spent a few hours each day in the crowded market places reading aloud and distributing gospels and tracts.

Weeks later in Old Delhi I saw these two evangelists standing on a street corner reading aloud from their religious books and trying to attract the attention of the bedraggled Indians, among whom were holy men "clothed" in nothing more than sifted ashes. I watched the performance of these two worthy American missionaries for an hour, and in that time I did not see a single Indian pay the slightest attention to the readings. Nor did I see one accept a proffered tract.

The Reverend and Mrs. Featherby were taking a new car back to India to replace their old one. The new automobile was large and comfortable, with four doors, and Mrs. Featherby told me with considerable emotion that she and her devout husband never attempted to select a new car themselves. They always entrusted such an important decision to the Lord, who seemed to have the happy faculty of selecting just the right make and style for their use. This close relationship with the Deity had been impressed upon me when I saw the automobile being lowered into the hold of the ship. In the back windows of each side of the car cardboard signs had been hung which read: "Christ Is Following." I thought to myself that it would be far safer to follow than to walk in front of that powerful automobile with the Reverend Featherby at the wheel. Their amity with the Divinity was further expressed by their bookplate. One dismal morning Mrs. Featherby suggested that I read a new American novel that she had in her cabin. When I opened the volume I was surprised to see an ornate bookplate with Old English lettering, which read: "Ex Libris—Jesus Christ." When I asked Mrs. Featherby about the significance of the bookplate, she explained that everything she and her husband possessed, including the automobile, actually belonged to Jesus, and she thought it only proper that the bookplate should convey this intimate association.

Of all the ships in which I had voyaged, the *Seminole* was the smallest and slowest. The maximum speed was 11.5 miles per hour, although the engine was seldom capable of pushing the vessel forward more than 7. At both Port Saïd and Port Sudan hasty repairs were made, but the speed of the ship was unaltered. Each evening the electric lights would refuse to function and the missionaries and I would have dinner by the light of two rusty oil lanterns suggestive of old sailing-ship days. At breakfast one morning we were greeted by a sign leaning carelessly against the revolving glass condiment cruets in the center of the table. It read, in the Chinese steward's best English: "No eat, stove broke." The stove, like the engine, was patched along the way and the voyage to India continued.

My missionary companions seemed never to be in agreement among themselves regarding their religious beliefs. On one point, however, they all agreed, and that concerned me: I had not been vaccinated for smallpox or inoculated against typhoid and typhus fevers before I left the United States, and this omission caused the thoughtful missionaries no end of anxiety. Under pressure I consented to be thoroughly immunized when we reached the port of Aden, on the southern tip of Arabia. When we finally arrived there, my religious friends lost no time in finding a local medical man who was willing to inoculate me against the prevailing distempers of India. After finishing his kind mission, the practitioner warned me that I might later suffer from nausea as his vaccines were old and rancid. No truer warning was ever given.

Early in December the *Seminole* arrived at Karachi. While awaiting the arrival of Sarangu Madhawa Rao, my guide, from Madras, I was the guest of Mr. Malkain of the Advain Paper Company, dealers in machinemade papers, and was entertained by him at the exclusive new Indian club. For many years, I was told, the English club of Karachi would not receive Indian guests, so the aristocratic Indians retaliated by building the finest and most elaborate club in the city and excluded all Britishers!

The day after I landed, Mr. Rao arrived. He was a young Hindu whom I was glad to welcome as a companion. He spoke not only English, but also Hindustani, Tamil, and Telugu. As cold weather was approaching and we wanted to reach Kashmir without delay, we left Karachi for the north the same evening. Kashmir had a special interest for me as the place where papermaking was first introduced into India during the craft's thousand-year journey from the Orient.

We knew that the papermaking center was near Srinagar, the capital, and that Rawalpindi was the nearest approach to this city by railway. The train journey took thirty-four hours through the Indian desert, and until we reached Lahore the country was desolate and distressing. This was my first experience of Indian railway sleeping-cars, which later became so familiar to me. At each station, travelers climbed into the bare, uncomfortable compartments with all manner of paraphernalia: ornamental brass teapots; German silver boxes containing small, lidded receptacles for the betel nut, lime, leaves, and spices so relished by the Indians; clay water bottles held upright in wooden racks; and heavy metal-bound trunks, each with several locks, which resembled the chests of Captain Kidd. They also brought ornate bedding-rolls and embroidered pillows of every shade.

There was so much of interest and amusement on Indian trains that I was lost in wonder and astonishment, and the discomforts were soon forgotten. On the trip to Rawalpindi one of my traveling companions was a serious young Mohammedan merchant on his way to Sailkot, where he was to be married. With him was an attentive male servant who supplied his master's every want. In the compartment the merchant had two large, shiny chests, each filled to the brim with an array of shoes, slippers, and clothing which defied description. During the daylight hours the young merchant occupied himself by trying on one pair of multicolored shoes or slippers after another, and with each new pair he would stretch his legs at full length so he could better admire the gorgeous footwear. Numerous pairs of thin, flowing silk pants, rainbow-hued shirts, and brocaded jackets were brought from the chests by the servant, only to be tried on and discarded, one after another, by the prospective bridegroom. At last he was arrayed in a preposterous outfit that seemed to please his sartorial taste in every way, and, with deep satisfaction, he sat contentedly amid his gay lounging-accessories. At Wazirabad he and his servant changed trains for Sailkot.

Indian railway stations were fascinating with their great throngs of white-robed people. Sitting in circles on the stone floors, they brewed tea by the blue blaze of cow-dung fires that gave off a pleasantly sweet aroma. The food sold to the travelers was mostly rice, vegetables, and goat meat, a sticky mass, laid upon broad green leaves. The displays of food were not always appetizing: outside one station I noticed a Hindu youngster reclining near a table laden with overripe fruit that was being offered for sale by his parents. The boy was evidently recovering from smallpox, and as he sat surrounded by the fruit I could not help seeing that he was picking the drying scabs from his face and head and casually tossing the scaly lamina onto his father's mellow grapes, oranges, and bananas. Fortunately I was well provided with a large wicker basket of

English whole-wheat biscuits, tinned fruit, and fish, supplemented by a bottle of Vichy water held erect in a stout wooden framework.

In traveling through India it was my experience that the people were reluctant to talk to strangers until the visitor's nationality was determined. Only when the Indians were certain that I was an American, and not a British subject, did they speak freely to me. In the sacred Ganges, it is said, there was an undercurrent of water running in the opposite direction from that which flowed on the surface of the river. This same undercurrent of unrest seemed to prevail within the mind of every educated Indian with whom I came in contact; rarely did his expression give an inkling of his innermost thoughts. Each Indian was slow to advance his ideas concerning freedom and independence, but, once aroused, he spoke in no uncertain terms of his hopes.

Before daylight of the morning of the third day after leaving Karachi, we reached Rawalpindi, situated on the banks of the river Leh, over seventeen hundred feet above sea level. After the long journey through the dry Indian desert I was encrusted with sand, and the yellow dust had even penetrated my camera case. Also, much to my chagrin, my bottle of Vichy water had been broken. Mr. Rao went around the town in search of a conveyance and a driver for the two-hundred-mile trip to Srinagar, and found Mr. Pestonjee, an elaborately turbaned Punjabi, who said he would drive us to the Kashmir capital for ninety rupees. He explained that the mountain road was narrow and steep and, as we would have to pass many oxcarts, it would be impossible to make the journey in one day. We would remain overnight in a dak house about halfway to Srinagar. The dak houses had been used in former years for the convenience of the mail-carriers on horseback.

# AN AUTOBIOGRAPHY

I had long heard of the beautiful Vale of Kashmir, but it had been no more than a romantic-sounding name; little had I realized the natural magnificence of this native Indian state. After being passed by the inspectors at the border, we traveled through winding mountain passes, climbing to almost seven thousand feet, then dropping to two or three thousand, only to rise again from one height to another in rapid succession. The temperature was twenty-six degrees, and a film of ice was forming on the mountain streams. The sparkling Jhelum River flowed rapidly through the valleys thousands of feet below the twisting roadway; the atmosphere was so clear that snow-capped mountains hundreds of miles distant were seen in distinct detail. In the low valleys the wide-spreading maple, birch, walnut, and plane trees had taken on full autumn coloring, and the silvery green of the pines, firs, and deodars gave a softness of texture and delicacy of shade, so that the landscape was unlike any other I had ever seen. On the far-off slopes of the valley and creeping up the sides of the mountains were orderly rice patches, and in the month of December these thousands of well-cultivated fields added a somber tone to the scene, which otherwise might have been almost too spectacular. The low houses of the peasants were of wood, stone, and mud, clinging to the sides of the mountains, in such harmony with the surroundings that not a single building appeared out of place.

Along the winding mountain passes our driver often stopped to permit scores of bullock carts to go by; all merchandise going from or coming to Kashmir was carried by these caravans. As dusk drew near, trains of oxcarts formed along the highway, as many as a hundred in a group, for huddled together there was less likelihood that they would be attacked by robbers. The huge wooden-wheeled carts laden with bales and boxes, the gray oxen munching the meager rice chaff, and the weary drivers clothed in somber red-brown robes, all illuminated by yellow campfires, made a picture that might have been seen on this same mountain route a thousand years earlier.

When we came in sight of the dak house where we were to spend the night, an oil lamp was burning in the window. The caretaker had been notified of our impending arrival, and a wood fire in the travelers' room was most welcome after the long drive through the cold mountain passes. After the servant had prepared a hot dinner of goat chops, rice, tea, and Kashmir cakes, I was glad to retire on the hard rope-bed, with stiff goatskin robes that were constantly sliding to the floor. Throughout the night I could hear the muffled agitation of the grouped caravans as the drivers and oxen tried to rest for their long journey in the morning. In dak houses the toilet requirements were a problem, and although the servant provided an earthenware bowl of water for bathing, I had to improvise all other arrangements.

Late the next evening we reached Srinagar, romantically situated in the mountains almost a mile above sea level. The ancient wood-and-mud houses, many with carved façades and balconies, occupied miles of frontage along the river with its seven picturesque wooden bridges. Although the summer hotel had been closed for the season, one room was opened for my comfort and a wood fire set to burning in the lofty apartment.

Nowshera, the papermaking center, was reached from Srinagar by driving through dirty, narrow, winding lanes and roads flanked on either side by dilapidated dwellings, vegetable and flesh markets open to flies and dogs, and tumble-down artisans' shops in which all the wood and metal utensils needed by the people were made and sold. As only Kashmiri was spoken, we had to find a local man who could also speak

Hindustani, for the language of Kashmir was as unfamiliar to Mr. Rao as to me. The papermakers' houses were hidden amid groups of ancient buildings, which we reached by walking along snake-like footpaths of black mud. Near a cluster of half-timbered houses with moss-covered dirt roofs we came upon dozens of chattering, jostling old men, all Mohammedans. Each man had a charcoal brazier hung from a girdle underneath his coarse brown robe for warming his hands and belly. The noise and excitement were disturbing; I could not understand why we had caused such seeming distemper. Through our interpreter we learned that the excited men were all papermakers, and they were selecting from their group a single craftsman who should have the privilege of making paper for the American visitor.

It was the cold season, and the "mills" were not regularly in operation. I was taken from house to house and had the opportunity of inspecting the dipping-vats, which had been drained for the winter. This enabled me to make measurements which otherwise would not have been feasible, as Kashmirian papermaking-vats were embedded in the earthen floors of the houses. Finally we were taken to a house where the vat had been filled with water and everything placed in readiness for making paper. The artisans had selected the oldest of their group to represent them in their ancient craft, and this bearded man of aristocratic bearing came forward and graciously bowed to me. He had been chosen to perform every step of the art for my inspection and study. It was evident that this was a proud day for him, not perhaps so much because he was to display his talents to a foreigner, but because all the skilled papermakers of Nowshera had elected him as their leader.

The old men were soon joined by dozens of children and

derelict dogs who crowded into the weathered building that housed the papermaking equipment. The two upper stories were used as living-quarters for the artisans' families, and I could see light-skinned women with elaborate metal and glass head ornaments peeking cautiously through the broken spindles of the shutters. Hundreds of years ago the house must have been of great beauty, for even in decay it had character and charm. There were shallow carvings around the windows and doorways and on the interior wooden posts. I made rubbings of some of the finest work, and the natives could not comprehend why anyone would be interested in surroundings that to them seemed so commonplace. Within the old house an improvised armchair was placed in front of the dipping-vat, and I was requested to sit in it for the exhibition of papermaking. My guide, the interpreter, and the Nowshera papermakers stood at my back; the babies and children, all encrusted with grime, played at my feet. No women were present, for in Kashmir it was not the custom for them to mingle publicly with men. Suddenly the assembled workers ceased their constant chatter and all was quiet. The low-beamed, dirt-floored room was gloomy as a cave. The exhibition was about to begin, and as I sat in the armchair I felt I was attending a well-staged play rather than a demonstration of papermaking in one of the farthest corners of the world.

The old worker made dozens of sheets of paper for my benefit. For every sheet formed, a small stone was placed in an earthen bowl. At the end of a day's work the stones represented the number of sheets of paper that had been made. After the paper had been couched, or laid, one sheet directly upon another, it would have been difficult to count the individual pieces.

After the papermaking demonstration, we left for Arach,

where the stamping-mill used in beating the rags was located. Before we left, however, I asked Mr. Rao to acquire specimens of all types of Kashmiri paper, as well as the various tools and moulds the workers used. When the poverty-stricken papermakers were aware that we wished to purchase paper, they ran in all directions to their millhouses, each man returning with bundles of paper from his own establishment. The paper was always rolled or folded and adapted only to limited local requirements. Each man wanted his paper to be used for specimens in my proposed book, and there was so much argument and controversy among the workers that we purchased all of the paper offered. Many transactions were consummated, which entirely satisfied the papermakers and left me with abundant quantities of paper, both unburnished and burnished. This welcome business completed, the workers accompanied us through the muddy paths to the waiting automobile. This attention was apparently a signal for every person in Nowshera to crowd around us as we took our leave. There were half-clothed men and women astride weak-kneed donkeys; beggars with emaciated babies whose scrawny hands were thrust toward us for alms; cripples hobbling on stumps of legs; men with palsy; blind people; children with skin diseases; dirty urchins whose distended bellies bespoke lack of nourishment, all hoping that a few pice might fall their way; half-wild dogs and screeching crows—all were there to see us off.

After our inspection and photographing of the old stamping-mills at Arach, Mr. Rao and I left for Sailkot, about four hundred miles south of Srinagar. With Mr. Saini, superintendent of the Department of Industries of the Punjab, as our local guide, we drove in a tonga to an outlying district of Sailkot, known as Nekapura, a locality where paper had been made for many centuries. The cottage mill was owned by

Mamudeen Khagjee, a Mohammedan, whose name had originally been derived from the Hindustani word *kaghazi,* meaning "papermaker." In most of the old papermaking districts of India the names of the papermaking families had been adopted from this Hindustani word, showing that the craft had been the family occupation for centuries. The making of paper was carried on by Mohammedans because the Hindus would have been reluctant to handle rags and other materials that in one way or another had come in contact with eaters of meat.

My notes and photographing completed, we went to the railway station heavily laden with great bundles of paper and all manner of papermaking equipment. The Eurasian stationmaster sounded the gong and we were on our way to Old Delhi by way of Ambala. The journey from Sailkot to Delhi took fifteen hours and brought us to the old city early in the morning.

Although Mr. Rao had been supplied with detailed information relative to the handmade-paper industry in Delhi, and we were certain that it continued, we had a great deal of difficulty in finding the paper merchant who had offered to guide us. The day of our arrival was a Mohammedan holiday, and the streets were clogged with humanity, but after an hour's search through cobbled passageways and courts we came upon the cluttered stationery shop of Dhoomi Mal Dharam Das, who had agreed to take us to the last remnant of the Old Delhi papermakers. After a long drive through jumbled streets and fly-infested markets, we arrived at our destination, still within the confines of the city. Alighting from the derelict automobile, we entered a gateway in a crumbling brick wall and I followed my guides through a maze of winding paths flanked by stone walls and ancient overhanging carved balconies. The pathway was almost impassable owing to the jostling of peddlers who, on this day of celebration, were selling oxhearts; the shiny blue-and-red muscular organs were piled in pyramids on flat, widespread wicker baskets. As my guides were Hindus, this scene must have been extremely revolting to them. Apparently only Mohammedans dwelt in this labyrinth of alleyways.

We finally came to an incised-stone entrance, desolate and neglected, which appeared to be the end of the paved walk, and after one more turn we were within the courtyard of the handmade-paper establishment. The owner and workers were out in the streets celebrating the holiday, but it was not long before they came into the millyard to greet us. We were introduced to the owner of the mill, Mohammed Sadrque Kaghzi—again the family name derived from *kaghazi*, "papermaker." His workers gave a demonstration of making paper in the age-old Delhi manner, and we acquired specimens of the paper and the tools that had been used in the demonstration. Although it was obvious that paper had been fabricated in this same courtyard for many generations, no one knew anything about its history. Mr. Kaghzi explained that he had gained his knowledge from his forebears, "who had made paper for a thousand years."

Throughout my travels in India my companions were reluctant to have me reside in an English-owned hotel or to permit me to purchase anything from a British shop. Most of the papermaking villages had no lodgings where I could remain overnight, and on numerous occasions the long-armed wooden chairs found in all Indian railway stations furnished the only available place to rest. When we would arrive in a city where a European-type hotel was located I would try to concoct excuses so that I might spend a night or two in moderate comfort, but my companions invariably insisted that I remain in Hindu lodgings, and such was the case in Old Delhi. The hostelry selected for me was in the oldest section of this ancient city, and occupied the third floor of a building with overhanging balconies, above cloth merchants and metal-working shops. The lodgings were reached by a wooden stairway from the crowded alley. Through the latticed windows of my bedroom I could look out over the seething city. One large room of the hotel served for both living- and dining-quarters. My bedchamber, along with numerous others, bordered this central room on three sides, with a red-curtained doorway leading to each sleeping-cubicle. At intervals in the arrangement of the door openings there were yellow-curtained recesses within which old-fashioned water closets had been set up. Perhaps the most unsavory feature of the combination dining- and living-room was the system of sewage disposal. This consisted of an open U-shaped miniature canal that ran around the tile floor past the dining-tables and lounging-chairs. Although the top edges of this shallow trough were level with the floor one had to be on the alert, for it formed a stumbling-place for the unwary. While having a meal it was disconcerting to hear the flushing action of one of the toilets and to be aware that within a few moments a somewhat unpleasant sight would flow alongside the dining-table through the open tile channel, en route to the downspout on the outside of the building. It seemed to me at the time that whoever planned this hotel had overlooked a few minor details that could have been arranged more tastefully.

While residing in Old Delhi I was overcome by a feeling of weakness and sickliness. My companions insisted that an elderly Hindu doctor be consulted, a man in whom they had great confidence. I felt that the ailment could not linger for long, and I dismissed the kind suggestion. After a few days, however, it became apparent that I had contracted something that required vigorous treatment, and I went in search of the Hindu physician who had been commended to me. After feverously wandering through the filthy alleys and streets of the old city, I found the doctor's lair hidden in a small, parched garden that was reached through a stone archway.

Before entering his small house, I looked through the shuttered door and saw the old fellow seated cross-legged on a voluminous gray pillow on a huge, round teakwood stool. His face was deeply furrowed, like a walnut shell; a thin beard of scarcely two dozen long white hairs protruded from his chin; his body and head were enveloped in white cotton cloths. Behind the doctor, within arm's reach, was a shelf of empty bottles of many sizes and shapes, varying in capacity from a few ounces to a half-gallon. As I entered the room and stood before the wise old Hindu, he barely raised his head, but he spoke to me kindly and in a whispering voice said: "You have amoebic dysentery or you would not have come; such is indeed serious." Without further observation, he thrust his scrawny fingers, suggestive of the claws of a vulture, in the direction of his collection of bottles, and with deliberation selected one of about a pint capacity. He then slowly pasted a narrow strip of paper on the bottle, extending from the base to the neck. With a pen dipped in black ink he scratched at right angles short lines, about a half-inch apart, throughout the length of the strip of paper. He next reached for a red clay jug, from which he filled the bottle with heavy black liquid that re-sembled the spent oil drained from an automobile. Without leaving his luxurious pillow he handed the filled pint bottle to me with the terse command that I drink the medicine every hour, from one inked line to the next. I took the obnoxious medicine from line to line. It tasted even worse than it looked. After a day's dosage, the nostrum had practically the same effect upon my ailment as if I had consumed a half-pound of plaster of Paris or devoured a cupful of mixed Portland cement. The most inconvenient feature of my sickness had been arrested. After finally recovering from the Hindu doctor's severe treatment, I left the cure to nature, but little did I realize that almost five years would elapse before I would be entirely free from all traces of the most disturbing malady I had ever encountered.

From Old Delhi we went to Agra. Visitors to this city were usually interested only in the Taj Mahal, but my thoughts were with papermaking. Our information suggested that there was one small cottage mill in the bazaar, to the rear of the Taj Mahal, in a settlement known as Taijang. All day we drove in a tonga through one dusty alley after another, and from house to house, seeking the papermakers of Agra. Wherever we inquired, the Indians shook their heads: nothing was known of paper ever having been made in Taijang. Finally a bent old man guided us to a tannery set well back in a dust-laden, grassless yard. The building was in the final stages of decay, surrounded by crumbling mud walls and tottering houses. Half-naked men and somberly dressed women peered through the crooked window openings; starving babies and children sank into the dry dust. At the doorway of one of the leaning hovels we were introduced to the last of the Agra papermakers—Old Wahzbuks, apparently in his eighties. He told us that no paper had been made in Agra or the surrounding country for many years, and that when the Taijang mill had been in operation, it had been owned by an old papermaking family named Chunna, of which not a single member remained. I asked Old Wahzbuks to permit me to photograph him, a request he graciously granted, saying that never before had he been so honored.

After having been in Agra for three days, we visited the Taj Mahal. The exterior was impressive, although I was surprised to find in the interior large sections of ordinary plaster painted in imitation of Italian marble.

In Agra we were told that the making of paper was carried on in the remote village of Kalpi, lying between Cawnpore and Jhansi. Thereupon we gathered together our nineteen pieces of luggage, consisting of bedding-rolls, water bottles, tiffin baskets, papermaking appliances, and bundles of paper, and entrained for Kalpi.

I was the first American to visit Kalpi, for unless a foreigner was interested in either handmade paper or the local production of a curiously sweet confection pierced by straws and held in flat mud dishes, there was nothing to attract him. It was about noon when the local train pulled into the little station near Kalpi, and after the coolies had unloaded our pile of baggage, the genial stationmaster presented himself and said that he would do anything within his power to make us comfortable while in his village. An easy chair in the compact waiting-room was provided for me while my guide, Mr. Rao, walked up the dusty road in search of Munnalal Khaddari, the master of the *vidyalay*, or school, where the craft of making paper by hand was taught. The Kalpi institute of papermaking had been established by Mohandas Karamchand Gandhi to develop this trade as a cottage industry. He hoped not only to give work to India's destitute, but also to reduce the importation of paper from Japan and the West, especially from Great Britain.

It seemed a long wait in the quiet little station for Mr. Rao's return. On that winter day the waiting-room was cool, and there was no need for the heavy woolen *pankha,* or large swinging fan, that was suspended overhead; but, as I sat in the long-armed chair, it was not difficult to imagine that during the summer months Kalpi could be extremely hot and enervating. Every little while the stationmaster, dressed in flowing white cotton, would come to the waiting-room to see if I was comfortable. I was interested in a torn, weather-stained notice, glazed and framed, that hung on the wall, a familiar object in all Indian village railway stations. The notice was the inventory of the furnishings of the waiting-room, and, for want of better amusement, I set down a transcript of the items in my notebook: "Four teak long-armed chairs; one iron jug; one notice board; one *pankha* with mat frill; one large teak table; one table for washing hands; one zinc bathing-tub; one iron-bound chest; one chamber pot." I was able to locate each and every object on the list, and I was gratified that nothing was missing.

After a short rest in the long-armed chair, I heard Mr. Rao at the door speaking Hindustani with several other Indian gentlemen who had returned with him. I was introduced to Munnalal Khaddari, the master of the Kalpi school of paper-making, and two of his instructors, Mr. Nagarajarao and Jagannath Prasad. After the thoughtful stationmaster had served tea, we left for the school. To reach it we walked through a thoroughfare ankle-deep in heavy black dust that was kept in agitation by the constant tread of innumerable bullocks' hoofs and the lumbering, wide-tired wheels of the overloaded carts. The Khaddari school stood on a low bank, the building being reached by five steps cut in the dry clay. A painted wooden signboard above the gateway gave the name. As we entered the small mud building, my attention was arrested by an earnest worker sitting before a simple loom on which he was weaving a grass-and-horsehair mould-cover for use in forming sheets of paper. As I sat on a bench in the cramped room, Mr. Khaddari and his helpers showed various examples of paper that had been made by the students, of which the instructors were obviously proud; their pride was even more pronounced, however, when they unfolded a copy of Mahatma Gandhi's weekly *Harijan*, which was printed on paper made in the Kalpi school. It was Gandhi's hope that every issue of this publication might be done on Indian hand-made paper, but up to this time only the one issue had been so printed. This unique edition appeared on July 17, 1937, and on page five of the eight-page quarto publication were these significant lines:

> NOTICE. The readers, we trust, will be glad to know that this issue of *Harijan* has been printed on handmade paper, of course as an experiment. The paper has been made in Kalpi (U.P.).
> Manager.

Although the school had only one copy of this coveted issue, Mr. Khaddari insisted that I add it to my collection of "paperi-ana." He also presented an inscribed copy of his own work, a sixteen-page octavo booklet, on modern papermaking by hand, the only treatise on this subject in the Hindustani language. During our stay at the school we were shown the entire proc-ess of making paper in the Kalpi manner, from the maceration of the raw materials to the burnishing of the finished paper.

Kalpi offered no sleeping-place for an Occidental visitor, nor was food available. I carried food and water, but the sleeping-arrangements presented a minor problem. The station-master again came to my rescue and placed my bedding-roll on two of the long-armed chairs in the railway waiting-room.

As night came on, my friends gathered around the station table, and in the light of a smoking castor-oil lamp we discussed papermaking, weaving, and the work of Mahatma Gandhi. One old craftsman brought a jug of warm buffalo milk that we drank from a communal hand-wrought brass bowl. There were a dozen or more men in the station speaking in both Hindustani and English; each in turn advanced his ideas for solving India's myriad problems, but at the last all were in accord that Mahatma Gandhi was the only one in India who could help them.

It was late when I finally fell asleep in the little railway station, for my mind was troubled. Was handwork, as Mr. Gandhi contended, the solution of India's difficulties? That lonely night in Kalpi I could not convince myself that there ever would be a solution.

Our visits to the papermaking districts of Kashmir, Sailkot, Old Delhi, and Kalpi had enabled me to inspect a number of handmade-paper mills and to become familiar with the details of Indian methods. Not until we were in Kalpi, however, was the political significance of the industry fully revealed to me, for in this village I first came in contact with Mahatma Gandhi's connection with papermaking as a Congress project.

From Kalpi we went to Wardha, where Gandhi made his home, and where the workshops of the Indian National Congress, including the original Gandhi school of papermaking, were located. Wardha was situated about six hundred miles south of Kalpi, and to reach this remote town we changed trains at Jhansi and Itarsi. Two nights were spent in the jolting, swaying sleeping-cars. The Wardha railway station did not in any manner suggest that this was the best-known village in all India. We drove in a tonga to the location of the numerous association buildings, known locally as Maganvadi. We had a letter to Mr. Kumarappa, author of the book *Why the Village Movement?* and principal of the school where the various handicrafts were taught. He was a pleasant, sincere gentleman, a former student at Columbia University. After an explanation of the cottage-industries movement, he went with us across the roadway to the school of papermaking which had been set up by Gandhi not only as a center for instruction but also as an agency for supplying information and help to other papermaking districts throughout India.

Upon our arrival in Wardha, Mr. Kumarappa said that it would not be possible to meet Gandhi, as he had only recently returned from Calcutta, where he had been under medical observation. Mr. Kumarappa himself had not seen him for more than two months, and only the previous week a most influential Chinese had been refused an audience. I explained that I had not come to Wardha to see Gandhi; my interest was in the papermaking school.

After the inspection of the school, we were taken to the administration building, where I met Mahadev Desai, editor of the Congress magazine, *Harijan,* and Gandhi's secretary and confidant. He likewise impressed upon me that it would not be possible to see Gandhi, although he expressed his willingness to give him my greetings and tell him of my keen interest in the papermaking school. Under Mr. Desai's guidance we went through the buildings of the Congress, including the museum under construction.

Just as Mr. Rao and I were about to take our leave, a young man hurriedly approached our group and handed Mr. Desai a message from Gandhi requesting that I go to his country retreat. Our friends were surprised, and I most of all. Without delay Mr. Desai summoned his car, a battered green Model-T Ford with a faded saffron, white, and emerald flag, the emblem of the Congress, flying from the radiator cap. I was placed in the back seat along with a basket of eggs, a case of California preserved peaches, and a small crate of dates, and we were off to the secluded home of the most influential and most beloved man in India. The antique car jogged along the rough, sun-baked road. We passed bullock carts whose drivers stubbornly refused to make way for the jolting Ford, but as there was no well-defined roadway I could see no need for argument. We drove about six miles through the dusty country, the dull, monotonous landscape broken only by a few scrubby bushes growing in the dry, hot sand. As we drove along, Mr. Desai looked out over the desolate scene and asked if there was any more beautiful countryside in America. He had an odd conception of my country, and was surprised to learn that in the United States there were actually large trees, running brooks, and open fields. He had pictured America as stripped of trees, the brooks and rivers polluted, and the entire area almost one continuous mass of factories and industrial buildings.

After a half-hour's drive we came to a long, low thatched house set close to the makeshift roadway. Some men were building fences, others were constructing a wide gate, and several stalwart workers were tugging at a long wooden pole attached to an old-fashioned sugar-cane press. We walked toward a modest group of small buildings within a fenced enclosure. Mr. Desai pointed to a newly built plaster house well away from the other buildings, and said that the Mahatma was within. I was asked to remain at the workshop to await a signal from Mr. Desai, who walked over to the plaster house. Within the workshop I could hear the hum of a sewing-machine and men talking in low voices. On the veranda there were baskets of vegetables, and also the eggs, tinned fruit, and dates that had come in the car. I had not been waiting long when a tall, lean Hindu came over to where I was sitting and asked if I would be willing to "treat" the eggs. He explained that Gandhi needed nourishment, but the Mahatma, like himself, was an orthodox Hindu and would not eat eggs unless they had first been rendered sterile. I readily consented to run a pointed darning-needle through each egg so that Gandhi's wish never to take life would not be broken.

An enormous hairy brown man in a breechcloth sat spinning on the workshop veranda. Another Hindu, of lesser proportions, was lying on a string bed, reading to the spinner. The book was in Hindustani, and the reclining man was translating it into English for the benefit of the huge brown artisan, who appeared incongruous alongside his delicate wooden spinning-wheel. The volume was a cookbook, and when I arrived the reader was translating a recipe for the preparation of cucumber soup. I listened all through this section and another dealing with the making of cheese from buffalo milk, until Mr. Desai appeared at the gateway of Gandhi's plaster house and beckoned me. As I walked toward the house, past Gandhi's outdoor rope-strung bed, I could see that in addition to the low doorway the house had a small, square window. Above the barred window, a well-porportioned replica of a fig tree, symbolic of horticulture, was modeled in the white plaster; neatly modeled spinning-wheels stood out in bold relief at either side of the window, and below it was a sculptured beehive with bees flying above—all emblems of the National Congress. The house was of one story, roofed with thatch, and was surrounded by a rail-and-picket fence with a crude turnstile entrance. As I passed through the turnstile, Mr. Desai came toward me and in a subdued voice requested that I remain with Gandhi only a few minutes and cautioned me to confine my conversation to papermaking. The

Mahatma was ill, he explained, and could not discuss political issues. Had I been politically minded, Gandhi would not have sent for me; his intense interest in the making of paper by hand and his knowledge that I was concerned only with this subject opened the way for my visit.

I entered the house, and there was Mahatma Gandhi on the flagstone floor, his frail body wrapped only in a cotton sheet. His head rested on a white pillow, and around his forehead was wound a gray cloth, held secure by a safety pin. Five or six of his disciples, both men and women, all Indians but one, reclined on the stone floor near him. Each member of this devoted group wrote down every word their prophet spoke. Gandhi looked up at me, and in a clear, soft voice said: "You are very tall, you must stoop to enter my poor home." He held his hands before his face, in the manner of the East, and then extended his right hand to me, and I knelt at his side and clasped his thin, bony hand between my hands. As I had hoped, Gandhi spoke only of Indian papermaking. He was pleased with the progress that had been made with this craft as one of the village industries. He mentioned the various processes of mould-making, beating, and forming the sheets of paper, and seemed to have a fair knowledge of the different procedures. In comparing papermaking with weaving, he said: "People could get along without paper, but could they exist without clothing?" It passed quickly through my mind that Gandhi himself was a perfect example of existing without clothing; also, as all of his disciples were at that very moment using paper to record his words, perhaps paper was even more important than cloth! I did not remain long in Gandhi's presence, as it was evident that talking was fatiguing to him; he had seen no other stranger since his return from Calcutta. As I arose to leave, he again extended his hand,

and I backed through the low doorway. I had indeed come in contact with a "Great Soul"—the meaning of *Mahatma*.

While visiting the Gandhi papermaking school in Wardha, we were given information regarding the other places where the making of paper by hand continued to be practiced.

After remaining in cosmopolitan Bombay for a few days' rest, we left in the afternoon for the native state of Hyderabad, where the craft of papermaking had survived for centuries. We reached Secunderabad the following morning. At the station we were met by Mr. Ratnam, of the Osmania University, who had been delegated by the Indian Industrial Commission to act as guide during our stay in Hyderabad. On our way to the inn he told us that the new Osmania University was the first institution in India to give university education through a vernacular; the second language was English, the study of which was compulsory. I was surprised to be told that when the foremost scholars of India were called upon to deliver an address in a native language, they found it expedient to compose the speech in English and then translate it into their own language—Urdu, Hindi, Tamil, Telugu, or whatever the required native tongue might be. Such a procedure was eloquent of the decadence of the native languages among the scholars of India. In the Osmania University the language was Urdu, and as it was difficult to procure modern textbooks in this language, the university had set up a large, well-equipped bureau of translation.

Everywhere I traveled in India I was impressed by the regard for college education. A degree was valued beyond wealth. In India, as in Germany, the degree to which a person was entitled was invariably placed after his name on business or visiting cards. I recall meeting a handsome young Indian who was so proud of even having worked toward the possible acquisition of a Doctorate of Philosophy that he had his card engraved to read: "Mr. —— ——, Ph.D. (Failed)." Another instance of a desire for prestige was the card of a young merchant I met in Sailkot who had been self-educated. On his business card his name appeared in bold lettering, followed by the brief assertion: "Subscriber to the London Times"—a distinction that no doubt carried considerable weight with his trade associates.

Coming to Hyderabad from modern Bombay, I was at once aware that we had reached a section of India where Western influence had not penetrated so deeply. Hyderabad had retained at least some of the ancient flavor and romance of the Mogul empire. His Exalted Highness, the Nizam, was of the Mohammedan faith, and ruled over one and a half million Moslems and eleven and a half million Hindus. The state had its own railways, army, and coinage. Although Hyderabad differed from other parts of India in many ways, it had the usual superabundance of beggars, poverty, and disease.

Mr. Ratnam told us that the papermaking center of Kagaziguda (Paper Village) was forty-three miles from Secunderabad and that the journey could not be made without discomfort. For our trip it was necessary to procure still another guide, a man familiar with the winding route to the village. We also found a young chauffeur willing to assume responsibility for our journey. With baskets of food and bottles of water, we left early in the morning for Kagaziguda. The first part of the highway was wide and smooth, but after a few miles the road began to narrow, until it was reduced to no more than a rutted right-of-way cut through the forest and underbrush. We drove over rocks, forded streams and swamps, and at last stuck fast in the thick, heavy mud. The local guide told us that we were fortunate in arriving at the finest time of year, for had we attempted to visit the paper districts of Hyderabad at any other period we would have been disappointed: it would have been impossible to reach them. Through ingenious manipulation and perseverance the chauffeur was at last able to extricate the automobile from the mire and carry us to within three or four miles of Kagaziguda. We walked the short distance to the remote locality, where I saw paper being made in the traditional manner, and where we made photographs of each step of the process. The papermakers of India, all living and working in inaccessible villages, had no conception of the eighteen-hundred-year history of their craft, and even in their own districts the local history was inaccurate.

During my investigations I was surprised to be told that neither the mill-owners or the workers had ever seen specimens of the fine handmade papers produced in Japan and Europe. Wherever I went in India, the artisans would ask me to describe the methods being used in another locality, perhaps not more than three hundred miles distant. The papermakers could not afford to travel, and the exchange of specimens of paper between districts was hampered not only by language difficulties, but also by the illiteracy of the workers. I found this same condition in China, although not to the same extent. While there were many dialects in China, there was but one system of writing and printing the spoken word. In India, however, there were many different alphabets and many distinct languages, which made intercourse difficult.

Before leaving the ancient hamlet of Kagaziguda, we were taken to see the many-storied juggernaut of the village. The enormous wooden contrivance was housed in a high brick building with an arched entrance open to the roadway. The papermakers' children were playing on the towering wheeled structure with apparently no thought of the sacredness of the lumbering vehicle. The heavy juggernaut was a dull "dragon's-blood" red; the stout wooden wheels with thick iron tires had sunk into the soft clay floor of the enclosure. This juggernaut was brought out only when the festival of *Rathaya-tra* was held in the district, a Hindu feast in which the god, or idol, Vishnu was placed in the huge carriage, which then was pulled by hundreds of Hindus through the roads. Contrary to belief, Hindu fanatics did not throw themselves in sacrifice beneath the sturdy wheels of these giant juggernauts. Such an act would have been a defilement that the gods would never have forgiven. It would have been considered unholy to be killed by a juggernaut or even to spill blood on so sacred a relic.

After leaving Secunderabad we first went to Beswada, where a number of years ago there had been handmade-paper mills in and near the city. We could not, however, find any activity of this kind in the district, and we resumed our journey to Rajahmundry, Mr. Rao's home town. In this coastal city of Madras I was royally entertained, and I shall long remember the hospitality of those gracious people. Through the kindness of Mr. Greenwood, an Englishman, I was housed in the long, rambling English club, which had but three members, the only English people in the district. Mr. Greenwood, whose wife was a charming Indian woman, was the superintendent of prisons of that section of Madras, and he asked regarding the possibility of making paper by hand in the jails. I explained that we had found the craft in practice in the prisons of Sailkot, a system that had been uninterrupted for many years. Mr. Greenwood believed that jail-made paper would find use in making the long, narrow, cowhide-bound account books used by the Madras merchants. I asked if his prisoners were incarcerated a sufficient length of time to make training worth while. He explained that there were many men serving long terms and even life sentences, and that only these prisoners would be put to work in the prison paper mill.

After 1870 considerable paper was made in Indian jails, and in some communities the industry was developed on such a large scale that the prisons became the major source of paper. In these places it was mandatory that jail-made paper be used in all public offices for vernacular writing. This competition was thought to be unfair by the free workers whose families for centuries had made paper in their cottage mills. Although the prices for jail-made paper were usually higher than those at which "free" paper could be sold, the independent workers became impoverished because the public offices were the best markets. In 1882, John Lockwood Kipling, the father of Rudyard Kipling and curator of Lahore Museum from 1875 to 1893, expressed himself strongly on the subject of jail-made paper: "The competition of the jails, none of which with all their resources have greatly improved on the best Sailkot stuff, has had an injurious effect on the manufacture. . . . District officers have frequently had occasion to complain of the quality of the paper they are compelled to buy, stating that they could better and more cheaply be served in the open market."

After a pleasant and profitable week in Rajahmundry, we left for the north to continue our investigations. The best route to the small papermaking villages in Munshiganj, Bengal, was from Calcutta, and although the distance of two hundred and fifty miles was insignificant by Indian standards, the journey was one of many inconveniences. The paper made in Munshiganj was known as Arial, named for one of the oldest papermaking villages. At the time of my visit the center of the craft was Kurmira, and the headquarters, where the finished paper was stored and sold, was near Autsahai. The closest post office was Purapara, the entire community lying within

Dhairpara, in the Dacca district. With the possible exception of Kashmir, I found this to be the most interesting papermaking settlement of India.

After securing a supply of whole-wheat biscuit, tinned fish and fruit, and bottles of pure water, we left Calcutta by night train, reaching Faridpur at daylight the following morning. At Faridpur we boarded a small steamboat that carried us along the Padma River to the fishing village of Talatalla, where we arrived in the early afternoon. Here we were met by Kiron Chandra Sen, head of Gandhi's papermaking project in the Munshiganj district. At Talatalla we awaited a smaller riverboat that took us on to another, even more primitive, fishing village, where we boarded a still smaller craft. We left this boat at the mouth of an almost hidden canal about midway between the hamlets of Pekabi-Bazar and Char Bairagadi. At the juncture of the grass-grown canal and the river we could see that a very small *dingi*, or skiff, with a curved rattan covering, was awaiting us. Our destination was Autsahai, and Mr. Sen had left nothing to chance. After our bedding-rolls, food, and water had been placed aboard the *dingi*, little space was left for the two guides and myself, but with the help of the old boatman who was to pole us up the canal we finally contrived to squeeze into the boat. The slow journey up the narrow canal was of unusual interest: at the crest of each steep bank of the waterway there were rambling settlements of mud houses, with the men, women, and children all engaged in the forming and baking of dark-clay bowls and pots for use in cooking. After we had traveled for several cramped hours in the *dingi*, the winding muddy canal became narrower and narrower, until even our tiny craft could go no farther. The remaining distance had to be covered on foot. After we disengaged ourselves from the pole-propelled boat and prepared for the last leg of our journey, I overheard Mr. Sen and the old boatman in an animated discussion, and I was afraid that something had arisen to endanger our trip. As the conversation was in Bengali, neither Mr. Rao nor I could understand what the disagreement might be. Finally, with a grave expression, Mr. Sen turned to me and said: "The boatman wishes to overcharge us; he is demanding four annas, an exorbitant charge for his few hours' work and the use of his *dingi*. The usual charge for this canal journey is but one anna." The gentle boatman had appealed to Mr. Sen, saying that the three men and the luggage had made a heavy load, that the day had been exceptionally warm, and that he had had to push all the way against the current. He had wished to charge us about nine cents, and our conscientious guide had objected. After the difficulty had been explained, I agreed with the boatman that a charge of four annas had been justified, and I asked Mr. Rao to give him the amount. As we said good-by to the old boatman, my latent Scottish generosity got the best of me, and without letting either of my guides know, I gave the old fellow a dozen or more extra annas. The average daily wage at that time in remote parts of Bengal was four annas.

Our baggage was soon balanced on the heads of two waiting coolies, who went ahead with orders to carry the burdens to Autsahai. Mr. Sen explained that not even a two-wheeled bullock cart could enter his village by the route we had to take. There were no roads, but only footpaths leading through wet black clay and over many arched wooden bridges, entirely impassable for any form of conveyance. The country was a network of rivers, streams, lakes, and swamps, all overgrown with an entangled mass of water hyacinths. During the rainy season, from the latter part of June until early September, the countryside was inundated, and all communication had to be by boat. After seemingly endless trudging through the slippery clay paths and over scores of frail bridges, many with missing footboards and broken handrails, we reached the edge of the village of Autsahai. Twilight had overtaken us, and I was relieved when Mr. Sen pointed to a cottage in the distance and said that it would be our home while in his village. Although the night was moist and cool, I was overheated from the long tramp, and the dew, almost as heavy as rain, had saturated my clothing. As we came closer to the cottage, I could see that many white-robed men were present, each carrying an old-fashioned square caster-oil lantern; myriad mosquitoes hovered around every yellow flame. The gentlemen came forward to greet the first Occidental who had ever visited their village on an unofficial mission. I was at once impressed by the dignity of these men; most of them were of middle age, some were patriarchal. As I stood among this group in the soft glare of the yellow lights, I was introduced to the leaders of the community—the librarian, the village doctor, the master of the school and his teachers, the president of the Union Board. All were there to wish us a pleasant sojourn in their village. I was delighted with these cultured men. Soon many more villagers arrived, until the dark countryside was alive with white-clad men, each with his own antique lantern. No women were present; it would have been presumptuous for them to have assumed equal station with their men. The crowd increased until there were more than a hundred men who had come to pay their respects. We had been at the cottage only a short time when I overheard the villagers quietly talking among themselves regarding "the meeting," a topic that seemed to concern everyone. I was anxious as to the part that I might have to play in "the meeting," but I knew that sooner or later I would understand.

After the welcome serving of hot tea and sugar-curds, most of the villagers left for their homes, promising to return early the following morning. I was tirèd, and suggested that I would be glad to retire. My bedding-rolls, which the coolies had carried on their heads, were spread on a wide wooden bench in the corner of one room of the dirt-floored cottage, which had been ingeniously constructed of bamboo. An adjoining room was piled high with bundles of handmade paper that had been produced in the district. Several of the older gentlemen remained with me while I prepared for bed, and when I removed my damp shoes they carefully covered them with bamboo mats, explaining that scorpions and tarantulas were abundant and delighted to spend the night hidden in shoes or slippers and then to surprise the owner in the morning by sinking their springlike claws into his feet. The caster-oil lamp was turned low, and as I tried to rest on the hard bed I was amused by watching the lizards crawl up and down the bamboo walls and across the rattan ceiling of the little room.

Throughout my stay in Autsahai the atmosphere remained cool and moist; at night the monkeys and birds chattered, dogs howled and barked, and I suspected that I heard the monotonous wailing of wild animals. To add to this confusion of tropical sounds, Mr. Rao talked in his sleep. Had he spoken in English, it might have been comforting, but unfortunately his nocturnal conversations were in his native tongue. Each morning at daylight the villagers began their trek to the cottage, and with little formality came into the room and sat around me on the improvised bed. Their hospitality knew no bounds; their gestures of welcome never ceased. Breakfast was served each morning in the ancient home of Asutosh

Gupta, a retired schoolteacher, who lived within the walled courtyard of the Marayan temple, which had been erected about 1635 by his ancestor, Har Mohan Gupta.

I suggested that we walk to Kurmira, a few miles distant, where the actual making of paper took place, but my hosts would not permit me to tramp the rough road to the mill: they insisted that the workers and the mill equipment be brought to me! Early one morning when we were returning from breakfast at the ancient Gupta house, we were greeted by eight old papermakers who had walked from Kurmira bearing on their heads the needed appliances for making paper. The bare yard around the Autsahai cottage was swiftly turned into a typical Bengal paper mill. A hole was dug in the earth to receive the huge baked-clay jar used in the maceration of the jute and hemp material. A large round earthenware dipping-vat was also embedded in the ground. The bamboo moulds, drying-frames, and finishing-tools had likewise been brought for use in the demonstration. The eight papermakers in their many-colored robes formed a picturesque group. These workers were of a lower caste than the aristocratic gentlemen who were entertaining us, and perhaps that was why they were not formally introduced. All the artisans bore the ancient surname Kaghazi ("Papermaker"); their given names were Munsubati, Arman, Lhahebali, Makbnl, Dibarbax, Samswrah, Ansn, and Ahammed. All were descendants of papermaking families who had carried on this trade for hundreds of years. These workers performed every branch of their craft for my edification, and I made many photographs and filled my notebook.

The papermakers in the Dacca district received from four to six annas a day; each vatman, working from twelve to sixteen hours, was required to mould about one hundred large sheets of paper. During the dry season, from nine to twelve families found their livelihood in papermaking, but only four or five families remained at work throughout the entire year. Aside from making paper, each family had a cow or two that gave a limited amount of milk and supplied dung-fuel for the cooking. Asutosh Gupta, who was the Autsahai village historian, assured me that a hundred years earlier, seven hundred and fifty families had been employed in making paper in this section of Bengal, and that had it not been for the intrusion of the papermaking-machine, a thousand families could still be earning their livelihood from this trade.

Even after the papermaking demonstration had been completed and the lowly descendants of the ancient Kaghazi family had returned to their own village of Kurmira, our instructive investigation in Autsahai did not end. With deference I was taken to the village dispensary, damp and cheerless, where the indigent people received surgical attention, and where medicines were distributed. It was distressing to see that many of the surgical instruments were covered with rust. We next visited the Union Board, an office where all matters relating to the community were transacted. The president, Prafulla Chandra Sen, gave me a handwritten booklet outlining the work of this bureau, from which I was surprised to learn that Autsahai had a population of 10,554, there being 6,333 Hindus and 4,221 Mohammedans, with a total assessment of 2,117 rupees, the Hindus contributing 1,512 rupees and the Mohammedans 605 rupees of the total amount. The manuscript enumerated ten temples and fifteen mosques, and listed the village needs: "one burning-ghat, more tube wells, one graveyard, one playground."

After completing our observation of the school, where only locally made paper was used, we walked through an overgrown path, past temples and mosques, to the library, a small structure on the edge of a lake, called a "tank." It contained about a thousand books, all suffering from mildew and mould. Two thirds of the volumes were in Bengali, the rest in English. A crude colored lithographic portrait of Mahatma Gandhi was the only picture in the library. In the enclosed yard there were two antique stone-carvings, one representing Ganesha and the other Shiva or Parvati, Hindu gods, that had been retrieved from the bottom of the tank where they had been thrown hundreds of years before.

As we left the library, I could see in the distance a great gathering of villagers, row upon row; the men and boys were sitting cross-legged on large Indian carpets; a small group of women and girls sat clustered together toward the rear. Every individual sat with dignity and decorum; not a sound disturbed the peace of the gathering. A table and three massive chairs had been placed before the assemblage of more than three hundred persons. I was suddenly aware of what had been meant by "the meeting"! I was shown to the middle chair, between Mr. Rao and the scholarly old schoolmaster. After a formal introduction, I did my best to address the villagers, although I was aware that only the more educated members of the group had a knowledge of English. The schoolmaster spoke next, and I could detect that he was giving a translation of my confused and disjointed talk. Mr. Rao was called upon to give an account of our Indian journeys, and although all of the villagers in the audience were Mr. Rao's own countrymen, he spoke to them in English, as his native language would not have been understood by a single person present.

During our days in Autsahai we had made many friends, and we were reluctant to leave. Our hosts suggested a different route for our return to the river on our way to Calcutta, a path that avoided the excessively long walk that had been necessary to reach the village. With Mano Ranjan Gupta as our guide, we started our early-morning walk over the slippery clay paths to Sabachani, the streamside hamlet, where a *dingi* was awaiting us. Our luggage, papermaking equipment, and bundles of paper, which had been carried from Autsahai on the heads of the bearers, had already been placed in the small boat. The boatman, a half-naked Hindu, stood with pole in hand ready to proceed. The day was warm, and all along the narrow canal the smells were almost offensive, suggesting damp clay, decaying vegetation, and human filth. We passed village after village where almost every person was engaged in making the same kind of dark-clay pottery that was being made along the other route. On one side of the waterway lived the Hindus, on the other the Mohammedans.

We floated noiselessly down the stream, the boatman's pole easily reaching the muddy bottom of the canal, which was overgrown with water hyacinth. With each stroke of the pole the wooden skiff went forward in an uncomfortable lurch. I had long known of the hostility between the Hindus and the Mohammedans, but not until this canal journey had I fully realized the significance of this age-old antagonism. At a bend in the snake-like canal an old half-starved cow had fallen into the water, and the sick animal was too weak to free herself from the sticky clay bottom. The Mohammedans, on their bank of the waterway, were determined to kill the cow and make use of the flesh, hide, and bones. The Hindus from their side loudly maintained that no human dare take the life of any animal. A heated argument rang out across the water. As the half-dead cow struggled, unaided, to free herself from the heavy mud, several dozen naked-necked vultures flew down from near-by trees and rested upon her protruding spine. And while the Hindus and Mohammedans continued their tirade, the repulsive birds sank their ugly beaks and claws deep and ripped the flesh from the bones of the limp and dying animal. The vultures had settled the argument. The old boatman plunged his long pole into the clay bottom of the canal, the boat gave a sudden lurch, and we continued silently down the narrow stream.

We were glad to leave the *dingi* when we reached Tarpasa late in the evening. It had been a long, cramped journey, but fortunately we had arrived in time for the large river steamboat that was to carry us on to Goalundo. The river was unusually wide at Tarpasa, and the rotting barge where the steamboat was to stop was well out in the water. From our small *dingi* the deck of the barge appeared alarmingly high, but with the aid of a rope we managed to climb aboard. There we were refreshed by hot tea while great flocks of screeching crows circled overhead. When the steamship arrived and pulled up to the barge, Mr. Rao and I went aboard, leaving Mr. Gupta to return to Subachani with the boatman. As we drifted down the wide river, Mr. Gupta vigorously waved his white blouse, our final farewell from the kindly people of Autsahai.

My travels and observations in India during 1937 and 1938 resulted in the quarto-size book entitled *Papermaking by Hand in India,* issued late in 1939. This edition of 370 signed and numbered copies was handsomely printed by Elmer Adler's Pynson Printers, New York. Mr. Adler and I would have preferred using Indian handmade paper for the text, but it was not suitable, being too uneven in thickness, texture, and finish. We felt that the Indians might resent the use of English-made paper, so after considerable deliberation we decided upon Swedish handmade paper for both text and illustrations. There were 130 pages of text hand-set in Baskerville type; 84

hand-printed photogravures; and 27 original specimens of native paper made in the various papermaking centers I had visited. The edition was bound by Gerhard Gerlach in three-quarters black calf, with cloth sides block-printed in India. The books were sold for thirty-six dollars a copy.

For the third time, a book that I had compiled was produced without physical exertion on my part. All that the Pynson Printers required was the manuscript for the text, the photographs for the illustrations, and the original samples of Indian paper. These were exceedingly simple requirements compared with having to set my own type, print the dampened sheets of handmade paper on the hand press, and finally dispose of the edition, all by my own efforts.

# ✤✤ XIII ✤✤

I N May 1936, several years before the publication of *Papermaking by Hand in India,* I received a letter from Dr. Karl Taylor Compton, President of the Massachusetts Institute of Technology, Cambridge. The letter was a complete surprise. Through Carl Tilden Keller, President of the Club of Odd Volumes, Boston, known among bibliophiles for his magnificent *Don Quixote* collection, Dr. Compton had learned of my work, and he had been purchasing the papermaking books as they appeared.

Dr. Compton was aware of the papermaking equipment and appliances that I had gathered in my travels to aid in making drawings and photographs for these books. He now proposed that this collection should become a museum of papermaking, and further suggested that the Massachusetts Institute of Technology would be the proper place for such a project. At that time, however, the thought of being connected with M.I.T. did not particularly appeal to me; I knew nothing about this great scientific institution along the Charles River; I had never been in Cambridge. In a later communication, dated December 15, 1936, Dr. Compton again urged me to join M.I.T. and outlined a ten-year agreement that the institute would be willing to make, giving me free rein to do any traveling, research, and book-printing I might wish to undertake.

It was not until the latter part of 1938, however, that I consented to follow Dr. Compton's plan, which ultimately resulted in the establishment of the Dard Hunter Paper Museum of the Massachusetts Institute of Technology.

By this time the William Barton Rogers building was almost completed, and the Paper Museum was installed in a large, well-proportioned exhibition gallery on the third floor of this classic structure at 77 Massachusetts Avenue. During the months when the hundreds of exhibits were being set up, Dr. Compton came often to the museum room, and always with words of encouragement. He was one of the world's most eminent physicists, scholars, and administrators, with a natural modesty and charm of manner that were most refreshing. It apparently required no effort for him to unbend to the mental level of the ordinary layman.

The Paper Museum was formally opened in the summer of 1939. There were 5,830 interested visitors during the first twelve months, and more than seven thousand the second year; after that time we stopped keeping a record. Many of our most enthusiastic visitors, even from distant parts of the country, made the journey to Cambridge especially to see the collection and were uninterested in other departments of the institute. Many appreciative letters were received, but probably none gave me more satisfaction than a note from Boston, dated March 4, 1941, written in longhand by Daniel Berkeley Updike, the reserved and scholarly founder of the Merrymount Press and author of *Printing Types, Their History, Forms, and Use.* He wrote:

I tried to find you on Sunday after our brief meeting, to tell you how much I enjoyed seeing your collection— so nicely, cheerily, and attractively installed. Many of the

choice Chinese papers are magnificent. I shall hope to see
the Museum again under more leisurely circumstances. In
the meantime all my congratulations on your achievement.

Of the visitors who came to the Paper Museum during the
early years, one stands out in my memory above all others.
It was a bright autumn morning with the usual number of
visitors, including some who showed genuine interest and a
few who gave only a cursory glance and departed as rapidly
as they had come. Among the earliest to arrive that morning
was a demure lady, probably eighty years of age, dressed in
plain black silk. She was alone. I wondered if she would find
the exhibits too specialized, and would soon tire of the history
of paper. But from my studio I soon saw that the frail little
woman in black was studying the contents of every display
case. An hour passed, and all this time she was so engrossed
that I hesitated to disturb her. It was apparent that the energetic octogenarian was reading every one of the hundreds of
labels; indeed, she was making copious notes upon a folded
sheaf of paper she had brought with her. As she had come early
in the morning and the lunch hour was at hand, I felt that I
should speak to her, even though I might be intruding. When
I entered the museum room from my adjoining studio, the
little old lady was intently bending over one of the long table
cases. As I came near, she rose to her full height of nearly
five feet and, thrusting out her hand, said: "I'm Karl's mother."
Although I had never before seen her, I realized that the
tireless little visitor was Mrs. Otelia Catherine Augspurger
Compton, mother of Karl Compton, President of M.I.T., Ar-
thur Holly Compton, Nobel Prize physicist, and Wilson Mar-
tindale Compton, President of Washington University. The

interest and enthusiasm shown by Mrs. Compton was gratifying and inspiring. Her visit gave me encouragement, and from that time on I felt that the establishment of the Paper Museum had been justified.

The museum was frequently visited by groups of interested professors and students from Harvard, Simmons, Wellesley, Boston University, and by members of paper and printing societies, and teachers and students from art schools. For the most part, however, the faculty and students of M.I.T. were apparently unable to grasp the significance of the collection. They probably thought that the museum had little to offer in highly developed scientific study. What the scientific-minded M.I.T. professors and students failed to realize, however, was that the origin and development of papermaking as shown in the museum was the basis of all civilization, and that had it not been for this craft the world would have been totally unable to exist. Without paper there would have been no scientists!

Although I had compiled a number of books covering specific techniques of papermaking as carried on in various parts of the world, the only general history had been the book printed and published in 1930 by William Edwin Rudge. My knowledge of papermaking by hand had naturally increased through the years, and most of my Asiatic traveling had been undertaken after the publication of the Rudge book; also, I had the store of illustrative material in the Paper Museum to draw upon. I felt that another general history should be issued. Using all my former books as background, I compiled a manuscript that was submitted to Alfred A. Knopf, New York, and to my surprise the material was accepted for publication. The first edition appeared in 1943 with the title *Papermaking: The History and Technique of an Ancient Craft*. The book was designed by William Addison Dwiggins. Although a history of papermaking would not be expected to appear on the best-seller list, the book was well received, and the edition eventually was exhausted. In 1947 Knopf issued a greatly enlarged edition with the same title; in this volume there were 648 pages, 317 illustrations, map, and diagram. The second edition of this work was my most comprehensive contribution to papermaking history and technique. Since the publication of these two editions I have received hundreds of letters from all parts of the world, as this book has had a wider circulation than any of my others.

While attending the Cleveland School of Art, my eldest son, Dard, Junior, under the guidance of Otto F. Egge, began the cutting of a fount of type, a task I had undertaken almost forty years earlier. Both of us cut the steel punches, struck and justified the matrices, and cast the individual types in hand moulds. Neither of us used prepared drawings, but cut the letters and ornaments directly into the ends of steel bars without preliminary outlines. We did, however, have fifteenth- and sixteenth-century book pages before us as we worked. Each fount required about three years to make, but it should be said that we did not work very steadily. Dard's type was first shown in a folio brochure issued in 1940, which described the making of the type and gave a photogravure illustration of the tools he had used. The actual specimen of the type was a full page in Latin. This publication was limited to 112 copies.

The second time this type was used was in printing a four-page folio of the first publication of Robert Frost's poem *A Considerable Speck,* issued without date by the Colonial Society, Boston. Both of these items were printed on the hand press in the workshop of the Paper Museum at M.I.T., on

Lime Rock handmade paper, with the limited amount of type that had been cast in a hand mould.

A short time after the printing of the type specimen and the Frost poem, we had a call at the museum from Alfred Hanson, the last remaining member of the old Hanson family that had established a type-foundry in Boston in 1872. Mr. Hanson had heard that we were making type by using fifteenth-century methods, but he could not understand our object in doing so. He explained that when the complete Hanson Foundry was sold to New Jersey interests, the Hanson family had felt justified in retaining certain drawings and diagrams of type-casting machines. With these detailed drawings in hand, Sandford H. Belyea, the former Hanson sales-manager, with M. Trolssas, a Norwegian machinist, as chief mechanic, began building the equipment for founding type. They had hoped that they could supply the printers of New England, as the old Hanson Foundry had done during its many years of activity. Unfortunately, however, after several years of arduous work in constructing type-casting machines and making moulds and matrices for casting type of various sizes and styles, the former Hanson sales-manager suddenly died, leaving the type-founding venture without its driving force. The reason for Mr. Hanson's visit to the Paper Museum was to ask my son and me to look at the newly set-up type-foundry before it was offered for sale as a going concern.

Mr. Hanson took us to a building in Purchase Street, in the old part of Boston, where we saw the new type-foundry, which had not been used except for preliminary experiments. There were four newly built casting-machines and every tool and appliance necessary for the manufacture of type for commercial use. Mr. Hanson explained that more than sixty thousand dollars had been spent in constructing the machines and getting the foundry ready to begin operating. We were offered the entire foundry for thirty thousand dollars. Although this figure was not unreasonable for a complete commercial type-foundry, we were not in a position to pay such an amount. We did not need the equipment, as our type-casting was done in hand moulds worth no more than fifteen or twenty dollars each; our entire equipment for making type by hand had cost no more than one hundred dollars. We frankly told Mr. Hanson that we could not purchase the foundry, and in taking our leave I jokingly said that one per cent of the amount asked would be about our limit. We left the type-foundry in Purchase Street with the thought that we would never see the equipment again.

After extensive advertising in printing-trade journals, Mr. Hanson apparently found that the demand for a type-foundry was exceedingly limited. Within two or three months he called by telephone stating that he would accept our offer. We could not recall that an offer had been made, but he was not slow to remind us that we had agreed to give one per cent of his price, or three hundred dollars. After this remarkable transaction had been completed, the equipment was transported to the workroom of the Paper Museum, where we found we had had acquired even more than had been first offered for thirty thousand dollars. The foundry included four new American and one used German type-casting machines, capable of casting all sizes of type from six to seventy-two point, as well as the wooden patterns that Mr. Trolssas, the mechanician, had used in making the heavy frames and smaller parts of the four machines. Also, there were dozens of moulds for all sizes of type, hundreds of matrices, matrix-adjusting machines, type-high and depth gauges, measuring-devices of all kinds, micrometers, planes for dressing types after casting, tool-grinders, shafting, pulleys, belting—in short, everything necessary for a complete commercial type-foundry.

During my curatorship of the Paper Museum, I was constantly reminded that, although I had traveled to distant countries in search of material for books dealing with European and Asiatic papermaking, I had long neglected the subject of pioneer papermaking in my own country. I therefore began to plan a book that would deal exclusively with the hand-made-paper makers of America—those untiring craftsmen who had so patiently struggled with limited skill and inadequate equipment to manufacture the paper needed by the Colonial printers for their books, pamphlets, newspapers, broadsides, and all sorts of ephemeral work.

In gathering material for this book we visited the sites of many pioneer mills, only to find that nothing remained even to suggest that an early paper mill had once existed there. Sometimes a filling-station, parking-lot, or an ugly modern building was occupying the original site. We found one instance of this sordid transformation when we were looking for the location of the earliest paper mill in Virginia, which had been established in 1744 by Benjamin Franklin and William Parks, Virginia's first printer. The acreage adjacent to the site of this historic mill was occupied by the sewage-disposal plant of the restored town of Colonial Williamsburg!

When I acquired the Lime Rock mill after the receivers' sale, a great many reams of paper that had been made by the Robertson family during the first two years of the mill's precarious existence remained in the drying-loft. This paper was well suited to printing a book on Colonial papermaking. The paper had been made by the methods that had been employed by the pioneer papermakers. It was transported to our small printing-shop in Chillicothe, where it was always possible to work without interruption. Two of the newly acquired type-casting machines were likewise shipped there, along with all the type-making appliances. It had been a hardship to cast by hand sufficient eighteen-point type for one folio page, all that had been needed for the type specimen and the Frost broadside. Now that we had the casting-machines, our task was greatly simplified, although we always operated the machines by hand; we never needed to use power. For casting type in a machine mould, however, the matrices were of slightly different proportions from those used in a hand mould. This made it necessary to strike a complete new set of copper matrices from the original hand-cut steel punches, one matrix for each of the upper- and lower-case letters, as well as for the points and ornaments.

When sufficient type for setting four folio pages had been cast and finished, and the handmade paper counted and sorted, we were ready to begin making the edition. This book was to have more pages and a greater number of illustrations than any book yet issued by our private press. I set the type from copious notes, and my son did the presswork. The printing was done on two hand presses. The larger one was used for printing two pages of text at one impression, and the smaller press for printing the facsimile reproductions. The initial letters in red and the text in black were printed at one impression; the initials, cut in brass, were inked separately and inserted in the chase after the text type had been inked.

As the book paper was unsized and unplated, like much of the earliest American paper, the presswork gave a great deal of difficulty. We always dampened the paper before printing, and as this particular paper had not been rendered impervious to moisture through gelatin sizing, no two sheets were precisely alike. Dard's type, like the paper, was well suited to the printing of this book, as it was bold in character and had the elusive qualities that only honest handwork can give. Bruce Rogers, the eminent typographical designer, thought so well of the type that he wanted to use it in a book he was planning, but we felt that it was best to retain it for our private press.

Toward the end of 1950, after several years of work, the edition was completed, and we gave the book the obvious title: *Papermaking by Hand in America.* The book had a hand-colored frontispiece; 326 pages; 96 facsimiles on specially made paper; 27 reproductions of early American watermarks made in imitation of the originals; and 42 full-size reproductions of old paper labels, printed on paper made to emulate the original labels in the Paper Museum. Some of the books were bound by Peter Franck, others by Arno Werner. Although it was stated in the colophon that there were 210 copies, it was only possible to assemble about 180. The available books were readily sold at the substantial price of one hundred and seventy-five dollars a copy. As we kept no record of time and costs, this figure was arbitrarily set, and naturally did not cover the actual expenditures. The bindings alone cost more than forty dollars each.

This book was reprinted commercially in an unlimited edition by the University of Pennsylvania Press, Philadelphia, in 1952, under the title: *Papermaking in Pioneer America,* after I had received the Rosenbach Fellowship in Bibliography. The reprint was an octavo with 192 pages of text and 22 illustrations of watermarks, and sold for a small fraction of the price of the original folio edition.

In November 1948, I reached sixty-five, the usual retiring age at the Massachusetts Institute of Technology. The president of the institute, however, requested that I remain as honorary curator for five more years, when a permanent home would be found for the collection. It was agreed that The Institute of Paper Chemistry, Appleton, Wisconsin, was the logical place to establish it on a perpetual basis, for there it would be seen by more people genuinely interested in the papermaking craft than anywhere else.

This organization had been founded for the specific purpose of carrying on research for the American paper industry and of preparing a limited number of students to enter paper mills as highly trained chemists and technicians. During October 1954, after sixteen years at M.I.T., the Paper Museum, consisting of more than twenty-five tons of material, was moved from the Charles Hayden Memorial Library building, where it had been housed since 1949, to The Institute of Paper Chemistry. Here the museum was permanently installed in the new general-activities building, in a large disaster-proof exhibition room especially designed for the purpose.

People who have not seen the paper collection often ask me how an entire museum can be devoted to such an ordinary substance as paper. It is difficult for the average person to comprehend that there could be any interest whatever in material so commonplace. Most people's contact with paper is limited to newspapers, magazines, packages, bags, toilet paper and paper money. It is surprising that many writers, teachers, professional people, even papermakers themselves, are often ignorant regarding the history of paper. On one occasion I overheard a college professor telling a well-known paper-mill executive that he should be proud of his age-old craft, and going on to explain that paper had been invented in Germany as early as the fourteenth century. The mill official was not slow to give his version, and told the professor that indeed his noble craft had been conceived in Egypt two thousand years before the birth of Christ!

Paper was invented during the early part of the second century of our era in Lei-yang, China, by the Chinese eunuch Ts'ai Lun, but it was not until A.D. 770, in Japan, that the first text-printing on paper was accomplished. These facts are substantiated in early Chinese and Japanese literature. It took more than a thousand years for papermaking to reach Europe, the first mill being set up in Valencia, Spain, in the twelfth century. The art of printing was introduced into Europe about three centuries later. Although printing in both the Orient and the Occident originated centuries after the invention of paper, the art of printing, historically and aesthetically, has always received vastly more attention than the more ancient and equally essential craft of making paper. There are numerous museums devoted to the graphic arts—type-making, typographical design, illustration, calligraphy, book-binding, and printing—but the long history of papermaking has been almost totally neglected. The Paper Museum was the first of its kind, but since its establishment in 1938, smaller collections have been established in Germany and Japan.

The material in the Paper Museum of The Institute of Paper Chemistry contains papermaking-moulds from all parts of the world, including the original type of *wove* mould such as Ts'ai Lun used when he invented paper; also, the original type of Chinese *laid* transfer mould, which shortly followed upon Ts'ai Lun's invention, and which is the basis for all modern papermaking, whether by hand or by machine. In addition to moulds from the papermaking centers of China, there are tools and equipment used in finishing the paper. There are also Chinese papers dating from the sixth century onward, with examples of early Chinese currency such as were seen by

Marco Polo, whose descriptions later gave Europeans the idea that paper could be used for money in lieu of metal. The museum has many specimens of all types of Chinese ceremonial papers for Buddhistic, Taoistic, and Lamaistic religious rites; also woodblocks formerly used in printing Chinese, Korean, Japanese, Tibetan, Mongolian, and Manchurian books. One of the exhibits in this section is an authentic specimen of the rare printed prayer—with the wooden pagoda in which it was kept—made in the eighth century for Empress Shōtoku of Japan. This, the world's first text-printing on paper, antedated the earliest movable-type printing in Europe by nearly seven hundred years. The walls of the museum are hung with Chinese colored screen and wall papers, each accompanied by the original series of woodblocks from which it was printed.

The Koreans were the first to make colored paper by placing the natural dyes directly with the vegetable fibers from which the sheets were made. They also formed the first envelopes, and so anticipated even the ingenious Chinese in these two important inventions. The museum has specimens of the earliest known Korean colored papers and examples of the first Korean imperial envelopes, the brilliant tones of which are still unfaded, testifying to the endurance of old vegetable dyes in contrast with modern paper dyes which soon lose their freshness.

The largest mould shown in the Japanese section of the museum is capable of forming sheets of paper that measure thirty by seventy inches. This paper is termed *shoji*, and is used in lieu of glass in the windows and doors of old-time Japanese houses. There are thousands of samples of Japanese papers, both plain and decorated, made by hand in the small family mills by using the inner barks of the mitsumata, gampi, and paper mulberry.

From India there are the various types of bamboo and grass moulds, and other papermaking-implements from the Punjab, Central and United Provinces, Hyderabad, Bengal, and the old paper center of Nowshera in the mountains of Kashmir. There are papers from all sections of India and from all periods, with examples of all the modern papers made in the schools sponsored by Gandhi.

Also there are moulds and appliances used by the papermakers of Siam, Indo-China, and Burma; as well as the beating-mallets and decorating-tools formerly used in Tonga, Samoa, Tahiti, the Marquesas, Hawaii, Celebes, Borneo, Solomon, New Guinea, Java, Sumatra, Central America, and Mexico, along with examples of both plain and decorated beaten-bark papers made in those localities.

Although papyrus and parchment are not paper, both have space in the museum, including an exhibition of parchment with full-size skins which show the progressive steps, beginning with the rough, hairy hide of the animal and going on through to the finished sheet of delicate parchment or vellum ready for the brush and quill of the calligrapher and illuminator. Papyrus and parchment were both used as writing-materials before the invention of paper, as were stone, clay, bone, bamboo, leaves, wood, lead, cloth, leather, and wax.

In one of the display cases there is an early laminated-paper falcon's coffin, made in Persia in a remote period. This was the forerunner of the built-up wallboard used so extensively in present-day house-construction. Also, there are various specimens of ancient pasteboard from Tibet and Mongolia. Laminated paper was used in Europe as early as 1772, as shown by a patent in the museum for making roofs of coaches, sedan chairs, wheeled carriages, panels for rooms, doors, cabinets, tables, bookcases, and tea trays of this material. The collection contains a manuscript by Lewis Charles Ducrest, dated August 12, 1788, which states that laminated paper was in use for "building houses, bridges, ships, boats, and all sorts of carriages." Practically every present-day use of paper had its counterpart in Asia or Europe hundreds of years ago.

There are early papers made from wood, straw, thistle stalks, cornhusks, leaves, conferva, turf, mallows, potatoes, aloe, willow, rush, cabbage stalks, wasps' nests, bamboo, hemp, and dozens of other vegetable fibers. The papers made from these unusual materials were experimental, having been made by European scientists in search of fibers to take the place of linen and cotton, the materials used almost exclusively in Europe for making paper up to the late eighteenth century. The first complete book to be printed in Europe on paper made from substances other than linen and cotton was issued in France in 1784: this paper was made from a mixture of grass, lime-tree bark, and other plant fibers. The earliest European volume in which the paper was made from a single material was published in Paris in 1786; one part of the edition was on paper made from the bark of the lime tree, and the remaining books of the edition were on paper fabricated from marsh mallow. The museum also has the first book printed on paper made from wood, another on paper made of straw, and a third volume printed on paper made from discarded, de-inked papers. These books by Matthias Koops were printed in London in 1800 and 1801. Koops might well be called the father of modern papermaking, for he was the first to build a paper mill for using wood pulp on a large commercial scale. But he was ahead of his time and went bankrupt in the venture. At the time (1800), the users of paper were not ready to accept wood-pulp paper, and continued to demand paper made from linen and cotton rags even for newspapers and other ephemeral printing. There is a noteworthy assemblage of Matthias Koops manuscript material in the collection. In fact, it includes all of the documents and business transactions found in the Westminster mill after its demise in 1802, including the excessively rare printed booklet listing the assets of the company when it was sold in bankruptcy. The Koops mill was never revived.

The Paper Museum covers watermarking by displaying the tools, equipment, and moulds used in this interesting craft, as well as specimens, from the original Italian line watermark of 1282 to the most elaborate light-and-shade marks of the twentieth century. The original experiments of Sir William Congreve include the first colored watermarks, of which he was the inventor. This collection embraces the actual watermarks made by Sir William in 1818 for the Bank of England in an effort to prevent the tremendous amount of counterfeiting practiced at that time. The present-day money papers of Great Britain show the influence of these early-nineteenth-century experiments.

Although the museum makes no attempt to carry the European exhibits beyond the period of making paper by hand, there is a small working model, founded on the original descriptions, of the first papermaking-machine, invented and patented in France in 1798 by Nicholas-Louis Robert. Owing to the disturbances in France at that time, however, the first machine capable of making usable paper was constructed in England and put into operation about 1804 at Frogmore Mill, Two Waters, Hertfordshire.

The most cumbersome exhibits in the museum are two full-size vats for the making of paper by hand in the European manner. One of these units was procured in Downton, Wiltshire, the other in Wookey Hole, Somerset, England. Both are set up at The Institute of Paper Chemistry, and each could be used for making about three reams of paper a day, provided that skilled workers were available, and power and water were supplied.

The gathering of the material in the Paper Museum has extended over a period of almost a half-century, and virtually every item was procured from the native workers in the locality of its origin. Two women worked almost a year cataloguing the material for ready reference. In the collection there are more than a thousand books and pamphlets in a dozen languages, all relating to some phase of old papermaking, watermarking, paper-decoration, paper mills, paper workers, paper uses, and kindred subjects. Although I have devoted my life to the obscure craft of making paper by hand, much research remains to be done. It is my hope that through the years to come the Paper Museum will be used by students, researchers, and writers who will find as much pleasure as I have found in a study of the ancient and honorable craft of papermaking.

# Bibliography

In my research work in the craft of papermaking, bibliographies have been particularly useful tools, and perhaps the present listing will also find use. As this bibliography extends over a period of more than forty years, some early material may have been overlooked. Prior to this listing, the most comprehensive bibliography of my work was published in 1953 in *Forschungsstelle Papiergeschichte*, when two European workers and I received Gutenberg Museum gold medals. The German publication, however, listed only about two-thirds as many titles as appear in the present bibliography, which is arranged chronologically.

Also included, under Part II, is a short list of articles relating to the actual making of the private-press books. These titles have been selected from several hundred publications in a dozen different countries. These are arranged under the names of the writers in alphabetical order.

## PART I

"The Modern Title Page." 8 illustrations. In *The British and Colonial Printer and Stationer*, Vol. LXVII, No. 26, pp. 413–14. London, December 29, 1910.

"The Lost Art of Making Books." 4 pages; 2 illustrations. In *The Miscellany*, Volume II, No. 1. Kansas City, Mo., 1915.

"Seventeenth-Century Type-making." 6 illustrations. In *The Quarterly Notebook*, pp. 45–54, Kansas City, Mo., 1915.

"The Characteristics of Handmade Paper." In *Paper Maker*

*and British Trade Journal.* International Number, London, 1916–17.

"Ancient Papermaking." 3 illustrations. In *The Miscellany,* Vol. II, No. 4, pp. 67–75. Kansas City, Mo., December 1915. In *Paper.* Vol. XXVI, pp. 18–19. New York, July 21, 1920. In *Paper and Paper Selling.* Vol. XXXIX, pp. 316–17. London, 1920.

*Handmade Paper and Its Watermarks, A Bibliography.* 22 pages. Technical Association of the Pulp and Paper Industry, New York, 1916.

"Paper for Artistic Printing." 2 illustrations. In *Scientific American,* No. 2119. New York, August 12, 1916.

"An American Handmade Paper Mill." 3 pages; 3 illustrations. In *Paper,* Volume XVIII, No. 24. New York, August 23, 1916.

"A Rare Book on Papermaking." 4 illustrations. In *Paper,* pp. 16–18. New York, September 15, 1920.

"Development of the Beating Engine." 5 illustrations. In *Paper Trade Journal,* Vol. LXXI, No. 9, pp. 36–40. New York, Nov. 4, 1920. In *World's Paper Trade Review,* pp. 2490–4. London, December 1920.

*Bibliographie de la Papeterie.* Translated from Charles Dumercy. In *Paper Trade Journal,* Vol. LXXII, No. 11, pp. 56–66, and No. 12, pp. 54–62. New York, March 10 and March 17, 1921.

"Watermarking Handmade Papers." 3 illustrations. In *Scientific American,* Vol. CXXIV, No. 13, pp. 248–9. New York, March 26, 1921. In *Paper,* Vol. XXVIII, pp. 12–13, 30. New York, June 29, 1921.

"A Bibliography of Marbled Papers." In *Paper Trade Journal,* Vol. LXXII, No. 18, pp. 52–8. New York, April 28, 1921.

"Ulman Stromer—First Chronicler of Paper." 3 pages; 5 illustrations. In *Paper,* Vol. XXVIII, No. 9. New York, May 4, 1921.

"Old Watermarks of Animals." 22 illustrations. In *Paper,* Vol. XXVIII, No. 25, pp. 12–25. New York, August 24, 1921. In *Worlds' Paper Trade Review,* Vol. LXXVI, pp. 1320–4. London, October 14, 1921.

"Laid and Wove." In *Printing Art,* Vol. XXXVIII, No. 1, pp. 33–40; 7 illustrations. Cambridge, Massachusetts, September 1921. In *Office Appliances,* Vol. XXXIV, No. 7, pp. 27–31; 7 illustrations. New York, January 1922. In *Smithsonian Report for 1921,* pp. 587–93; 6 illustrations. Government Printing Office, Washington, D.C., 1923. In *American Exporter,* pp. 82–3; 3 illustrations. New York, 1923.

"The Watermarking of Portraits, Ancient and Modern." 11 illustrations. In *The Inland Printer,* Vol. LXVIII No. 1, pp. 51–3. Chicago, October 1921. In *Indian Print and Paper.* Vol. V, pp. 22–5. Calcutta, March 1940.

"Making a Book." 2 illustrations. In *Illustrated World,* Vol. XXXVI, No. 6, pp. 873–5. Chicago, February 1922.

"Handmade Paper Through the Ages." 2 illustrations. In *The Pulp & Paper Magazine of Canada,* Vol. XXIX, No. 27, pp. 3–4. Gardenville, Quebec, 1922.

"A Maker of One-Man Books." 4 illustrations. In *The Mentor,* Vol. X, No. 2, pp. 30–2. New York, March 1922.

"One-Man Book Production." 2 illustrations. In *The Library World,* Vol. XXV, Nos. 290–1, pp. 239–42. London, August-September 1922.

"The Couching Material Used by the Old Papermakers." In *Alfelco Facts.* Vol. II, pp. 3–7. Albany, N.Y., October 1923.

*Old Papermaking.* Frontispiece of Marlborough Mill by Ralph M. Pearson; 112 pages; 57 illustrations in black and white; 25 illustrations in color; 9 specimens of old paper. Quarto;

200 copies. Bound in marbled boards by Charles Youngers. Mountain House Press, Chillicothe, Ohio, 1923.

"Symbolism in Paper Markings." In *Paper,* Vol. V, No. 33, pp. 3–6. New York, December 20, 1923.

"Features of Early Papermaking." In *The American Printer,* Vol. LXXIX, No. 2, pp. 27–30. New York, July 20, 1924.

*The Literature of Papermaking,* 1390–1800. 48 pages; 22 illustrations; 24 reproductions of old title pages. Folio; 180 copies. Loose sheets in portfolio. Mountain House Press, Chillicothe, Ohio, 1925.

"Handmade Paper." 17 illustrations. In *The Manufacture of Pulp and Paper,* J. N. Stephenson, editor, pp. 1–31. New York and London, 1925.

"Complete Bookmaking." 4 illustrations. In *Popular Mechanics Magazine,* pp. 557–60. Chicago, April 1926.

"About Handmade Paper and Deckle Edges." 3 illustrations. In *The American Printer,* pp. 31–3. New York, April 20, 1926.

"Fifteenth-Century Papermaking." 6 illustrations. In *Ars Typographica,* Vol. III, No. 1, pp. 37–51. New York, July 1926.

"Making Paper in the South Sea Islands." 3 illustrations. In *The American Printer,* Vol. 83, No. 3, pp. 33–6. New York, September 1926. In *Pulp and Paper Magazine of Canada,* Vol. XXV. Gardenville, Quebec, May 5, 1927.

*Primitive Papermaking.* Frontispiece of Mountain House Press, 1852; 48 pages; 35 illustrations in black and white; 1 illustration in color; 10 photographs; 31 specimens of primitive paper. Folio; 200 copies. Sheets held in portfolio. Mountain House Press, Chillicothe, Ohio, 1925.

"About the Book, Primitive Papermaking." 1 illustration. In *The American Printer,* pp. 64–5. New York, December 1927.

"The Romantic History of Papermaking." 2 illustrations. In

# BIBLIOGRAPHY

*The Paper Industry*, Vol. X, pp. 2160–2. Chicago, March 1929.

"Watermarks." 1 full-page plate. In *Encyclopædia Britannica*, 14th edition, p. 424. London and New York, 1929.

*Papermaking Through Eighteen Centuries*. 358 pages; 215 illustrations. Press of William Edwin Rudge, New York, 1930.

*Papermaking in the Classroom*. 80 pages; 46 illustrations. Manual Arts Press, Peoria, Illinois, 1931.

"Peregrinations & Prospects." 12 pages; 1 illustration. In *The Colophon*, Part 7. Pynson Printers, New York, 1931.

*Old Papermaking in China and Japan*. 72 pages; 19 illustrations in black and white; 11 illustrations in color; 15 specimens of old Oriental paper; 3 examples of bark. Folio; 200 copies. Bound by Peter Franck. The Mountain House Press, Chillicothe, Ohio, 1932.

"Adventures in Bookmaking." 6 illustrations. In *The Pacific Printer and Publisher*, pp. 24–8. San Francisco, California, August 15, 1933.

"Handmade Paper and Its Relation to Modern Printing." 20 illustrations. In *The Dolphin, A Journal of the Making of Books*, No. 1, pp. 116–27. Limited Editions Club, New York, 1933.

*A Papermaking Pilgrimage to Japan, Korea, and China*. 150 pages; 68 photogravure illustrations; 50 specimens of paper. Quarto; 375 copies. Bound by Gerhard Gerlach. Pynson Printers, New York, 1935.

"Making Books on Papermaking." 5 pages; 3 illustrations. In *The Paper Mill and Wood Pulp News*, Vol. LIX, No. 14. New York, April 4, 1936.

*Papermaking in Southern Siam*. 40 pages; 17 illustrations; specimens of paper. Quarto; 115 copies. Bound by Peter Franck. The Mountain House Press, Chillicothe, Ohio, 1936.

# BIBLIOGRAPHY

"The Use and Significance of Ancient Watermarks." In *Paper and Printing Digest*. Chicago, December 1936; January, February, and March 1937.

*Chinese Ceremonial Paper*. 82 pages; 44 photogravure illustrations; 40 specimens of spirit-paper and gods; three folding plates. Quarto; 125 copies. Bound by Peter Franck. The Mountain House Press, Chillicothe, Ohio, 1937.

"The Story of Paper." 36 illustrations. In *The Natural History Magazine*, Vol. XL, No. 3, pp. 577–97. American Museum of Natural History, New York, 1937.

*The Story of Early Printers*. 27 pages. A booklet describing an exhibit of printing for Chillicothe Newspapers, Inc. Chillicothe Gazette Press, Chillicothe, Ohio, 1938.

"Papermaking." 17 illustrations. In *A History of the Printed Book*, No. 3, pp. 345–70. Edited by Lawrence Wroth. Limited Editions Club, New York, 1938.

*The Paper Museum*. 8 pages; frontispiece. 200 copies. Paper Museum Press, Massachusetts Institute of Technology, Cambridge, Mass., 1939. Reprinted by The Institute of Paper Chemistry. 8 pages; frontispiece; folding Museum Guide Chart. Appleton, Wisconsin, 1954.

"Chang Shan-tse, Artist-Poet." 2 illustrations. In *Asia Magazine*, Vol. XXXIX, pp. 696–7. New York, December 1939.

*Papermaking by Hand in India*. 130 pages; 84 photogravure illustrations; 27 specimens of Indian paper. Quarto; 375 copies. Bound by Gerhard Gerlach. Pynson Printers, New York, 1939.

"Lost and Not Lost." 4 illustrations. In *Technology Review*, Vol. XLII, No. 3, pp. 109–26. Massachusetts Institute of Technology, Cambridge, Mass., January 1940.

"Handmade Paper Moulds." In *Paper Industry and Paper World*, Vol. XXI, pp. 1164–9. Chicago, 1940.

# BIBLIOGRAPHY

"The Papermaking Moulds of Asia." 19 illustrations. In *Gutenberg Jahrbuch*, pp. 9–24. Mainz, 1940.

*Romance of Watermarks, with a Biographical Sketch of the Author by Katherine Fisher.* 36 pages; 3 illustrations. 200 copies. The Stratford Press of E. F. Gleason, Cincinnati, Ohio, n.d.

*A Specimen of Type—An Experiment in Typefounding by Dard Hunter, Jr., by Employing the Same Methods and Materials Used During the Earliest Centuries of the Craft.* 8 pages; 1 photogravure illustration. 112 copies. The Paper Museum Press, Cambridge, Mass., 1940.

*Before Life Began, An Autobiography—1883–1923.* 120 pages; Watermark frontispiece. 219 copies. The Rowfant Club, Cleveland, Ohio, 1941.

*The Aztec and Mayan Papermakers.* Victor W. von Hagen. Introduction by and dedicated to Dard Hunter. New York, 1943.

"An Era in Papermaking—The Story of Dr. Jacob Christian Schäffer." 5 illustrations. In *Journal of the New York Botanical Garden*, Vol. XLIV, No. 523, pp. 149–59. New York, July 1943.

*Papermaking: The History and Technique of an Ancient Craft.* Pages 398, xxiii; 162 illustrations; map and 2 specimens of paper. First edition. Alfred A. Knopf, Inc., New York, 1943.

"Ohio's Pioneer Paper Mills." 15 illustrations. In *Antiques,* Ohio number, Vol. XLIX, No. 1, pp. 36, 39, 66. New York January 1946.

"Fifty Years a Binder, The Story of Peter Franck." 11 illustrations. In *Print*, Vol. IV, No. 4, pp. 29–36. Woodstock, Vt., 1946.

"Some Notes on Oriental and Occidental Paper and Books." 16 illustrations. In *The Paper Maker*, No. 2, pp. 3–14. Wilmington, Del., 1946.

# BIBLIOGRAPHY

*Papermaking: The History and Technique of an Ancient Craft.* Pages 610, xxxvii; 317 illustrations; 2 folding plates. Enlarged second edition. Alfred A. Knopf, Inc., New York, 1947.

*Papermaking in Indo-China.* 110 pages; 19 photographic illustrations; 2 specimens of Indochinese paper. Quarto; 182 copies. Bound by Peter Franck. The Mountain House Press, Chillicothe, Ohio, 1947.

"Elbert Hubbard and *A Message to Garcia.*" In *The New Colophon*, Vol. I, No. 1, pp. 27–35. New York, January 1948.

"The World's Most Important Material—Paper—Its Origins and History." 24 illustrations. In *The Illustrated London News*, Vol. CCXVII, No. 5813, pp. 437–40. London, September 16, 1950.

*Papermaking by Hand in America.* 326 pages; 96 facsimile illustrations; 27 reproductions of early watermarks; 42 full-size reproductions of old paper labels in the Paper Museum. Folio; 180 copies. Bound by Peter Franck and Arno Werner. The Mountain House Press, Chillicothe, Ohio, 1950.

*The Handmade Papers of Japan.* Thomas and Harriet R. Tindale. Foreword by Dard Hunter, pp. 11–17. 4 volumes. Tokyo, 1950.

"Early Papermaking in America." 14 illustrations. In *Gutenberg Jahrbuch 1950*, pp. 31–40. Mainz, 1950.

*De Papierwereld* (with Jan Poortenaar and C. Pels). 254 pages; 102 illustrations; numerous specimens. Naarden, Holland, 1951.

"American Paper Labels." 17 illustrations. In *Gutenberg Jahrbuch 1951*, pp. 30–3. Mainz, 1951.

*Papermaking in Pioneer America.* 192 pages; 24 illustrations. The University of Pennsylvania Press, Philadelphia, Pa., 1952.

# BIBLIOGRAPHY

"Rosamond Loring's Place in the Study and Making of Decorated Papers." In *Decorated Book Papers*. Harvard University Press, Cambridge, Mass., 1952.

"The Early Paper Mills of Ohio." 8 illustrations. In *The Briquet Album II*, pp. 85–96. The Paper Publications Society, edited by E. J. Labarre. Hilversum, Holland, 1952.

"Handmade Papermaking." 17 illustrations. In *The Manufacture and Testing of Paper and Board*, pp. 628–54. Edited by J. Newell Stephenson. New York, Toronto, London, 1953.

## PART II

Ballou, Robert: "The Story of Dard Hunter." 5 pages; 6 illustrations. In *Ben Franklin Monthly*, Vol. XXI, No. 3. Chicago, March 1923.

Bertieri, Raffaello: *"Les artistes du livre,"* pp. 83–92; 5 illustrations. *"Artista del libro,"* pp. 465–77; 2 illustrations. In *Il Risorgimento Grafico*, respectively Année VIII, No. 11, and Anno XVIV, No. 10, Milan, Italy, November 1911 and October 1921.

Brewer, Reginald: *About Dard Hunter*. 2 illustrations. In *The Delightful Diversion, The Whys and Wherefores of Book Collecting*, pp. 103–5. New York, 1935.

Clark, Neil M.: "A Fifteenth-Century Art Revived." In *American Magazine*, Vol. CIV. New York, November 1927.
——: "Paper Detective." *The Saturday Evening Post*, Vol. CCVI. Philadelphia, Pa., February 27, 1954.

Crawford, Nelson Antrim: "The Books of Dard Hunter." In *The American Mercury*, Vol. XI, No. 8. New York, August 1924.

Elliott, Harrison: "A Visit to Dard Hunter." 2 illustrations. In *The American Printer*, Vol. XXVIII, No. 6, pp. 27–30. New York, March 20, 1926.

Focus: *"En Modern Gutenberg-Son."* 2 illustrations. In

# BIBLIOGRAPHY

*Nordisk Boktryckare Konst.*, Vol. XXIII, No. 7, pp. 215–17. Stockholm, July 1922.

Gress, Edmund G.: *"A Modern Printer-Craftsman,"* 3 pages; 2 illustrations. *"Sketches and Impressions of an American Printer,"* pp. 36–8. In *The American Printer*, respectively December 20, 1921, and March 5, 1924. "A Modern Printer-Craftsman" reprinted in *The Publishers' Circular*, Vol. CXVI, No. 2905, London, March 4, 1922, and *The British Printer*, Vol. XXXV, No. 210, London, March–April 1923.

Guthrie, James: "A Maker of Books." In *The Scottish Nation*. Glasgow and Edinburgh, August 1923.

Hellman, Geoffrey T.: *Dard.* In *The New Yorker*, Vol. XII, No. 10, pp. 10–11. New York, April 25, 1936.

Hinrichsen, Steen: *"Enspaeder-Naturen Dard Hunter."* In *De Grafiske Fag.* Copenhagen, June 1948.

Ingersoll, Walter: "A Unique Printing Plant." In *The Inland Printer*, Vol. CXX. Chicago, February 1948.

Johnson, L.: "One-Man Books." In *Industrial Educational Magazine*, Vol. XXVII. Peoria, Illinois, February 1926.

Karnosh, Louis Joseph: *Bibliomania or the Madness of Book Collecting.* 40 pages. The Rowfant Club, Cleveland, Ohio, 1939.

Kieser, Paul W.: "Dard Hunter, Artisan." In *The Inland Printer*, Vol. CIX. Chicago, November 1943.

Levison, Lois C.: "A Maker of Books." 20 pages. In *Quarto Club Papers*, MCMXXVII–MCMXXVIII. New York, 1929

Meiner, Annemarie: *"Das Buch und seine Ausstattung."* In *Börsenblatt für den Deutschen Buchhandel*, Nr. 147, R. 75, 98 Jahrgang, pp. 618–20. Leipzig, July 1931.

Newton, A. Edward: "The Book, *Old Papermaking*, 1923." In *This Book Collecting Game*, pp. 109–10. Boston, 1928.

Pearson, Ralph M.: "An Artist in the Making of Books." 2 il-

# BIBLIOGRAPHY

lustrations. In *Personality Magazine,* Vol. I, No. 6, pp. 34–40. Garden City, N.Y., 1928. In *The American Scrap Book The Year's Golden Harvest of Thought and Achievement,* Pages 195–8. New York, 1928.

Philpott, A. J.: *A Lesson in Papermaking by Dard Hunter.* 12 pages; 61 copies. The Club of Odd Volumes, Boston, 1934.

Renker, Armin: *"Dard Hunter: Erinnerungen und Ausblicke."* In *Imprimatur, IV,* pp. 56–64. 1933.

Ruohomaa, Kosti: *"Dard Hunter—His Book."* In *Friends Magazine,* General Motors, Detroit, January 1955.

Shay, Felix: *"Dard Hunter."* In *Elbert Hubbard of East Aurora,* pp. 152–4. New York, 1926.

Siberell, Lloyd Emerson: "Dard Hunter, The Mountain House and Chillicothe." In *The Ohio State Archaeological and Historical Quarterly,* Vol. XLIV, No. 2, pp. 238–44. Columbus, Ohio, April 1935.

Tolman, R. P.: "Printing Recognized at the National Museum." 14 illustrations. In *The American Printer,* pp. 31–6. September 20, 1923.

Voorn, H.: *"Dard Hunter: Schrief de geshiedonis der Amerikianse Papierindustrie."* In *Papierwereld,* Nr. 7, S. 314. Amsterdam, 1951.

Wheelwright, William Bond: "The World's Greatest Museum of Paper." In *The Paper Maker,* Vol. XIX, No. 2. Wilmington, Delaware, 1950.

# Index

# INDEX

# INDEX

# INDEX

*iv*

# INDEX

# INDEX

# INDEX

*vii*

# A NOTE ON THE AUTHOR

DARD HUNTER was born in Steubenville, Ohio, on November 29, 1883, of a family of printers and publishers. He attended Ohio State University, the Graphische Lehr- und Versuchsanstalt and Kunstgewerbe Schule, Vienna, and the Royal Technical College of Finsbury, London. Originally a printer, he early became interested in paper and papermaking, and studied this craft in all parts of the world. This quest took him to nearly every papermaking country of Europe; to China, Japan, Korea, Indo-China, Siam, Malaya, the Philippines, the Netherlands East Indies, and the papermaking centers of India; to Mexico, Africa, Arabia, New Zealand, and many of the islands of the South Pacific Ocean.

Additionally, Dard Hunter has been a zealous craftsman in every aspect of bookmaking—author, illustrator, type-designer, punchcutter, founder, papermaker, and printer. He has produced books in which every step, from writing to the finished volumes, has been his own work. For many years he maintained a studio in his home in Chillicothe, Ohio, where he issued limited editions of books thus produced. He is also author of several commercially published books, of which the most important is: *Papermaking: The History and Technique of an Ancient Craft* (Second Edition, 1947). In his travels he assembled an amazingly complete collection of papermaking tools and equipment from all parts of the world. In 1939 this collection was established in the Massachusetts Institute of Technology, Cambridge, as the Dard Hunter Paper Museum; in 1954 it was permanently moved to The Institute of Paper Chemistry, Appleton, Wisconsin.

# A NOTE ON THE TYPE

The text of this book was set on the Linotype in Fairfield, the first type-face from the hand of the distinguished American artist and engraver Rudolph Ruzicka. In its structure Fairfield displays the sober and sane qualities of a master craftsman whose talent has long been dedicated to clarity. It is this trait that accounts for the trim grace and virility, the spirited design and sensitive balance of this original type-face.

Rudolph Ruzicka was born in Bohemia in 1883 and came to America in 1894. He has designed and illustrated many books and has created a considerable list of individual prints—wood-engravings, line-engravings on copper, aquatints.

The book was composed, printed, and bound by Kingsport Press, Inc., Kingsport, Tennessee. Paper manufactured by S. D. Warren Company, Boston. Typography and binding designs by Rudolph Ruzicka.